Lecture Notes in Computer Science   6029

Commenced Publication in 1973
Founding and Former Series Editors:
Gerhard Goos, Juris Hartmanis, and Jan van Leeuwen

Editorial Board

David Hutchison
  Lancaster University, UK
Takeo Kanade
  Carnegie Mellon Universi
Josef Kittler
  University of Surrey, Guil
Jon M. Kleinberg
  Cornell University, Ithaca, NY, USA
Alfred Kobsa
  University of California, Irvine, CA, USA
Friedemann Mattern
  ETH Zurich, Switzerland
John C. Mitchell
  Stanford University, CA, USA
Moni Naor
  Weizmann Institute of Science, Rehovot, Israel
Oscar Nierstrasz
  University of Bern, Switzerland
C. Pandu Rangan
  Indian Institute of Technology, Madras, India
Bernhard Steffen
  TU Dortmund University, Germany
Madhu Sudan
  Microsoft Research, Cambridge, MA, USA
Demetri Terzopoulos
  University of California, Los Angeles, CA, USA
Doug Tygar
  University of California, Berkeley, CA, USA
Gerhard Weikum
  Max-Planck Institute of Computer Science, Saarbruecken, Germany

Peter Müller (Ed.)

Advanced Lectures on Software Engineering

LASER Summer School 2007/2008

 Springer

Volume Editor

Peter Müller
ETH Zurich
ETH Zentrum, RZ F2, 8092 Zurich, Switzerland
E-mail: peter.mueller@inf.ethz.ch

Library of Congress Control Number: 2010926406

CR Subject Classification (1998): D.2, F.3, D.3, K.6, C.2, D.1

LNCS Sublibrary: SL 2 – Programming and Software Engineering

ISSN	0302-9743
ISBN-10	3-642-13009-7 Springer Berlin Heidelberg New York
ISBN-13	978-3-642-13009-0 Springer Berlin Heidelberg New York

springer.com

© Springer-Verlag Berlin Heidelberg 2010
Printed in Germany

Typesetting: Camera-ready by author, data conversion by Scientific Publishing Services, Chennai, India
Printed on acid-free paper   06/3180

Preface

Only five years after its inception, the LASER Summer School on Software Engineering has established itself among the premier training schools for PhD students and professionals from the industry. Each year, the summer school focuses on an important software engineering topic. This book contains selected lecture notes from the LASER Summer Schools 2007 and 2008, both of which focused on correctness—Applied Software Verification in 2007 and Concurrency and Correctness in 2008.

From the 2007 summer school on Applied Software Verification, this volume contains contributions by Tony Hoare on the verification of fine-grain concurrency and transactions, by Benjamin Morandi, Sebastian Bauer, and Bertrand Meyer on the SCOOP model for concurrent object-oriented programming, by Rustan Leino and Peter Müller on the Spec# programming and verification system, and by Natarajan Shankar on verification in the Prototype Verification System PVS. From the 2008 summer school on Concurrency and Correctness, the volume includes lecture notes by Tryggve Fossum on multi-core chip design.

I would like to thank the lecturers and their co-authors, who devoted much time to contributing to this volume. I am grateful to Marieke Huisman, Ling Liu, Rosemary Monahan, Matthew Parkinson, Sarvani Vakkalanka, and Hagen Völzer for their valuable feedback on drafts of the papers and to Marlies Weissert for her assistance in preparing the proceedings. Last but not least, I would like to thank Bertrand Meyer and his team for making the LASER Summer School such an enjoyable experience.

February 2010   Peter Müller

Table of Contents

Fine-Grain Concurrency

Tony Hoare

Microsoft Research, Cambridge

Abstract. I have been interested in concurrent programming since about 1963, when its associated problems contributed to the failure of the largest software project that I have managed. When I moved to an academic career in 1968, I hoped that I could find a solution to the problems by my research. Quite quickly I decided to concentrate on coarse-grained concurrency, which does not allow concurrent processes to share main memory. The only interaction between processes is confined to explicit input and output commands. This simplification led eventually to the exploration of the theory of Communicating Sequential Processes.

Since joining Microsoft Research in 1999, I have plucked up courage at last to look at fine-grain concurrency, involving threads which interleave their access to main memory at the fine granularity of single instruction execution. By combining the merits of a number of different theories of concurrency, one can paint a relatively simple picture of a theory for the correct design of concurrent systems. Indeed, pictures area great help in conveying the basic understanding. This paper presents some on-going directions of research that I have been pursuing with colleagues in Cambridge – both at Microsoft Research and in the University Computing Laboratory.

1 Introduction

Intel has announced that in future each standard computer chip will contain a hundred or more processors (cores), operating concurrently on the same shared memory. The speed of the individual processors will never be significantly faster than they are today. Continued increase in performance of hardware will therefore depend on the skill of programmers in exploiting the concurrency of this multi-core architecture. In addition, programmers will have to avoid increased risks of race conditions, non-determinism, deadlocks and livelocks. And they will have to avoid the usual overheads that concurrency libraries often impose on them today. History shows that these are challenges that programmers have found difficult to meet. Can good research, leading to good theory, and backed up by good programming tools, help us to discharge our new responsibility to maintain the validity of Moore's law?

To meet this challenge, there are a great many theories to choose from. They include automata theory, Petri nets, process algebra (many varieties), separation logic, critical regions and rely/guarantee conditions. The practicing programmer might well be disillusioned by the wide choice, and resolve to avoid theory completely, at least until the theorists have got their act together. This paper aims at just such a synthesis.

P. Müller (Ed.): LASER Summer School 2007/2008, LNCS 6029, pp. 1–20, 2010.

I have amalgamated ideas from all these well-known and well-researched and well-tested theories. I have applied them to the design of a structured calculus for low-overhead fine-grain concurrent programming. My theory of correctness is equally well-known: it is based on flowcharts and Floyd assertions. They provide a contractual basis for the compositional design and verification of concurrent algorithms and systems.

The ideas that I describe are intended to be an aid to effective thinking about concurrency, and to reliable planning of its exploitation. But it is possible to imagine a future in which the ideas can be more directly exploited. My intention is that a small collection of primitive operations will be simple enough for direct implementation in hardware, reducing the familiar overheads of concurrency to the irreducible minimum. Furthermore, the correctness of the designs may be certified by future programming tools capable of verifying the assertions that specify correctness. And finally, the pictures that I draw may help in education of programmers to exploit concurrency with confidence, and so enable all users of computers to benefit from future increases in hardware performance. But I leave to you the judgement whether this is a likely outcome.

2   Sequential Processes, Modeled by Flowcharts

I will start with a review of the concept of a flowchart. It is a graph consisting of boxes connected by arrows. Each box contains basic actions and tests from the program. On its perimeter, the box offers a number of entry and exit ports. Each arrow connects an exit port of the box at its tail to an entry port of the box at its head.

Execution of the program is modelled by a control token that passes along the arrows and through the boxes of the flowchart. As it passes through each box, it executes the actions and tests inside the box. In a sequential program there is only one token, so entry of a token into a box strictly alternates with exit from the box. Furthermore, there is no risk of two token passing down the same arrow at the same time. We will preserve an analogue of this property when we introduce concurrency.

The example in Figure 1 shows the familiar features of a flowchart. The first box on the left has two exits and one entry; it is the purpose of the test within the box to determine which exit is taken by the token on each occasion of entry. The two arrows on the right of the picture fan in to the same head. After the token has passed through a fan-in, it is no longer known which of the two incoming arrows it has traversed.

As shown in Figure 2, the execution control token starts at a designated arrow of the flowchart, usually drawn at the top left corner of the diagram. We regard the token as carrying the current state of the computer. This includes the names and current values of all the internal variables of the program, as well as the state of parts of the real world that are directly connected to the computer. In this simple example, we assume the initial state on entry of the token ascribes the value 9 to x.

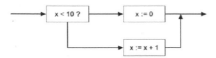

Fig. 1. A flowchart

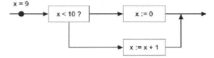

Fig. 2. A flowchart with token – 1

As shown in Figure 3, execution of the test in the first box causes the token to exit on the lower port, without changing the value of x. In Figure 4, execution of the code in the next box increases the value of x by 1.

Fig. 3. A flowchart with token – 2   **Fig. 4.** A flowchart with token – 3

In this sequence of diagrams, I have taken a snapshot of the passage of the token along each arrow. There is actually no storage of tokens on arrows, and conceptually, the emergence of a token from the port at the tail of an arrow occurs at the same time as entry of the token into the port at the head of the arrow.

The previous figures showed an example of a conditional command, selecting between the execution of a **then** clause and an **else** clause. Figure 5 shows the general structure of a conditional command. It is general in the sense that the boxes are empty, and can be filled in any way you like. Notice that all the boxes now have one entry and two exits. The exit at the bottom of each of each box stands for the throw of an exception, implemented perhaps by a forward jump.

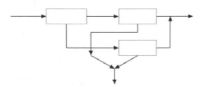

Fig. 5. Conditional flowcharts

Figure 6 shows another useful generalisation of the concept of a flowchart, the structured flowchart: we allow any box to contain not only primitive commands of a program but also complete flowcharts. The pattern of containment must be properly nested, so the perimeters of different boxes do not intersect. Wherever an arrow crosses the perimeter between the interior and the outside of a containing box, it creates an entry or exit port, which is visible from the outside. Connections and internal boxes enclosed within the perimeter are regarded as externally invisible. Thus from the outside, the entire containing box can be regarded as a single command. The sole purpose of structuring is to permit flowcharts to be composed in a structured and modular fashion. The containing boxes are entirely ignored in execution.

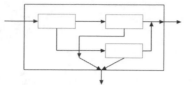

Fig. 6. A structured flowchart

For convenience of verbal description, we will give conventional names to the entries and exits of each box as shown in Figure 7. The names are suggestive of the purpose of each port. In our simple calculus there will always be a start entry for initial entry of the token, a finish exit for normal termination, and a throw exit for exceptional termination. The names are regarded as local to the box. In pictures we will usually omit the names of the ports, and rely on the position of the arrow on the perimeter of the box to identify it.

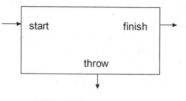

Fig. 7. Port names

The ports of the enclosing boxes also have names. In fact, we generally use the same names for the enclosing box as well as the enclosed boxes. This is allowed, because port names inside boxes are treated as strictly local. The re-use of names emphasises the structural similarity of the enclosing box to the enclosed boxes. For example, in Figure 8, the enclosing box has the same structure and port names as each of the enclosed boxes. In fact, the whole purpose of the calculus that we develop is to preserve the same structure for all boxes, both large and small.

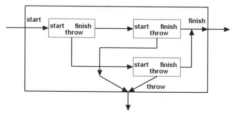

Fig. 8. Structured naming

The notion of correctness of a flowchart is provided by Floyd assertions, placed on the entries and exits of the boxes. An assertion is a boolean condition that is expected to be true whenever a token passes through the port that it labels. An assertion on an entry port is a precondition of the box, and must be made true by the environment before the token arrives at that entry. The assertion on an exit port is a post-condition of the box, and the program in the box must make it true before sending the token out on that exit. That is the criterion of correctness of the box; and the proof of correctness is the responsibility of the designer of the program inside the box.

Figure 9 shows our familiar example of a flowchart, with assertions on some of the arrows. The starting precondition is that x is an odd number. After the first test has succeeded, its postcondition states that x is still odd and furthermore it is less than 10. After adding 1 to x, it is less than 11, and 1 more than an odd number. The postcondition of the other branch is obviously that x is 0. On both branches of the conditional, the postcondition on the extreme right of the flowchart states that x is even, and less than 11.

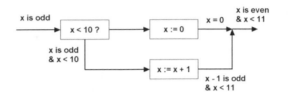

Fig. 9. Flowchart with assertions

Let us examine the principles that have been used in this informal reasoning. The criterion of correctness for an arrow is very simple: the assertion at the tail of the arrow must logically imply the assertion at the head. And that is enough. As Floyd pointed out, a complete flowchart is correct if all its boxes and all its arrows are correct. This means that the total task of correctness proof of a complete system is modular, and can be discharged one arrow and one box at a time.

There is a great advantage in Floyd's method of formalising program correctness. The same flowchart is used both for an operational semantics, determining the path of the token when executed, and for an axiomatic semantics, determining the flow of implication in a correctness proof. There is no need to prove the consistency of the two presentations of semantics.

Fig. 10. Arrow. The arrow is correct if $P \Rightarrow R$.

We allow any number of arrows to be composed into arbitrary meshes. But we are not interested in the details of the internal construction of the mesh. We are only interested whether any given arrow tail on the extreme left has a connection path of arrows leading to a given arrow head on the extreme right. We ignore the details of the path that makes the connection. Two meshes are regarded as equal if they make all the same connections. So the mesh consisting of a fan-in followed by a fan-out is the same as a fully connected mesh, as shown in Figure 11. Wherever the mesh shows a connection, the assertion at the tail on the left must imply the assertion at the head on the right. The proof obligation can be abbreviated to a single implication, using disjunction of the antecedents and conjunction of the consequents.

Fig. 11. Equal meshes. The mesh is correct if P v Q $\Rightarrow$ R & S.

We will now proceed to give a definition of a little calculus of fine-grain concurrent programs. We start with some of the simplest possible boxes and flowcharts. The first example in Figure 12 is the simple skip action which does nothing. A token that enters at the start passes unchanged to the finish. The throw exit remains unconnected, with the result that it is never activated.

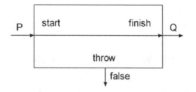

Fig. 12. Skip action. The box is correct if P $\Rightarrow$ R.

The proof obligation for skip follows directly from the correctness condition of the single arrow that it contains. The false postcondition on the throw exit indicates that this exit will never be taken. Since false implies anything, an exit labelled by false may be correctly connected to any entry whatsoever.

The purpose of a throw is to deal with a situation in which successful completion is known to be impossible or inappropriate. The throw is usually invoked conditionally. Its definition is very similar to that of the skip, and so is its correctness condition. A flowchart for the throw action is shown in Figure 13.

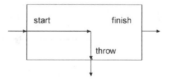

Fig. 13. Throw action

The operators of our calculus show how smaller flowcharts can be connected to make larger flowcharts. Our first operator is sequential composition. We adopt the convention that the two operands of a composite flowchart are drawn as boxes inside an enclosing box that describes the whole of the composed transaction. The behaviour of the operator is determined solely by the internal connections between the ports of all three boxes. It is essential in a compositional calculus that the definition does not depend on the contents of its operand boxes. This rule is guaranteed if the internal boxes contain nothing, as shown in Figure 14.

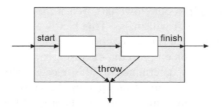

Fig. 14. Sequential composition

To assist in proof of correctness, there should in principle be assertions on each of the arrows. However, the permitted patterns for these assertions are completely determined by the correctness principle for the arrows of a flowchart, so there is no need to mention them explicitly.

Sequential composition has many interesting and useful mathematical properties. For example, it is an associative operator. All the binary operators defined in the rest of this presentation will also be associative. Informal proofs of these and similar algebraic properties are quite simple. Just draw the flowcharts for each side of the equation, and then remove the boxes that indicate the bracketing. The two flowcharts will then be found to be identical. They therefore have identical executions and identical assertions, and identical correctness conditions.

Figure 15 shows the sequential composition of three transactions, with the gray box indicating that the brackets are placed to the left.

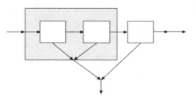

Fig. 15. Asssociativity proof (left association)

And Figure 16 shows the same three processes with bracketing to the right. You can see that the flowcharts remain the same, even when the enclosing gray box moves. The apparent movement of the throw arrow is obviously not significant, according to our definition of equality of meshes of arrows.

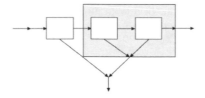

Fig. 16. Asssociativity proof (right association)

In conventional flow-charts, it is prohibited for an arrow to fan out. Thus the thick arrow in Figure 17 would not be allowed. But we will allow fan-out, and use it to introduce nondeterminism into our flowchart. When the token reaches a fan-out, it is not determined which choice it will make. This fact is exploited in the definition of a structured operator for nondeterministic choice between two operands. Whichever choice is made by the token on entry to the enclosing gray box, the subsequent behaviour of the program is wholly determined by the selected internal box. The other one will never even be started. The programmer must be prepared for both choices, and both must be correct. Non-determinism can only be used if the programmer genuinely does not care which choice is made. This is why non-determinism is not a useful operator for explicit use by programmers. We define it here merely as an aid to reasoning about the non-determinism that is inevitably introduced by fine-grain concurrency.

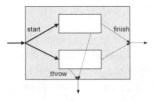

Fig. 17. Non-determinism

Note that non-determinism is associative, but it has no unit. It is symmetric: the order in which the operands are written does not matter. It is idempotent: a choice between two identical boxes is the same as no choice at all. Finally, sequential composition, and most other forms of composition distribute, through nondeterminism. The proof of this uses Floyd's principle, that two flowcharts which have identical correctness conditions have the same meaning.

3   Concurrent Processes, Modeled by Petri Nets

We now extend our notation for flowcharts to introduce concurrency. This is done by one of the basic primitives of a Petri net, the transition. As shown in Figure 18, a transition is drawn usually as a thick vertical bar, and it acts as a barrier to tokens passing through. It has entry ports on one side (usually on the left) and exit ports on the other. The transition transmits tokens only when there are tokens ready to pass on every one of its entry ports. These tokens are then replaced by tokens emerging simultaneously from every one of the exit ports. Note that transitions in themselves do not store tokens: the firing of a transition is an atomic event. We will later introduce Petri net places as primitive devices to perform the storage function.

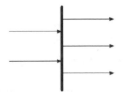

Fig. 18. Petri net transition

As shown in Figure 19, if there is only one entry arrow, the transition is geometrically like a fan-out, since it contains two (or more) exit arrows. It is used to transmit a token simultaneously to a number of concurrent threads. It is therefore called a fork.

The other simple case of a transition is a join, as shown in Figure 20. It has only one exit port, and two or more entries. It requires tokens on all its inputs to pass through it simultaneously, and merges them into a single token. It thereby reduces the degree of concurrency in the system.

Fig. 19. Petri net fork   **Fig. 20.** Petri net join

The simple cases of forks and joins are sufficient to reconstruct all the more complicated forms of a Petri net transition. This is done by connecting a number of transitions into a mesh, possibly together with other arrows fanning in and fanning out. A mesh with transitions is capable of absorbing a complete set of tokens on some subset of its entry arrows, delivering tokens simultaneously to some subset of its exit arrows. These two subsets are said to be connected by the mesh. In the case of a mesh without transitions, the connection is made between singleton subsets. Two general meshes are regarded as equal if they make exactly the same connections between subsets. So the mesh shown in Figure 21 is equal to the mesh shown in Figure 22. If there were places between the transitions, the equivalence would not hold.

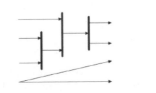

Fig. 21. Petri net mesh – 1   **Fig. 22.** Petri net mesh – 2

An inappropriate mixture of transitions with fan-in and fan-out of arrows can lead to unfortunate effects. Figure 23 shows an example corner case. A token at the top left of the mesh can never move through the transition. This is because the fan-out delivers a token at only one of its two heads, whereas the transition requires a token at both of them. As a result, the whole mesh has exactly the same effect as a mesh which actually makes only one connection. We will design our calculus of concurrency to ensure that such corner cases will never arise.

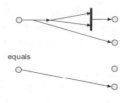

Fig. 23. A corner case

In the design of fine-grain concurrent programs, it is essential to keep account of the ownership of resources by the threads which update them. We will therefore regard each token as carrying with it a claim to the ownership (i.e., the write permissions and read permissions) for just a part of the state of the computer; though for simplicity, we will largely ignore read permissions. Obviously, we will allow a box to access and update only the resources carried by the token that has entered the box. The addition of ownership claims to the tokens helps us to use Petri nets for their initial purpose, the modelling of data flow as well as control flow through the system.

In Figure 24, the ownership of variables x and y is indicated by writing these names on the token which carries the variables. Figure 25 is the state after firing the transition. The resources claimed by the token are split into two or more disjoint parts (possibly sharing read-only variables); these parts are carried by the separate tokens emerging from the fork.

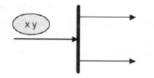

Fig. 24. Token split: before

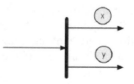

Fig. 25. Token split: after

In Figure 24 and Figure 25, token at entry carries whole state: {x y}; at the exits, each sub-token carries a disjoint part of the state.

The Petri net join is entirely symmetric to the fork. Just as the fork splits the ownership claims of the incoming token, the join merges the claims into a single token. In Figure 26 and Figure 27, each sub-token carries part of the state at entry; at exit, the token carries whole state again.

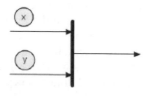

Fig. 26. Token merge: before

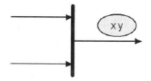

Fig. 27. Token merge: after

What happens if the incoming tokens make incompatible claims on the same resource? Fortunately, in our structured calculus this cannot happen. The only way of generating tokens with different ownership claims is by the fork, which can only generate tokens with disjoint ownership claims. As a result, the claims of each distinct token in the entire system are disjoint with the claims of all the others. The join transition shown above preserves this disjointness property. So no resource is ever shared between two distinct tokens.

We allow the assertion on an arrow of a Petri net to describe the ownership claims of the token that passes along the arrow. For simplicity, we will just assume that any variable mentioned in the assertion is part of this claim. In reasoning with these assertions, it is convenient to use a recently introduced extension of classical logic, known as separation logic; it deals with assertions that make ownership claims.

Separation logic introduces a new associative operator, the separated conjunction of two predicates, usually denoted by a star $(P * Q)$. This asserts that both the predicates are true, and furthermore, that their ownership claims are disjoint, in the sense that there is no variable in common between the assertions. The ownership claim of the separated conjunction is the union of the claims of its two operands.

In a program that uses only declared variables without aliasing, the disjointness of the claims can be checked by a compiler, and separation logic is not necessary. The great strength of separation logic is that it deals equally well with pointers to objects in the heap. It allows any form of aliasing, and deals with the consequences by formal proof. However, our example will not illustrate this power of separation logic.

The axiom of assignment in separation logic is designed to prevent race conditions in a fine-grain concurrent program. It enforces the rule that the precondition and the postcondition must have the same claim; furthermore, the claim must include a write permission for the variable assigned, and a read permission for every variable read in the expression that delivers the assigned value. In the displayed axiom of assignment (Figure 28) we have exploited the common convention that a proposition implicitly claims all variables that it mentions. So the precondition and postcondition claim x and y. Because of disjointness, R must not claim x or y. For simplicity, we have failed to distinguish read and write permissions.

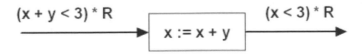

Fig. 28. Axiom of assignment

Separated conjunction is used to express the correctness condition for Petri net transitions. The assertion at the entry of a must imply the separated conjunction of all the assertions at the exits. In Figure 29, the disjointness of P and Q represents the fact that the outgoing tokens will have disjoint claims.

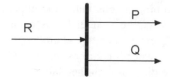

Fig. 29. Correctness condition of fork: $P \star Q \Rightarrow R$

As mentioned before, the join is a mirror image of the fork. Accordingly, the correctness condition for a join is the mirror image of the correctness condition for a fork.

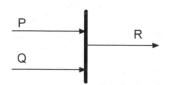

Fig. 30. Correctness condition for join: $P \star Q \Rightarrow R$

There is a problem here. What happens if $P \star Q$ is false, even though both P and Q are both true? This would mean that the execution of the program has to make falsity true when it fires. But no implementation can do that – it is a logical impossibility. Fortunately, the rule of assignment ensures that P and Q must be consistent with each other. The details of the consistency proof of separation logic are beyond the scope of this paper.

The first example of the use of transitions in our calculus is the definition of the kind of structured (fork/join) concurrency introduced by Dijkstra. In Figure 31, the fork on the left ensures that both the threads labelled T and U will start together. The join on the right ensures that they will finish together. In between these transitions, each of the threads has its own token, and can therefore execute concurrently with the other. By definition of the fork and join, the tokens have disjoint claims. Since a thread can only mention variables owned by its token, the rule of assignment excludes the possibility of race conditions. It also excludes the possibility of any interaction whatsoever between the two threads.

In Figure 31, I have not allowed any possibility of a throw. The omission will be rectified shortly.

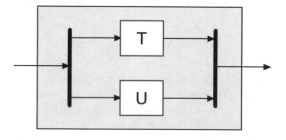

Fig. 31. Concurrent composition. There is no connection between T and U.

Figure 32 is a simple example of a concurrent program. The precondition says that x and y have the same parity. One thread adds 2 to x, and the other multiplies y by 7. Both these operations preserve parity. So the same precondition still holds as a postcondition. Although this is obvious, the proof requires a construction, as shown in Figure 33. The construction introduces an abstract or ghost variable z to stand for the parity of x and y. A ghost variable may appear only in assertions, so it remains constant throughout its scope. For the same reason, a ghost variable can be validly shared among threads (though it may not be either read or written). When it has served its purpose, the ghost variable may be eliminated by existential quantification in both the precondition and the postcondition.

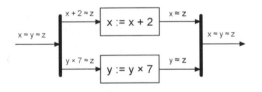

Fig. 32. A concurrent composition example. $x \approx y$ means $(x - y)$ mod $2 = 0$ (their difference is even).

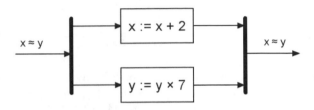

Fig. 33. Ghost variable z

Proof: $x \approx y \Rightarrow x + 2 \approx y \times 7$
$x \approx y \approx z \Rightarrow (x + 2 \approx z) \star (y \times 7 \approx z)$

We now return to the example of the structured concurrency operator and remove the restriction on throws. In Figure 34, the throw exits of T and U are connected through a new join transition to the throw exit of the composition. As a result, the concurrent combination throws just when both the operands throw. This still leaves an unfortunate situation when one of the operands attempts to throw, whereas the other one finishes normally. In an implementation, this would manifest itself as a deadlock.

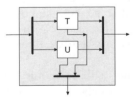

Fig. 34. Concurrency with throw. To avoid deadlock, T and U must agree on their exits.

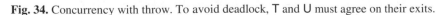

A solution is to adopt an even more complicated definition of concurrent composition. It ensures that a throw will occur when either of the operands throws, even if the other one finishes. As shown in Figure 35, this is achieved by additional joins to cover the two cases when the threads disagree on their choice of exit port.

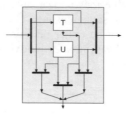

Fig. 35. Deadlock avoided. Disagreement on exit leads to throw.

In Figure 36, note the four encircled fan-outs in the arrows at the exits of the operands T and U . Each of these introduces non-determinism. However, it is non-determinism of the external kind that is studied in process algebras like CCS and CSP. It is called external, because the choice between the alternatives is made at the head of the arrow rather than at the tail. On reaching the fan-out, the token will choose a branch leading to a transition that is ready to fire, and not to a transition that cannot fire. In Figure 36, we have ensured that at most one of the alternative transitions can be ready to fire. Thus the diagram is in fact still completely deterministic, in spite of the four fan-outs.

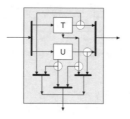

Fig. 36. Fan-out gives external non-determinism

The calculus that we have described so far is not capable of exploiting fully the power of multi-core architecture. The reason is that the same rules that prohibit race conditions also prohibit any form of communication or co-operation among the threads. To relax this restriction, it is necessary to establish some method of internal communication from one thread to another. For the purpose of exploiting multi-core architecture, the highest bandwidth, the minimum overhead and the lowest latency are simultaneously achieved by use of the resources of the shared memory for communication. Communication takes place when one thread updates a variable that is later read by another.

Of course, race conditions must still be avoided. This is done by the mechanism of a critical region, which enables the programmer to define a suitable level of granularity for the interleaving of operations on the shared resource by all the sharing threads. A critical region starts by acquiring the shared resource and ends by releasing it, through new entry ports introduced into our calculus for this purpose. Inside a critical region, a thread may freely update the shared resource together with the variables that it owns permanently. Race conditions are still avoided, because the implementation ensures that at any time at most one thread can be in possession of the critical region. A simple implementation technique like an exclusion semaphore can ensure this.

In our Petri net model, a shared resource is represented by a token which carries ownership of the resource. In order to access and update the shared resource, a thread must acquire this token, which is done by means of a standard join between the control token and a token carrying ownership of the resource. After updating the shared state within the critical region, the thread must release the token, by means of a standard fork. The standard rules of ownership are exactly appropriate for checking critical regions defined in this way, since the token that travels through the region will carry with it the ownership of both the local variables of the thread and the variables of the shared resource. These can therefore be freely updated together within the critical region.

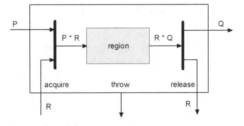

Fig. 37. Critical region. R is the resource invariant.

Note that the body of the critical region has no acquire or release ports. This intentionally prohibits the nesting of critical regions. Furthermore, I have disallowed throws from within a critical region. To allow throws, the definition of a critical region requires an additional fork transition to ensure that the resource token is released before the throw exit. This means that the programmer must restore the resource invariant before the throw.

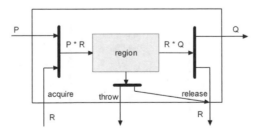

Fig. 38. Critical region with throw

Addition of new ports into a calculus requires extension of the definition of all the previously defined operators. In the case of the new acquire and release ports, the resource is equally accessible to all the operands, and the standard extension rule is to just connect each new entry port of the enclosing block for the operator by a fan-out to the like-named new entry ports of both the operands; and connect every new exit port of each operand via a fan-in to the like-named port on the enclosing block. Figure 39 shows only the new ports and additional arrows that are to be added to every operator defined so far. It ensures that the new ports can be used at any time by either of the operands.

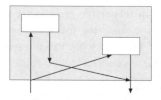

Fig. 39. New ports

A shared resource is introduced by exactly the same operator which introduces multiple threads. The token that owns the resource is created by the fork on the left of Figure 40. It then resides at a place (denoted by a circle) specially designated for it within the Petri net. The resource token is acquired by its users one at a time through the acquire entry at the beginning of each critical region, and it is released after use through the release exit at the end of each critical region. It then returns to its designated place. If more than one user is simultaneously ready to acquire the resource token, the choice between them is arbitrary; it has to be made by the semaphore mechanism that implements exclusion. This is the way that shared memory introduces don't-care non-determinism into a concurrent program.

The assertion R in this diagram stands for the resource invariant. As shown in Figure 39, it may be assumed true at the beginning of every critical region, and must be proved true at the end. It thus serves the same role as a guarantee condition in the rely/guarantee method of proving concurrent programs.

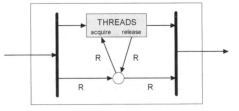

Fig. 40. Resource declaration. Petri net place: ○ stores a token.

Figure 41 caters for the possibility of a throw, in the usual way.

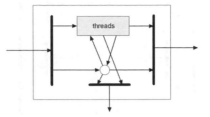

Fig. 41. Resource declaration with throw

Figure 42 is an extremely simple example of concurrency with critical regions. Two threads share a variable x. One of them assigns to it the value 2, and the other one assigns the value 7. Because the variable is shared, this has to be done in a critical region Each thread is nothing but a single critical region. As a result, the two critical regions are executed in arbitrary order, and the final value of x will be either 2 or 7. The easiest proof is operational: just prove the postcondition separately for each of the two interleavings. But in general, the number of interleavings is astronomical. So we want to ask whether our assertional proof system capable of proving this directly in a more abstract way?

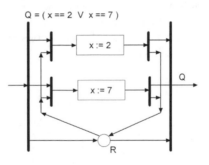

Fig. 42. Example – 1

The answer seems to be yes, but only with the help of a ghost variable t, introduced to record the termination of one of the threads. The variable obviously starts false. By conditioning the resource invariant on t, its truth is assured at the beginning. Both critical regions leave the resource invariant R true. And one of them sets t true. Thus at the end, both t and R are true. Thus Q is also true at the end.

But the question arises, who owns t? It has to be joint ownership by the resource and the first thread. Such jointly owned variables can be updated only in a critical region, and only by the thread that half-owns it. The resource owns the other half. When the resource and the thread have come together in the critical region, full ownership enables the variable to be updated. This is adequate protection against race conditions. Fractional ownership is a mechanism also used for read-only variables in recent versions of separation logic.

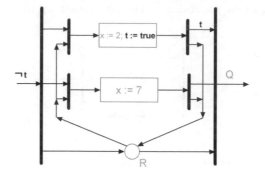

Fig. 43. Example – 2. Q = x ε {2, 7} and R = t ⇒ Q.

4 Other Features of a Calculus

Recursion is the most important feature of any programming calculus, because it allows the execution of a program to be longer than the program itself. Iteration is of course an especially efficient special case of recursion. Fortunately, Dana Scott showed how to introduce recursion into flowcharts a long time ago. Just give a name X to a box, and use the same name as the content of one or more of the interior boxes. This effectively defines an infinite net, with a copy of the whole box inserted into the inner box. For this reason, the pattern of entry and exit ports of the recursive call must be the same as that of the outer named box. That is a constraint that is easily enforced by use of a calculus like one we have described.

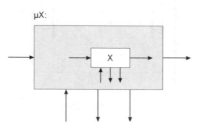

Fig. 44. Scott recursion

A variable can be represented by a place pre-loaded with a token that owns the variable. This token joins the main control token on entry to the block, which can use the variable as required. It is forked off again on exit from the block, so that it is never seen from the outside. A place is needed at the finish to store the token after use. Let us use the same place as stored the token at the beginning.

The assertions on the arrow leading from and to the place should just be the proposition true, which is always true. This means that nothing is known of the value of the variable immediately after declaration. It also means that its value on termination is irrelevant. This permits an implementation to delay allocation of storage to the variable until the block is entered, and to recover the storage or exit.

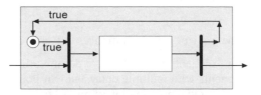

Fig. 45. Variable declaration – 1

Figure 46 extends the diagram to show what happens on a throw. The variable still needs to be retained inside the box after an exception.

The Petri net fork is a direct implementation of an output from one thread of a system to another. It simply transfers ownership of the message (together with its value) to the inputting process. It does not copy the value. It does not allocate any buffer. Overhead is therefore held to a minimum. If buffers are desired, they can be modelled as a sequence of Petri net places.

Just as output was a fork, input is a join at the other end of an arrow between two threads. Note that the output is synchronised with the inputting process. In a sympathetic architecture (like that of the transputer), the operations of input and output can be built into the instruction set of the computer, thereby avoiding software overhead altogether.

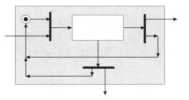

Fig. 46. Variable declaration – 2

The introduction of arbitrary arrows communicating ownership among threads can easily lead to deadlock. Absence of deadlock can be proved by the methods of process algebra, and we will not treat it here. Fortunately, the use of non-nested critical regions is a disciplined form of communication which is not subject to deadlock. A simple hierarchy of regions can extend the guarantee to nested regions.

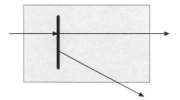

Fig. 47. Output

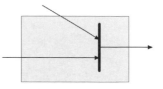

Fig. 48. Input

5 Conclusion

The main conclusions that may be drawn from this study are:

1. Flow-charts are an excellent pictorial way of defining the operational semantics of program components with multiple entry and exit points. Of course, they are not recommended for actual presentation of non-trivial programs.
2. Floyd assertions are an excellent way of defining and proving correctness of flowcharts. Consistency with an operational semantics for flowcharts is immediate.
3. Petri nets with transitions extend these benefits to fine-grain concurrent programs. The tokens are envisaged as carrying ownership of system resources, and permissions for their use.
4. Separation logic provides appropriate concepts for annotating the transitions of a Petri net. The axiom of assignment provides proof of absence of race conditions.
5. Critical regions (possibly conditional) provide a relatively safe way of using shared memory for communication and co-operation among threads.
6. Although they are not treated in this paper, rely/guarantee conditions provide a useful abstraction for the interleaving of critical regions.
7. Pictures are an excellent medium for defining the operators of a calculus. They are readily understood by programmers who are unfamiliar with programming language semantics (some of them even have an aversion to syntax).

Of course, there is abundant evidence, accumulated over many years, of the value of each of these ideas used separately. The only novel suggestion of this presentation is that their combined use may be of yet further value in meeting the new challenges of multi-core architecture.

Acknowledgment. Thanks to Robert Floyd, Carl Adam Petri, Cliff Jones, Simon Peyton Jones, Tim Harris, Viktor Vafeiadis, Matthew Parkinson, Wolfgang Reisig and Steve Schneider. Even though there are no references, it is a pleasure to express my thanks to those who have inspired this work, or helped its progress.

Compensable Transactions

Tony Hoare

Microsoft Research, Cambridge, England

Summary. The concept of a compensable transaction has been embodied in modern business workflow languages like BPEL. This article uses the concept of a box-structured Petri net to formalise the definition of a compensable transaction. The standard definitions of structured program connectives are extended to construct longer-running transactions out of shorter fine-grain ones. Floyd-type assertions on the arcs of the net specify the intended properties of the transaction and of its component programs. The correctness of the whole transaction can therefore be proved by local reasoning.

1 Introduction

A compensable transaction can be formed from a pair of programs: one that performs an action and another that performs a compensation for that action if and when required. The forward action is a conventional atomic transaction: it may fail before completion, but before failure it guarantees to restore (an acceptable approximation of) the initial state before the transaction, and of the relevant parts of the real world. A compensable transaction has an additional property: after successful completion of the forward action, a failure of the next following transaction may trigger a call of the compensation, which will undo the effects of the forward action, as far as possible. Thus the longer transaction (this one together with the next one) is atomic, in the sense that it never stops half way through, and that its failure is adequately equivalent to doing nothing. In the (hopefully rare) case that a transaction can neither succeed nor restore its initial conditions, an explicit exception must be thrown.

The availability of a suitable compensation gives freedom to the forward action to exercise an effect on the real world, in the expectation that the compensation can effectively undo it later, if necessary. For example, a compensation may issue apologies, cancel reservations, make penalty payments, etc. Thus compensable transactions do not have to be independent (in the sense of ACID); and their durability is obviously conditional on the non-occurrence of the compensation, which undoes them. Because all our transactions are compensable, in this article we will often omit the qualification.

We will define a number of ways of composing transactions into larger structures, which are also compensable transactions. Transaction declarations can even be nested. This enables the concept of a transaction to be re-used at many levels of granularity, ranging perhaps from a few microseconds to several months -- twelve orders of magnitude. Of course, transactions will only be useful if failure is rare, and the longer transactions must have much rarer failures.

P. Müller (Ed.): LASER Summer School 2007/2008, LNCS 6029, pp. 21–40, 2010.

The main composition method for a long-running transaction is sequential composition of an ordered sequence of shorter transactions. Any action of the sequence may fail, and this triggers the compensations of the previously completed transactions, executed in the reverse order of finishing. A sequential transaction succeeds only if and when all its component transactions have succeeded.

In the second mode of composition, the transactions in a sequence are treated as alternatives: they are tried one after another until the first one succeeds. Failure of any action of the sequence triggers the forward action of the next transaction in the sequence. The sequence fails only if and when all its component transactions have failed.

In some cases (hopefully even rarer than failure), a transaction reaches a state in which it can neither succeed nor fail back to an acceptable approximation of its original starting state. The only recourse is to throw an exception. A catch clause is provided to field the exception, and attempt to rectify the situation.

The last composition method defined in this article introduces concurrent execution both of the forward actions and of the backward actions. Completion depends on completion of all the concurrent components. They can all succeed, or they can all fail; any other combination leads to a throw.

2   The Petri Box Model of Execution

A compensable transaction is a program fragment with several entry points and several exits. It is therefore conveniently modelled as a conventional program flowchart, or more generally as a Petri net. A flowchart for an ordinary sequential program is a directed graph: its nodes contain programmed actions (assignments, tests, input, output, ... as in your favourite language), and its arrows allow passage of a single control token from the node at its tail to the node at its head. We imagine that the token carries with it a value consisting of the entire state of the computer, together with the state of that part of the world with which the computer interacts. The value of the token is updated by execution of the program held at each node that it passes through. For a sequential program, there is always exactly one token in the whole net, so there is never any possibility that two tokens may arrive at an action before it is complete.

In section 6, we introduce concurrency by means of a Petri net transition, which splits the token into separate tokens, one for each component thread. It may be regarded as carrying that part of the machine resources which is owned by the thread, and communication channels with those parts of the real world for which it is responsible. The split token is merged again by another transition when all the threads are complete. The restriction to a single token therefore applies within each thread.

A structured flowchart is one in which some of its parts are enclosed in boxes. The fragment of a flowchart inside a box is called a block. The perimeter of a box represents an abstraction of the block that it contains. Arrows crossing the perimeter are either entries or exits from the box. We require the boxes to be either disjoint or properly nested within each other. That is why we call it a structured flowchart, though we relax the common restriction that each box has only one entry and one exit arrow. The boxes are used only as a conceptual aid in planning and programming a transaction, and in defining a calculus for proving their correctness. In the actual execution of the transaction, they are completely ignored.

We will give conventional names to the entry points and exit points of the arrows crossing the perimeter of the box. The names will be used to specify how blocks are composed into larger blocks by connecting the exits of one box to the entries of another, and enclosing the result in yet another box. This clearly preserves the disjointness constraint for a box-structured net.

One of the arrows entering the box will be designated as the *start* arrow. That is where the token first enters the box. The execution of the block is modelled by the movement of the token along the internal arrows between the nodes of the graph that are inside the box. The token then can leave the box by one of its exit points, generally chosen by the program inside the box. The token can then re-enter the box again through one of the other entry points that it is ready to accept it. The pattern of entering and leaving the block may be repeated many times.

In our formal definition of a compensable transaction, we will include a behavioural constraint, specifying more or less precisely the order in which entry and exit points can be activated. The behavioural constraint will often be expressed as a regular expression, whose language defines all permissible sequences of entry and exit events which may be observed and sequentially recorded.

We will introduce non-determinism into our flowchart by means of the Petri net place. A place is drawn as a small circle (Figure 2.1) with no associated action. It may have many incoming arrows and many outgoing arrows. The place is entered by a token arriving along any one of its entries. The next action (known as a firing) of the place is to emit the token just once, along any one of its exit arrows. The token arriving at the exit of the place may have originated at any one of its entries. The strict alternation of entries and exits of a place may be formally described by the regular expression

$$(l + m + n) ; (r + s + t)$$

where l, m, n name the entries of the place, and r, s, t name the exits.

Technical note: in general, a Petri net place is capable of storing a token. In our restricted calculus this capability is exploited only once (in section 6). In fact, we may regard a token as passing instantaneously (as a single event) through any sequence of consecutive states. Of course, a regular expression cannot model this simultaneity.

If the place has only a single exit arrow, it acts as a normal fan-in, and has the same function as in a conventional flowchart. If there are many exits, the place acts as a fan-out. The choice of exit arrow on each occasion of entry is usually determined by the current readiness of the block at the head of the exit arrow to accept entry of the token. But if more than one block is ready, the choice is non-deterministic, in the usual sense of don't-care or demonic non-determinism. It is the programmer's responsibility to ensure that all choices are correct; and the implementation may choose any alternative according to any criterion whatsoever, because it is known that correctness will not be affected. For example, efficiency and responsiveness are among the more desirable of the permissible criteria.

We follow Floyd's suggestion that the arrows in a flowchart should be annotated with assertions. Assertions are descriptions of the state of the world (including the state of the machine), and the programmer intends that they should be true of the world value carried by the control token, whenever it passes along the annotated arrow. An assertion on an arrow which enters a box serves as a precondition for the block, and it is the responsibility of the surrounding flowchart to make it true before transmitting the token to that entry. An assertion on an exit arrow from the box serves as a postcondition, and it is the responsibility of the block itself to make it true before transmitting the token through that exit.

The correctness of the composed flowchart may be determined locally in the usual way, by considering the assertions on each arrow and on each place. For an arrow which connects a single exit point to a single entry (usually on another box), the exit assertion of the box at the tail of the arrow must logically imply the entry assertion of the box at its head. For a place, the rule is a natural extension of this. A place is correct if the assertion on *each* one of its entry arrows logically implies *every* one of the assertions at the heads of its exit arrows. In other words, the verification condition for a place is that the disjunction of all the tail assertions implies the conjunction of all the head assertions (see Figure 2.1, where the upper case letters stand for the arrows annotated by the corresponding lower case letter). Thus overall correctness of the entire flowchart can be proved in a modular fashion, just one arrow or place or action at a time.

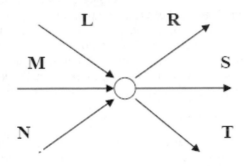

Correctness condition: $L \vee M \vee N \Rightarrow R \wedge S \wedge T$
Behaviour: $(l + m + n) ; (r + s + t)$

Fig. 2.1. A Petri net place

The intention of drawing a box of a structured flowchart is that the details of the flowchart inside the box should be irrelevant to the rest of the flowchart that lies outside the box. From the outside, you only need to know three items: (1) the names of the entry and exit points; these are used to specify how the box is connected into its environment (2) the assertions on the arrows that enter and leave the box; and (3) the constraints that govern the order of entry and exit events, by which the token enters and leaves the box along the arrows that cross the perimeter. If two boxes have the same assertions and the same set of behaviours, we define them to be semantically equivalent.

This rule of equivalence may be applied to just a single place. As a result, any complete collection of linked Petri net places, in which all the entries are connected to all the exits, can be replaced by a single place, -- one that has all the same entries and the exits, but the internal arrows are eliminated. Figure 2.2 therefore has the same semantics as Figure 2.1.

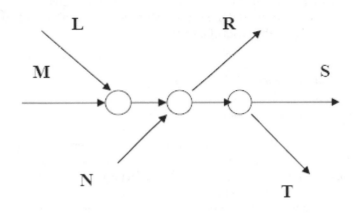

Correctness condition: $L \lor M \lor N \Rightarrow R \land S \land T$
Behaviour: $(l + m + n) ; (r + s + t)$

Fig. 2.2. The same place as Figure 2.1

3   Definition of a Transaction

A compensable transaction is a special kind of box in a Petri net. It is defined as a box whose names, behaviour and assertions satisfy a given set of constraints. The first constraint is a naming constraint.

A transaction box has two entry points named *start* and *failback* (which triggers a compensation), and three exit points named *finish, fail* and *throw*. The intended function of each of these points is indicated by its name, and will be more precisely described by the other constraints. When a transaction is represented as a box, we introduce the convention that these entries and exits should be distributed around the perimeter as shown in Figure 3.1. As a result, our diagrams will usually omit the names, since the identity of each arrow is indicated by its relative position on the perimeter of the box.

A more significant part of the formal definition of a transaction is a behavioural constraint, constraining the order in which the token is allowed to enter and exit the block at each entry and exit point. The constraint is conveniently defined by a regular expression:

start ; (finish ; failback)* ; (fail + throw + finish)

This expression stipulates that the first activation of the transaction is triggered by entry of the token at the *start* point. The last de-activation of the transaction is when the token leaves at any one of the three exit points. In between these two events, the transaction may engage in any number of intermediate exits and entries. On each iteration, it finishes successfully, but is later required to compensate by a *failback* entry, triggered by failure of the following sequentially composed transaction. The number of occurrences of *finish* followed by *failback* is not limited, and may even be zero. Typical complete behaviours of a transaction are:

> *start, finish*
> *start, finish, failback, fail*
> *start, finish, failback, finish*
> *start, finish, failback, finish, failback, throw*

The final constraint in the definition of a transaction governs the assertions on its entry and exit points. This constraint expresses the primary and most essential property of a transaction: that if it fails, it has already returned the world to a state that is sufficiently close to the original initial state.

Sufficient closeness might be defined in many ways, but we give the weakest reasonable definition. Our simple requirement is that on failure the world has been returned to a state which again satisfies the initial precondition of the transaction. More precisely, the assertion on the *fail* exit, must be the same original precondition that labels the *start* entry point. Similarly, on *failback* the transaction may assume that the postcondition that it previously established on finishing is again valid. These standard assertional constraints are indicated by the annotations in Figure 3.1. There is no constraint on the assertion E labelling the *throw* exit.

Many of the constructions of our calculus of transactions can be applied to transactions which satisfy weaker or stronger assertional constraints than the standard described above. For example, a transaction may be *exactly* compensable if on failure it returns to exactly the original state (where obviously the state of the world must be defined to exclude such observations as the real time clock). A weaker constraint is that the postcondition of failure is merely implied by the precondition. Finally, there is the possibility that the transaction has no assertional constraint at all. We will not further consider these variations.

In drawing diagrams with many boxes, the assertions on the arrows will often be omitted. It is assumed that in concrete examples they will be restored in any way that satisfies the intended assertional constraint, and also satisfies the local correctness criterion for assertions, which apply to all arrows and all places.

That concludes our semantic definition of the concept of a transaction. The flowchart gives an operational semantics, describing how the transactions are executed. The assertions give an axiomatic semantics, describing how the transactions are specified and proved correct. The interpretation of a flowchart makes it fairly obvious that the operational and the axiomatic definitions are in close accord.

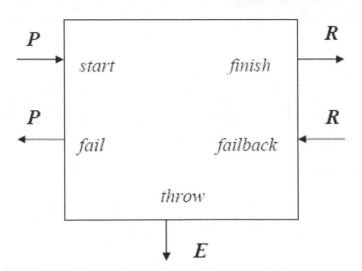

Fig. 3.1. Entry and exit names

4   A Calculus of Transactions

In this section we will define a small calculus for design and implementation of transactions. They are built up by applying the operators that we define to smaller by building them from smaller component transactions. The ultimate components are ordinary fragments of sequential program. Our semantic definitions will mainly use the pictorial representation shown in Figure 3.1. But for the sake of completeness, here is a more conventional syntax.

<transaction> ::= <composed transaction> | *<primitive transaction>*
<primitive transaction> ::= **succeed** | *fail* | *throw* |
                                          <transaction declaration>
<transaction declaration> ::= [*<forward action>* **comp** *compensation>*]
<forward action> ::= <ordinary program>
<compensation> ::= <ordinary program>
<composed transaction> ::= <sequential composition>
           | *<alternative composition>* | *<exception block>* |
              <non-deterministic choice>
<sequential composition>::= <transaction> ; *<transaction>*
<alternative composition> ::= <transaction> **else** *<transaction>*
<exception block> ::= <transaction> **catch** *< transaction>*
<non-deterministic choice> ::= <transaction> **or** *< transaction>*

The shortest primitive transactions are those that do nothing. There are three ways of doing nothing: by succeeding, by failing, or by throwing. Definitions for these transactions are given diagrammatically in Figure 4.1, where the small unconnected arrows will never be activated. The leftmost example does nothing but succeed, and this can obviously be compensated by doing nothing again. The other two examples do nothing but fail or throw. These will never be called upon to compensate.

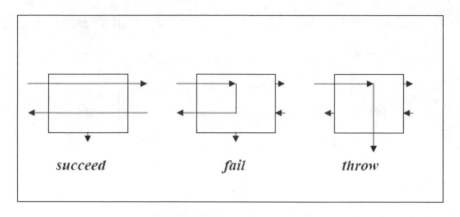

Fig. 4.1. Primitive Transactions

Longer running transactions are constructed by composing smaller ones in sequence, or as alternatives, or as a non-deterministic choice, or by try/catch clauses. In all cases, the result of the composition of compensable transactions will also be a compensable transaction. The semantics of each construction will be explained diagrammatically as a box that encloses the boxes representing the components. Some of the exit arrows of each component box will be connected to some of the entry arrows of the other component box, and thereby become internal arrows that can be ignored from outside. Entries and exits on the surrounding box are connected to remaining exits and entries of the component boxes, often ones that share the same name. Where necessary, places may be introduced to deal with fan-in and fan-out.

The basic primitive fine-grained transaction is declared by specifying two sections of normal sequential code (Figure 4.2). The first of them T performs the required action as control passes from the *start* on the left to the *finish* on the right. The second section of code U specifies how the action should be compensated as control passes back from the *failback* on the right to the *fail* on the left. Either the action or the compensation can throw, on detecting that neither progress nor compensation is possible. The fan-in of the *throw* arrow indicates that it is not known from the outside which of the two components has actually performed the throw. This fan-in of throws is common to most of the operators defined below, and will sometimes be omitted from the diagrams

The first definition of the constructions for non-primitive transactions will be sequential composition, which is shown in Figure 4.3. The outer block denoting the whole composition starts with the *start* of the first component block **T**. The *finish* of this block triggers the *start* of the second component block **U**. The *finish* of the second block finishes the whole sequential composition. A similar story can be told of the backward-going failure path, which performs the two compensations in the reverse order to the forward operations. This is what makes the composed transaction compensable in the same way as its components are. Furthermore, the sequential composition will satisfy the behavioural constraint for transactions, simply because its components do so.

There should be assertions on each of the arrows. However, the permitted patterns for these assertions are completely determined by the correctness principle for flow-charts, so there is no need to mention them explicitly.

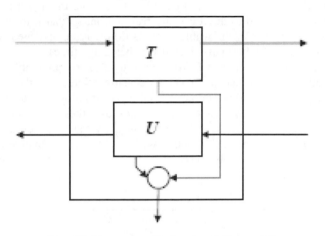

Fig. 4.2. Transaction Declaration: [*T comp U*]

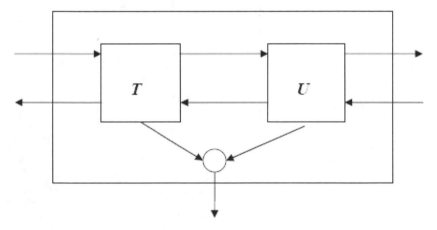

Fig. 4.3. Sequential Composition: *T ; U*

This definition of sequential composition is associative and has **succeed** as its unit. A simple proof of associativity is obtained by drawing the diagram for a sequential composition with three components, and adding an extra box, either around the two left operands or around the two right operands. It is easy to see that this represents the two different bracketings of the associative law. The flowchart itself remains the same in both cases.

The definition of sequential composition states that failure of any component transaction of the sequence will propagate inexorably to the left, until everything that has ever been done since the beginning of time has been undone. This is not always desirable. The *else* operator shown in Figure 4.4 gives a way of halting the stream of failures and compensations. It reverses again the direction of travel of the token, and tries a different way of achieving the same eventual goal.

At most one of these alternatives will actually take effect. The first of them is tried first. If it fails (having compensated of course), the second one is started. If this now succeeds, control is passed to the following transaction, so that it too may try again. As a result, the *finish* exit of the whole composition may be activated twice, or even more often if either of the alternatives itself finishes many times.

Note the fan-in at the *finish* exit: from the outside it is impossible to distinguish which alternative has succeeded on each occasion. Note also the fan-out of the *failback* arrow. In spite of this fan-out, the *else* construction is deterministic. When failback occurs, control may pass to the *failback* of either of the alternatives. The selection of destination will always be determined by the behavioural constraint on the component boxes. As a result, control will pass to the alternative that has most recently finished, which is obviously the right one to perform the appropriate compensation.

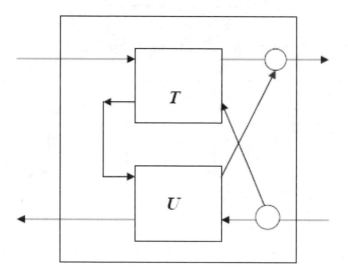

Fig. 4.4. Alternative Composition: *T else U*

In the uncertain world in which computers operate, especially in the vicinity of people, it is quite possible that a transaction that has failed once may succeed when it is simply tried again. But clearly the programmer should control how often to repeat the attempt. For example, suppose it is known that the transaction *U* is strictly compensable. Then the transaction

succeed else succeed else succeed; U

merely causes *U* to be repeated up to three times – that is, up to three times more often than this transaction itself is repeated by its own predecessors.

The *else* operator is associative with unit *fail* . The proof is no more difficult than that for sequential composition.

Because of its deterministic order of execution, the *else* command is asymmetric. Sometimes the programmer does not care which choice is made, and it is acceptable to delegate the choice to the implementation. For this reason, we introduce an *or* constructor, which is symmetric but non-deterministic. Its pictorial definition is very regular, but too cluttered to be worth drawing explicitly. Each entry of the outer box fans out to the like-named entry of both inner boxes. Each exit from the outer box fans in from the like-named exits of the two inner boxes. The non-determinism is introduced by the fan-out of the *start* arrow, which leads to two entries that are both ready to accept the token. After the start, the behavioural constraint ensures that the rejected alternative will never obtain the token. Note that the *fail* arrow of the whole box fans in from the *fail* arrows of both its operands. This shows that the whole box may fail if **either** of its two operands fails. In this respect, non-determinism differs from (and is worse than) the **else** construction, which guarantees to recover from any single failure.

There is yet a third form of choice between alternatives, which plays the role of the external choice in a process algebra. It is denoted by [] in CSP or + in CCS. External choice is slightly more deterministic than *or*, and a bit less deterministic than *else*. Like *or* it is symmetric. Like *else* it recovers from any single failure. It is defined by means of an *else* , where the order of trying the operands is non-deterministic.

$$T \,[]\, U \;=\; (\,T \; else \; U\,) \; or \; (\,U \; else \; T\,)$$

A picture of this operator would have to contain two copies of each of the operands; it is not worth drawing. A conventional equational definition is to be preferred.

This construction $T \,[]\, U$

- fails if both U and T fail
- does U if T fails
- does T if U fails
- chooses non-deterministically if neither fails
- may throw if either T or U can do so.

A *catch* is similar to an *else* in providing an alternative way of achieving the same goal. The difference is that the first operand does not necessarily restore its initial state, and that the second operand is triggered by a *throw* exit instead of a *fail* exit from the first operand. A throw is appropriate when the first operand has been unable either to restore the initial state or to finish successfully. The catching clause is intended to behave like the first operand should have done: either to complete the compensation and fail, or to succeed in the normal way, or else to throw again to some yet more distant catch. Note that the catching clause does not satisfy the assertional constraint for a compensable transaction, because the assertion at its *start* is not the same as the assertion at its *fail* exit.

5   Nested Transactions

We have described in the previous section how a primitive transaction can be declared by specifying a forward action together with its compensation. In the elementary case, both of these are ordinary sequential programs. In this section we will also allow the forward action to be itself a long-running transaction (which we call the child transaction), nested inside a larger parent transaction declaration, as shown in Figure 5.1. As before, the compensation **U** of the parent transaction is an ordinary sequential program, and is triggered from the *failback* entry of the parent transaction. As a result, the *failback* entry of the child transaction **T** is never activated. As a result, when the parent transaction is complete, an implementation can discard the accumulated child compensations, and recover the stack frames and other declared resources of the child transactions.

Nested transactions can be useful as follows. When a long sequence of transactions all succeed, they build up a long sequence of compensations to be executed (in reverse order) in the event of subsequent failure. However, at a certain stage there may be some much better way of achieving the compensation, as it were in a single big step right back to the beginning, rather than in the sequence of small steps accumulated by the child transactions. The new single-step compensation is declared as the compensation for the parent transaction. An example can be taken from a word processing program, where each child transaction deals with a single keystroke, and undoes it when required to compensate. However, when the parent document is complete, any subsequent failure will be compensated by restoring the previous version of the whole document.

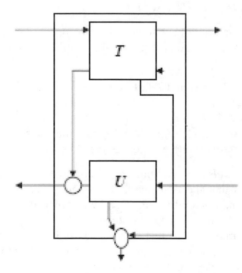

Fig. 5.1. Nested Transaction Declaration

When the child transactions have all finished, their *failback* entries will never subsequently be activated, because (when necessary) the parent compensation is called instead. As a result, at the *finish* of the parent transaction an implementation can simply discard the accumulated child compensations, and recover the stack frames that they occupied.

In addition to stack frames, there may be other resources which need to be released by the child transactions on completion of the parent transaction. In the case of failure, the compensation can do this. But if all the child transactions succeed, we need another mechanism. To provide this requires a significant extension to our definition of a transaction. We add to every transaction (the child transactions as well as the parent) a new entry point called *finally*, placed between the *start* and the *fail*, and a new exit point called *complete*, placed between the *finish* and the *failback*. The nestable transaction declaration therefore takes a third operand, a *completion* action; it is entered by the *finally* entry and exited by the *complete* exit.

When transactions (parents or children) are composed sequentially, their completions are also composed sequentially, like their compensations, by connecting the *complete* exit of the left operand to the *finally* entry of the right operand. So the connecting arrows between completions go from left to right, and the completions are executed in the same order as the forward actions, rather than in the reverse order.

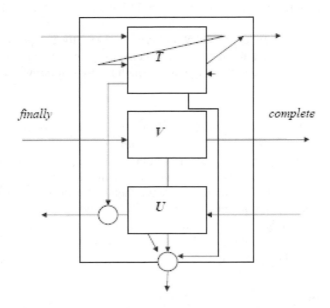

finally

complete

Fig. 5.2. Nesting with Completion [*T finally V comp U*]

In Figure 5.2, the child transaction is denoted T , the parent compensation is U , and the parent completion is V. The child transaction also has a *finally* entry and a *complete* exit, and a completion action, which is not shown explicitly in the diagram. In the case that the child is not a transaction, an ordinary sequential program can be artificially made into a transaction by adding a completion action that does nothing. In that case, the definition of a nested transaction becomes equivalent to that of an un-nested one.

When the whole child transaction has finished, the completions accumulated by the child transactions are triggered. That is indicated in Figure 5.2 by the transverse arrow from the *finally* exit of the child transactions T to the new *finally* entry of the child transactions themselves. It executes the completion actions of all the children, in the same order as the execution of forward actions of the children.

Another benefit of the introduction of completion actions is to implement the *lazy update* design pattern. Each child makes a generally accessible note of the update that it is responsible for performing, but lazily does not perform the update until all the child transactions of the same parent have successfully finished. On seeing the note, the forward action of each subsequent child takes account of the notes left by all previously executed children, and behaves as if the updates postponed by all previous children had already occurred. But on completion of the parent transaction, the real updates are actually performed by the *completion* code provided by each component child transaction. As a result, the rest of the world will never know how lazy the transaction has been. The completion codes will be executed in the same sequence as the forward actions of the children. Compensations for lazy transactions tend to be rather simple, since all that is required is to throw away the notes on the actions that should have been performed but have not yet been.

Introduction of the new *finally* entry and *complete* exit for completion actions requires an extension to the definition of the behavioural constraint on transactions. Note that a completion is not allowed to fail, though it may still throw.

$$start \; ; \; X$$

where $X = fail + throw + (finish \; ; \; (\; finally \; ; \; (\; complete + throw \;)$
$$+ failback \; ; \; X \;))$$

The definition of sequential composition and other operators needs to be adapted to accommodate the addition of new entry and exit points for the completion actions. The adaptations are fairly obvious, and we leave them to the interested reader.

The nesting of transactions may seem unpleasantly complex, but the concept of nesting is essential to deal with the wide range of granularity at which the concept of atomicity can be applied. Many kinds of transaction will last a few microseconds, whereas others may last a few months.

6 Concurrency

The Petri net place has provided a mechanism for fan-in and fan-out of the arrows of a flowchart. Each activation (firing) of the place involves the entry of a single token along a single **one** of the entry arrow, and the exit of the same token along any **one** of its exit arrows. As a result, a place always maintains the number of tokens in the net – in our treatment so far, there has only been just one token.

Introduction and elimination of tokens from the net is the purpose of the other primitive element of a Petri net, the transition. This too provides a form of fan-in and fan-out, but its behavioural rule is conjunctive rather than disjunctive, universal rather than existential. Each firing of a transition requires the entry of a token on **all** of its entry arrows, and the emission of a token on **all** of its exit arrows. The notation used for transitions is shown in Figure 6.1.

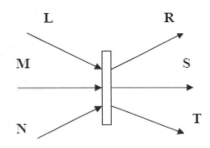

Correctness condition: **L & M & N ⇒ R & S & T**

Behaviour: *(l ‖ m ‖ n) ; (r ‖ s ‖ t)*

Fig. 6.1. Petri net transition

If there is only one entry to a transition, it acts as a fan-out: its firing will increase the number of tokens travelling simultaneously in the network. This could certainly lead to confusion if one of the tokens ever meets another at the same place. By allowing only limited and well-structured forms of composition, our calculus will confine each token to a disjoint region of the net, and ensure that tokens meet only at the entry to a transition, which is what is intended. Often, such a meeting place is a fan-in; it has only one exit, so that it reduces the number of tokens in the system.

It is possible to think of all the entry and exit events for a transition as occurring simultaneously. However, in representing this simultaneous behaviour as a regular expression, it is common to use a total ordering of events, in which any causal event occurs before its effect. Furthermore, arbitrary interleaving is commonly used to record sequentially events that occur simultaneously. The regular expression (P ‖ Q) will stand for the set of all interleavings of a string from P with a string from Q . Thus the behavioural constraint on a transition in Figure 6.1 is that the arrival in any order of a token on all of the entry arrows will trigger the emission of a token on each and every one of the exit arrows, again in any order.

The correctness of a transition obviously requires that **all** the assertions on all the exit arrows must be valid at the time of firing. In this respect, the transition is like a place. It differs from a place in the precondition that **all** the assertions on the entry arrows may be assumed to be true when the transition fires. Thus the correctness condition on a transition is that the conjunction of all the entry assertions must logically imply the conjunction of all the exit assertions. In general, there is a possibility that the conjunction will be inconsistent; but we will design our calculus carefully to avoid this risk.

The semantics of the Petri net transition is given in terms of its correctness condition and its behaviour. Thus it satisfies the same equivalence criterion as the place: any acyclic network of pure transitions (in which every external exit is reachable from every external entry) is equivalent to a single transition with exactly the same external entry and exit arrows, but omitting the internal arrows.

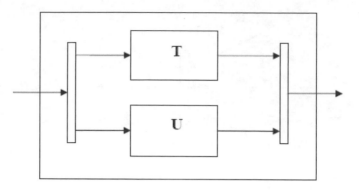

Fig. 6.2. Parallel composition: T ‖ U

We will explain the concept of well-structured concurrency first in the context of ordinary programs, which have only a single entry and a single exit arrow. Concurrent composition of two such programs is made to satisfy the same constraint, as shown in Figure 6.2. This shows how two sections of code **T** and **U** will start simultaneously and proceed concurrently until they have both finished. Only then does the concurrent combination finish.

It is evident from the diagram (and from the structured property of boxes) that the only meeting point of the two tokens generated by the fan-out transition on the left will be at the final fan-in transition on the right, where they are merged. The diagram can easily be adapted to deal with three or more threads. But this is not necessary, because the rules of equivalence for transitions ensure that concurrent composition is both an associative and a commutative operator.

The proof of correctness of concurrent threads should be modular in the same way as proof of correctness of all the other forms of composition. In order to make this possible, some disjointness constraints must be placed on the actions of the individual threads. The simplest constraint is that no thread can access any variable updated by some other concurrent thread. This same constraint must also be applied to the assertions used to prove correctness of each thread. The token which travels within a thread can be regarded as carrying the variables and owned by that thread, together with their values.

In simple cases, the constraint on disjointness can be enforced by a compile-time check on the global variables accessed by a thread. But in general, the use of indirect addressing (for example, in an object-oriented program) will make it necessary to prove disjointness by including some notion of ownership into the assertion language. Separation logic provides an elegant and flexible means of expressing disjointness of ownership, and establishing it by means of proof. However, we will not pursue this issue further here.

The disjointness constraint is effective in ensuring consistency of the final assertions of the threads when they all terminate together. It also avoids race conditions at run time, and so prevents any form of unwanted interference between the activities of the threads. However, it also rules out any form of beneficial interaction or cooperation between them. In particular, it rules out any sharing of internal storage or communication channels. A safe relaxation of this restriction is provided by atomic regions (or critical sections). This is defined as a section of code inside a thread, which is allowed to access and update a shared resource. The implementation must guarantee (for example by an exclusion semaphore) that only one thread at a time can be executing inside an atomic region, so race conditions are still avoided. The overall effect of multiple threads updating the shared resource includes an arbitrary interleaving of the execution of their complete atomic regions.

The Petri net formalisation of an atomic region models a shared resource as a token, which may be regarded as carrying the current state and value of the resource. At the beginning of an atomic region, a thread acquires ownership of this token in order to access and update the shared resource; and at the end of the region the shared resource is released. Of course, execution of the region also requires the normal sequential token of the thread that contains it.

An atomic region is defined (Figure 6.3) as a sort of inverse of concurrent composition, with a fan-in at the beginning and a fan-out at the end. For simplicity, we assume that there is only a single shared resource, consisting of everything except the private resources of the currently active individual threads. In most practical applications, many separate resources will need to be declared, but we shall not deal with that complexity here.

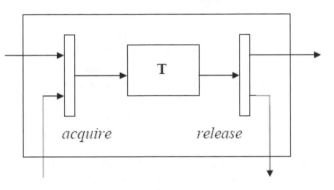

Fig. 6.3. Atomic Region: atomic[T]

The definition of an atomic region requires the introduction of another entry and another exit into the standard repertoire. The entry carries the suggestive name *acquire*, and the exit is called *release*. The new entries and exits require extension of the behavioural constraint, by inserting (*acquire;release*)* between every entry and the next following exit. The definition of all the operators of our calculus must also be extended: but this is very simple, because in each diagram defining an operator, all the *acquire* entries are connected via a fan-out place, and all the *release* exits are connected via a fan-in place.

The declaration of a sharable resource is shown in Figure 6.4. The token that represents a resource is created by means of a transition fan-out. The block **T** contains all the multiple threads that are going to share the resource. When all of them have finished, the token is therefore merged again. The assertion **R** is known as the resource invariant: it must be true at the beginning of **T** and at the end of every atomic region within **T**. Conversely, **R** may be assumed true at the end of the whole block **T**, and at the beginning of every atomic region within it. Note that in this diagram the place is expected to store the token between successive executions of the atomic regions.

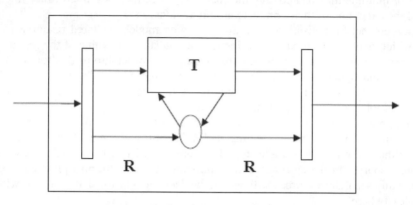

Fig. 6.4. Resource Declaration: resource R in T

The explicit statement of a resource invariant permits a very necessary relaxation of the restriction that the assertions used within the threads of **T** may not refer to the values of the variables of the shared resource, for fear that they are subject to concurrent update by concurrent threads. The relaxed restriction states that all of the assertions private to a thread (initial, internal or final) may mention the values of the shared resource, but only in a way that is tolerant of interference. This means that the local assertions of each thread must also be an invariant of every atomic region that may be invoked by the other threads.

A direct application of this proof rule would require proof of each thread to know all the internal assertions in every other thread -- a serious violation of the principal of locality of proof. A stronger but more modular condition is that each thread must prove locally that all its assertions are invariant of any section of code **X** that leaves **R** invariant. The details of the formalisation will not be elaborated here.

The definition of concurrent composition given in Figure 6.2 applies to fragments of ordinary program with a single entry and a single exit. Our final task is to apply the same idea to compensable transactions, with many more entries and exits. The basic definition of concurrency of transactions introduces a transition to fan out each entry of the concurrent block to the two (or more) like-named entries of the components; and similarly, it introduces a transition to fan in the like-named exits of the components to relevant exit of the whole composition (Figure 6.5). This means that the compensations of concurrent transactions will also be executed concurrently in the same way as their forward actions.

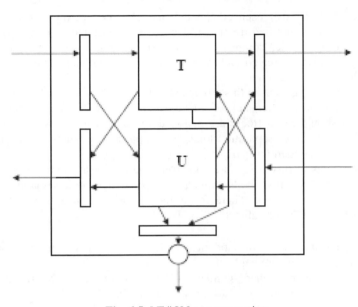

Fig. 6.5. [T ‖ U] as a transaction

This scheme works well, provided that both components agree on which exit to activate on each occasion -- either they both finish, or they both fail, or they both throw. The availability of a shared resource enables them to negotiate an agreement as required. However, if they fail to do so, the result is deadlock, and no further action is possible. It may be a good idea to complicate the definition of concurrency of transactions to avoid this unfortunate possibility automatically, by doing something sensible in each case. Four additional transitions are needed to implement the necessary logic.

(1) if one component **T** finishes and **U** fails, these two exits are fanned in by a transition, whose exit leads to the *failback* of the successful **T** .

(2) Similarly, if **U** finishes and **T** fails, the *failback* of **U** is invoked.

(3) In the case that **T** performs a throw but **U** does not, the whole construction must throw. This involves connecting **U**'s *finish* and *fail* exits via a place to a transition that joins it with the *throw* exit of **T** .

(4) A similar treatment deals with the case that **U** performs a throw.

7 Conclusion

This paper gives a simple account using Petri nets of long-running transactions with compensations. The account is also quite formal, in the sense that the nets for any transaction composed solely by the principles described can actually be drawn, programmed and executed by computer. The assertions on the arrows give guidance on how to design correctness into a system of transactions from the earliest stage. The correctness principle for places and transitions serves as an axiomatic semantics, and shows how to prove the correctness of a complete flowchart in a modular way, by proving the correctness of each component and each connecting arrow separately. Thus we have given a unified treatment of both an operational and an axiomatic semantics for compensable, composable and nestable transactions. Simple cases of concurrency can also be treated, but more work, both theoretical and experimental, is needed to deal with more general cases.

The more surprising ideas in this article are (1) use of the precondition of a transaction as the criterion of adequacy of an approximation to the initial state that the compensation should reach (there are many more complicated ways of doing this); and (2) the suggestion of separation logic as an appropriate language for annotating the transitions of a concurrent Petri net.

The deficiencies of this article are numerous and obvious. There are no transition rules, no deductive systems, no algebraic axioms, no denotational semantic functions, no proofs and no references. There is far more work still to be done by anyone sufficiently interested in the subject.

Acknowledgements. The ideas and presentation of this paper have been greatly improved by the helpful comments of:

Michael Butler, Ernie Cohen, Tim Harris, Niels Lohmann, Jay Misra, Eliot Moss, Matthew Parkinson, Simon Peyton Jones, Viktor Vafeiadis.

SCOOP – A Contract-Based Concurrent Object-Oriented Programming Model

Benjamin Morandi[1], Sebastian S. Bauer[2], and Bertrand Meyer[1]

[1] Chair of Software Engineering, Swiss Federal Institute of Technology Zurich,
Switzerland
`firstname.lastname@inf.ethz.ch`
`http://se.inf.ethz.ch/`
[2] Institut für Informatik, Ludwig-Maximilians-Universität München, Germany
`sebastian.bauer@pst.ifi.lmu.de`
`http://www.pst.ifi.lmu.de/`

Abstract. SCOOP is a concurrent object-oriented programming model based on contracts. The model introduces processors as a new concept and it generalizes existing object-oriented concepts for the concurrent context. Simplicity is the main objective of SCOOP. The model guarantees the absence of data races in any execution of a SCOOP program. This article is a technical description of SCOOP as defined by Nienaltowski [11] and Meyer [7,9,10].

1 Introduction

In a semaphore based concurrent programming model it is the responsibility of developers to ensure proper synchronization between threads. With respect to safety, no undesirable interference between threads must occur. In general, this is a global property of a program that requires global analysis. With respect to liveness, every thread should progress eventually. Again, this is a global property. Another issue comes from the limited reusability of classes. A class whose instances should be accessed by multiple threads must be annotated with correct synchronization code. In general, a class that is not annotated accordingly can only be used sequentially.

SCOOP stands for *Simple Concurrent Object-Oriented Programming*. This name captures what SCOOP is all about – a simple object-oriented programming model for concurrency. SCOOP is simple because it introduces only few new concepts on top of an object-oriented programming model. This makes SCOOP simple to understand. SCOOP is simple because it helps to avoid common correctness and liveness issues due to improper synchronization. SCOOP is also simple because a class does not need to be annotated with synchronization code before it can be used in a concurrent program. This fosters reusability. SCOOP is simple because it supports sequential reasoning on concurrent programs. There are many reasons why SCOOP is simple and the following sections will explain in more details where the simplicity is coming from. The risk of simplicity is

P. Müller (Ed.): LASER Summer School 2007/2008, LNCS 6029, pp. 41–90, 2010.

the loss of expressiveness on account of too many restrictions. SCOOP preserves object-oriented expressivity because it generalizes existing object-oriented concepts in the concurrent context. Sequential programs are treated as a subset of a concurrent programs. As presented here, SCOOP builds on Eiffel [4]; however, it is possible to extend other object-oriented programming models with SCOOP. The key requirements of such an programming model are the presence of contracts and a static type system.

SCOOP has gone through several iterations of refinement. The initial model was proposed by Meyer [7,9,10]. Nienaltowski worked on consistency and usability of the model. The following sections provide a concise description of the SCOOP model as presented by Nienaltowski in his PhD dissertation [11]. The next section shows an introductory example to give a brief overview on SCOOP. The remaining sections cover the details. Sections 3, 5 and 6 describe the essence of the computational model. Sections 4, 8, 9, and 10 define the type system. Section 7 describes the impact of SCOOP on contracts and sections 11, 12, and 13 discuss advanced object-oriented mechanisms. We conclude with section 14 on limitations and future work.

2   Example

This section introduces an implementation of a producer-consumer scenario written in SCOOP. The concepts introduced in this example will be explained in depth in the following sections.

A producer-consumer application consists of a number of producers and a number of consumers. Both producers and consumers have access to a shared fixed-size buffer. Producers store elements in the buffer and consumers retrieve elements from the buffer. A producer must not be allowed to add elements to the buffer if it is full. A consumer must not be allowed to remove elements from an empty buffer. The access to the buffer must be restricted to one actor at a time.

Listing 1.1. producer class

```
1 class PRODUCER[G]

3 inherit
    PROCESS
5
  create
7   make

9 feature {NONE} -- Initialization
    make (a_buffer: separate BOUNDED_QUEUE[G])
11      -- Create a producer with 'a_buffer'.
    do
```

```
13      buffer := a_buffer
      ensure
15      buffer = a_buffer
      end
17
   feature -- Basic operations
19   step
         -- Produce an element and store it in 'buffer'.
21   local
         l_element: G
23   do
         l_element := ...
25      store (buffer, l_element)
      end
27
   feature {NONE} -- Implementation
29   buffer: separate BOUNDED_QUEUE[G]
         -- The buffer.
31
      store (a_buffer: separate BOUNDED_QUEUE[G]; a_element: G)
33         -- Store 'a_element' in 'a_buffer'.
      require
35      a_buffer_is_not_full: not a_buffer.is_full
      do
37      a_buffer.put (a_element)
      ensure
39      a_element_is_added: a_buffer.count = old a_buffer.count + 1
      end
41 end
```

Listing 1.2. consumer class

```
1 class CONSUMER[G]

3 inherit
   PROCESS
5
   create
7   make

9 feature {NONE} -- Initialization
   make (a_buffer: separate BOUNDED_QUEUE[G])
11      -- Create a consumer with 'a_buffer'.
      do
```

```
13      buffer := a_buffer
        ensure
15      buffer = a_buffer
        end
17
   feature -- Basic operations
19  step
           -- Consume an element from 'buffer'.
21  local
        l_element: G
23  do
        retrieve (buffer)
25      l_element := last_element
        ...
27  end

29 feature {NONE} -- Implementation
     buffer: separate BOUNDED_QUEUE[G]
31     -- The buffer.

33   retrieve (a_buffer: separate BOUNDED_QUEUE[G])
              -- Retrieve an element from 'a_buffer' and store it in '
                 last_element'.
35       require
             a_buffer_is_not_empty: not a_buffer.is_empty
37       do
             last_element := a_buffer.item
39           a_buffer.remove
           ensure
41           last_element_is_set: last_element = old a_buffer.item
             a_buffer_is_decreased: a_buffer.count = old a_buffer.count - 1
43       end

45   last_element: G
   end
```

Producers and consumers repeatedly perform a sequence of actions. Producers store elements into the buffer and consumers retrieve elements from the buffer. Producers and consumers can therefore be modeled as processes. Both of the classes inherit from a class *PROCESS*, which is not shown here. The class *PROCESS* offers a deferred feature *step*, which gets called over and over again as soon as the feature *live* is called. Therefore the main activities of producers and consumers are enclosed by their respective implementations of *step*.

Both producers and consumers operate on a shared buffer attached to *buffer*. The type **separate** *BOUNDED_QUEUE[G]* of these two features is of interest.

The class type $BOUNDED\_QUEUE[G]$ specifies the nature of the buffer: It is a bounded queue with elements of a type G. The keyword **separate** is a SCOOP specific addition to the type system. In SCOOP every object is associated to a processor that is responsible for the sequential execution of instructions on that object. One object can only be associated to one processor, but one processor can be responsible for multiple objects. The **separate** keyword defines that the object attached to the entity of such a type can potentially be handled by a different processor than the processor of the current object. In the absence of this keyword the object must be handled by same processor as the current object. If two objects are on different processors then the two processors can execute features on these objects in parallel. In this example, we want to achieve this for the buffer. Features on the buffer should be executed in parallel to the features on producers and consumers. Thus the buffer needs to be on its own processor. This is reflected in the type of the buffer.

The problem description asks for mutual exclusion on the buffer. In SCOOP locks are granted on the granularity level of processors. Locking a processor means exclusive access to all the objects handled by the processor. Prior to its execution, every feature automatically requests the locks on all the processors of the attached formal arguments. The feature cannot be executed until all the requested locks got granted. In the producer and consumer classes it is therefore necessary to enclose the calls to the buffer in features taking the buffer as an attached formal argument in order to satisfy the exclusivity requirement. For this purpose, the producer class has a feature *store* that takes the buffer and the element as formal arguments. A call to *store* gets delayed until the producer acquired the lock on the buffer. Note that the lock on the element is already given because the missing **separate** keyword in the type of the element implies that the element and the producer are on the same processor. Next to the locks there is another constraint that must be satisfied before *store* can be executed. The feature has a precondition asking for the buffer not to be full, as specified. As the buffer is shared among different producers and consumers, the responsibility to satisfy the precondition is also shared among the different producers and consumers. The precondition therefore turns into a wait condition as *store* needs to wait for the precondition to be satisfied. In summary, *store* can only be executed when the precondition is satisfied and the necessary locks are acquired. A similar argument is true for the feature *retrieve* of the consumer. In the next section, we start with an elaboration on the computational model of SCOOP.

3   Processors, Objects, and the Scheduler

Processors and objects are the basic computational units in SCOOP. A processor is an autonomous thread of control capable of executing features on objects. Every processor is responsible for a set of objects. In this context, a processor is called the handler of the associated objects. Every object is assigned to exactly one processor that is the authority of feature executions on this object. If a processor q wants to call a feature on a target handled by a different processor p then q needs to send a feature request to processor p. This is where the request queue of processor p comes into place. The request queue keeps track of features to be executed on behalf of other processors. Processor q can add a request to this queue and processor p will execute the request as soon as it executed all previous requests in the request queue. Processor p uses its call stack is used to execute the feature request at the beginning of the request queue. Before processor q can add a request, it must have a lock on processor p's request queue. Otherwise another processor could intervene. Once processor q is done with the request queue of processor p it can add an unlock operation to the end of the request queue. This will make sure that the request queue lock of p will be released after all the previous feature requests have been executed. Similarly, processor p must have a lock on its call stack to add features to it. To simplify this, every processor starts with a lock on its own call stack. Section 5 on the semantics of feature calls and feature applications will explain the interaction between processors in more details. In conclusion, a processor and its object form a sequential system. The overall concurrent system can be seen as a collection of interacting sequential systems. A sequential system can be seen as a particular case of a concurrent system with only one processor.

Definition 1 (Processor). *A processor is an autonomous thread of control capable of supporting the sequential execution of instructions on one or more objects. Every processor has the following elements:*

- *Handled objects: It keeps track of the handled objects.*
- *Request queue: It keeps track of features to be executed on objects handled by the processor. Requests in the request queue are serviced in the order of their arrival.*
- *Call stack: It is used for the application of features.*
- *Locks: It contains all the locks held by the processor, as defined in definition 2.*

Definition 2 (Processor locks). *For every processor there exists a lock on the request queue and a lock on the call stack. A lock on the request queue grants permission to add a feature request to the end of the request queue. A lock on the call stack grants permission to add a feature request to the top of the call stack. Initially every processor has a lock on its own call stack and its request queue is not locked.*

Definition 3 (Processor loop). *A processor loops through the following sequence of actions:*

1. *Idle wait: If both the call stack and the request queue are empty then wait for new requests to be enqueued.*
2. *Request scheduling: If the call stack is empty but the request queue is not empty then dequeue an item and push it onto the call stack.*
3. *Request processing: If there is an item on the call stack then pop the item from the call stack and process it.*

- *If the item is a feature request then apply the feature.*
- *If the items is an unlock operation then unlock the request queue of the processor.*

In the standard case, every processor keeps the lock on its own call stack. A processor needs this lock to dequeue items from the request queue and put them on the call stack, as described in definition 3. Normally, only the request queue is used for the communication between different processors. Section 5 will show how this can be different. In the following we will introduce an abstraction under the assumption that every processor keeps its call stack lock. In this abstraction we call the request queue lock on a processor p simply the lock on p. As long as the call stack lock on a processor p is in possession of p, a request queue lock on p in possession of a processor q means that processor p will be executing new feature requests in the request queue exclusively on behalf of q. This means that a request queue lock grants exclusive access to all the objects handled by p. Transferring this insight to our abstractions, a lock on processor p denotes exclusive access to the objects handled by p. We used the abstraction in the beginning of the article, as it is easier to begin with. In the remaining sections we will not make use of this abstraction anymore.

As stated earlier, there is only one processor that can execute features on a particular object. As a consequence, any execution of a SCOOP program is free ob low-level data races that occur when multiple processors access an attribute of an object at the same time and there is at least one write access. Proposition 1 expresses this fact.

Proposition 1. *A SCOOP system is free of low-level data races.*

As mentioned, a request queue can only be accessed by a processor that is in possession of the corresponding request queue lock. The execution of a feature requires access to request queues of other processors. Therefore it is necessary to obtain request queue locks prior to the execution of a feature so that these request queues can be accessed during the execution. There might be more than one processor whose current feature request requires a particular lock. This is where the scheduler comes into place. The scheduler is the arbiter for feature requests. More details on this will be given in section 5. The model permits a number of possible scheduling algorithms. Scheduling algorithms differ in their level of fairness and their performance. In this article we do not focus on a particular instance. More information on particular scheduling algorithms can be found in Nienaltowski's dissertation [11].

Definition 4 (Scheduler). *The scheduler is responsible for scheduling feature applications.*

Processors bring a new dimension to feature calls because feature calls can either happen within one processor or from one processor to another. Thus feature calls can be separate or non-separate depending on the location of the client and the target object.

Definition 5 (Separateness). *Objects that are handled by different processors are separate from each other. All the objects on the same processor are non-separate from each other. A feature call is separate if and only if the target and the client objects are separate. A references to a separate object is called a separate reference.*

4   Types

4.1   Definition

In SCOOP two objects are either separate or non-separate with respect to each other. The separateness depends on the location of the two objects. Throughout the following sections, the relative location of one object to another object will be of importance. Thus there needs to be a way of computing this information. SCOOP uses a refinement of the Eiffel type system to keep track of the relative locations. The Eiffel type system is based on detachable tags and classes. The detachable tag defines whether an entity is allowed to be void or not. In SCOOP the detachable tag has an additional meaning. Section 5 will show that only objects attached to attached entities will be locked. In order to argue about separateness the type system must accommodate the locality of objects in addition to the existing type components. The following definitions refine the definitions in section 8.11 of the Eiffel ECMA standard [4].

Definition 6 (Type). *A type is represented as a triple $T = (d, p, C)$ with the following components:*

- *The component d is the detachable tag as described by definition 7.*
- *The component p is the processor tag as described by definition 8.*
- *The component C is the class type.*

A type is always relative to the instance of the class where the type is declared. An actual generic parameter is always relative to the instance of the class where the corresponding formal generic parameter is declared.

Definition 7 (Detachable tag). *The detachable tag d captures detachability and selective locking.*

- *An entity can be of attached type, formally written as $d = !$. Entities of an attached type are statically guaranteed to be non-void. Only request queues of processors handling arguments of attachable type get locked.*
- *An entity can be of detachable type, formally written as $d = ?$. Entities of detachable type can be void. Request queues of processors handling arguments of detachable type do not get locked.*

Definition 8 (Processor tag). *The processor tag p captures the locality of objects accessed by an entity of type T.*

- *The processor tag p can be separate, formally written as $p = \top$. The object attached to the entity of type T is potentially handled by a different processor than the current processor.*
- *The processor tag p can be explicit, formally written as $p = \alpha$. The object attached to the entity of type T is handled by the processor specified by α. Definition 9 shows how a processor can be specified explicitly.*
- *The processor tag p can be non-separate, formally written as $p = \bullet$. The object attached to the entity of type T is handled by the current processor.*
- *The processor tag p can denote no processor, formally written as $p = \bot$. It is used to type the void reference.*

Note the difference between a separate type and a separate object. A separate object is on a different processor. An entity of a separate type stores a potentially separate object.

Definition 9 (Explicit processor specification). *A processor can be specified explicitly either in an unqualified or a qualified way. An unqualified explicit processor specification is based on a processor attribute p. The processor attribute p must have the type $(!, \bullet, PROCESSOR)$ and it must be declared in the same class as the explicit processor specification or in one of the ancestors. The processor denoted by this explicit processor specification is the processor stored in p. A qualified explicit processor specification relies on an entity e occurring in the same class as the explicit processor specification or in one of the ancestors. The entity e must be a non-writable entity of attached type and the type of e must not have a qualified explicit processor tag. The processor denoted by this explicit processor specification is the same processor as the one of the object referenced by e.*

Explicit processor tags support precise reasoning about object locality. Entities declared with the same processor tag represent objects handled by the same processor. The type system takes advantage of this information to support safe attachments and safe feature calls. A qualified explicit processor specification can only be defined on a non-writable entity of attached type to facilitate static type checking. Possibly void or writable entities would require an analysis of the runtime behavior. This would make static type checking unfeasible. The type of the entity e must not have a qualified explicit processor tag itself. This restriction prevents dependency cycles among processor tags.

4.2   Syntax

SCOOP extends the Eiffel type syntax to incorporate the enhanced type definition.

Definition 10 (Type syntax)

$type \triangleq$
     $[detachable\_tag]$

$[separate]$ $[explicit\_processor\_specification]$
$class\_name$ $[actual\_generics]$

$detachable\_tag$ ≜
    $attached$ | $detachable$

$explicit\_processor\_specification$ ≜
    $qualified\_explicit\_processor\_specification$ |
    $unqualified\_explicit\_processor\_specification$

$qualified\_explicit\_processor\_specification$ ≜
    ">" $entity\_name$ "." $handler$ ">"

$unqualified\_explicit\_processor\_specification$ ≜
    ">" $entity\_name$ ">"

The absence of both the attached *and* detachable *keyword implies an attached type.*

The SCOOP syntax change is minimal and ensures backward compatibility to plain Eiffel programs. Definition 10 anticipates a change in the syntax of the detachable tag which is not yet part of the Eiffel ECMA standard [4].

Example 1 (Type syntax). Listing 1.3 shows a couple of attributes along with their types. The comments attached to the attributes explain what is meant by the syntax.

Listing 1.3. type syntax example

```
   a: BOOK                                  -- (!, •, BOOK)
 2 b: separate BOOK                         -- (!, ⊤, BOOK)
   c: separate <p> BOOK                     -- (!, p, BOOK)
 4 d: attached BOOK                         -- (!, •, BOOK)
   e: attached separate BOOK                -- (!, ⊤, BOOK)
 6 f: attached separate <a.handler> BOOK    -- (!, a.handler, BOOK)
   g: detachable BOOK                       -- (?, •, BOOK)
 8 h: detachable separate BOOK              -- (?, ⊤, BOOK)
   i: detachable separate <p> BOOK          -- (?, p, BOOK)
10
   p: PROCESSOR
```

4.3   Explicit and Implicit Types

Every entity has an explicit type. It is the type as written in the code. Thanks to the qualified explicit processor specifications, every attached and non-writable entity also has an implicit type. This is stated in definition 11. **Current** is one of these attached and non-writable entities and consequently it has an implicit type. The explicit type of **Current** is shown in definition 12. Definition 13 justifies the processor tag $\perp$. It is used to define the type of the void reference. Hereby, the standard Eiffel class *NONE* is used as the class type, because it is at the bottom of the class hierarchy.

Definition 11 (Implicit type). *An attached non-writable entity e of type $(!, p, C)$ also has an implicit type $(!, e.handler, C)$.*

Definition 12 (Explicit type of the current object). *In the context of a class C, the current object has the type $(!, \bullet, C)$.*

Definition 13 (Explicit type of the void reference). *The void reference has the type $(?, \perp, NONE)$.*

4.4   Expanded Types

Every object is either of reference type or of expanded type. Instances of classes annotated with the keyword **expanded** are objects of expanded type. Other objects are of reference type. The difference between the two categories affects the semantics of attachment. An attachment of an object of a reference type to an entity stores the reference to the object in the entity. An attachment of an object of expanded type copies the object and attaches it to the entity. Section 7.4 of the Eiffel ECMA standard [4] explains this in more details. Due to the copy semantics, an expanded object is never attached to more than one entity and thus expanded objects do not get aliased. One can think of expanded objects to be part of the object to which they are attached. Thus expanded objects are defined to be non-separate. Furthermore, an entity of expanded type never contains the void reference. Thus an expanded type is always an attached type. This leads to the validity definition 14 for expanded types. Syntactically this rule prohibits the use of separate annotations and the question mark as the detachable tag.

Definition 14 (Expanded type validity). *A type T based on an expanded class E is valid if an only if it is attached and non-separate, i.e. $T = (!, \bullet, E)$.*

4.5   Formal Generic Parameters

Formal generic parameters are type parameters for generic classes. A generic derivation must be used to get a type from a generic class. In a generic derivation each formal generic parameter must be substituted by a type, which is the actual generic parameter. Optionally, every formal generic parameter can have a constraint on the actual generic parameter used in the generic derivation. Such a constraint allows the generic class to make assumptions on a formal generic parameter. An implicit generic constraint is used if no explicit constraint is given. In the presence of the new type system the implicit constraint as described in section 8.12.7 of the Eiffel ECMA standard [4] must be generalized. For compatibility with the existing rule the implicit constraint must be attached and have the class type ANY. The class ANY is the root class in the Eiffel class hierarchy. An implicit type should be as general as possible. The separate processor tag is most general and thus definition 15 makes use of it.

Definition 15 (Implicit formal generic parameter constraint). *The constraint of a formal generic parameter is the explicit constraint if present. Otherwise the implicit constraint is* $(!, \top, ANY)$.

4.6   Soundness

SCOOP extends the Eiffel type system with information about object locality. This information can be used to determine whether an object is separate or non-separate. To be sound, the type system must ensure that this information is accurate at all times for all entities. In conjunction with the justifications of the rules and mechanisms, the following sections provide arguments on why the type system is sound. One component of soundness is the absence of traitors as defined in definition 16. However, the absence of traitors does not imply full soundness. Soundness must also be guaranteed for types with explicit processor specifications.

Definition 16 (Traitor). *A traitor is an entity declared as non-separate but pointing to a separate object.*

We defer a full soundness proof to later work as described in section 14.

5   Feature Call and Feature Application

A processor p can call features on objects that are either handled by p or by another processor q. A non-separate call is executed by p itself. For a separate call, processor p needs to ask processor q to execute the feature. In this section we will take a closer look at the steps involved in a feature call and in the subsequent execution, which we call the feature application. As we will see, a separate call can be asynchronous, but a non-separate call is always synchronous. Every feature call happens in the context of a feature application. For this reason we will start with the description of the feature application and then describe the feature call. In the end we will present an example to illustrate once again how the two concepts work together. In terms of contracts, this section only describes the runtime aspects of contracts. A more detailed picture will be given in section 7. The definitions presented in this section generalize the definitions in section 8.23 of the Eiffel ECMA standard [4].

5.1   Feature Application

We start in a situation where a processor p wants to apply a feature request f on a target x. The execution of f will require a number of request queue locks.

Furthermore, the precondition of f must be satisfied before f can be executed. These two prerequisites are established in the synchronization step. This step involves the scheduler. Processor p will wait until the scheduler gives the green light and then execute f. After the execution, the postcondition must be checked. If f is a query then the result must be returned. Finally the obtained request queue locks must be released. Definition 17 captures these steps.

Definition 17 (Feature application). *The application of feature f on target x, requested by a client processor p_c, results in the following sequence of actions performed by the supplier processor p_x:*

1. *Synchronization: Involve the scheduler to wait until the following synchronization conditions are satisfied atomically:*
   - *All the request queues of processors that handle arguments of an attached type in f are locked on behalf of p_x.*
   - *The precondition of f holds.*
2. *Execution*
   - *If f is a routine then run its body.*
   - *If f is an attribute then evaluate it.*
3. *Postcondition evaluation: Every query in the postcondition must be evaluated by its target handler. The result must be combined by p_x if it is involved in the postcondition. Otherwise any involved processor may be used.*
4. *Result returning: If f is a query then return the result to p_c. Results of expanded type need to be imported by the client handler p_c.*
5. *Lock releasing: Add an unlock operation to the end of each request queue that has been locked in the synchronization step.*

Synchronization. Before a feature can be applied there are some synchronization constraints to be fulfilled. First, the supplier processor must have atomically acquired all the required request queue locks. The formal argument list of f indicates which request queues must be locked. If a formal argument is declared as attached then the corresponding request queue gets locked. If a formal argument is declared as detachable then the corresponding request queue does not get locked. Note that the feature call rule in definition 22 will show that p_x could already have some locks through a chain of lock passing operations. It is not necessary to reacquire these locks. The selective locking mechanism has advantages over an eager locking mechanism where all the request queues get locked. The likelihood of deadlocks is decreased thanks to fewer locks. Selective locking supports a precise specification of resources needed by a routine and it makes it possible to pass an argument without locking the corresponding request queue. There is a reason why the detachable tag is used to encode selective locking. Assuming a formal argument would be detached then it is not clear how locking should be defined on a detached formal argument. Thus it makes sense to restrict locking to attached formal arguments. This leads to the generalized semantics of the detachable tag. As a second synchronization constraint, the precondition of f must hold. Note that if f is a routine that was called in qualified way and not as a creation procedure then the invariant is part of the precondition, as described in section 8.9.26 of the Eiffel ECMA standard [4]. A violated precondition clause can either cause an exception or it can lead to waiting. Section 7 will show that only unsatisfied controlled precondition clauses cause an exception.

Locking before executing ensures that processor p_x can access the locked request queues without interference caused by other processors. Thus processor p_x can make separate calls without interference as long as all calls are on objects handled by the corresponding processors. There is the assumption that each call stack lock of the argument processors is either in possession of its own processor or in possession of p_x. We will see later why this assumption is always given as we take a look at lock passing. Non-separate calls can also be executed without interference. As we will see, a non-separate call is handled over the call stack of p_x and does not involve the request queue of p_x. A new feature request is simply added to the top of the call stack. No other processor can interfere in this process. In conclusion, there are a number of safe targets which we call controlled. For safety reasons we only allow these targets in feature calls. Definitions 18 and 19 capture this restriction in terms of the type system.

Definition 18 (Controlled expression). *An expression exp of type $T_{exp} = (d, p, C)$ is controlled if and only if exp is attached, i.e. $d = \text{!}$, and exp satisfies at least one of the following conditions:*

- *The expression exp is non separate, i.e. $p = \bullet$.*
- *The expression exp appears in a routine r that has an attached formal argument farg with the same handler as exp, i.e. $p = farg.handler$.*

The second condition of definition 18 is satisfied if and only if at least one of the following conditions is true:

- The expression *exp* appears as an attached formal argument of r.
- The expression *exp* has a qualified explicit processor specification *farg.handler* and *farg* is an attached formal argument of r.
- The expression *exp* has an unqualified explicit processor specification p, and some attached formal argument of r has p as its unqualified explicit processor specification.

Definition 19 (Valid target). *Call $exp.f(\overline{a})$ appearing in class C is valid if and only if the following conditions hold:*

- *The expression exp is controlled.*
- *The expression exp's base class has a feature f exported to C, and the actual arguments $\overline{a}$ conform in number and type to the formal arguments of f.*

Definitions 18 and 19 apply to invariants, preconditions, postconditions and the routine bodies of a class. In case of an invariant, there is no enclosing routine. Thus an invariant can only contain non-separate calls. As a further consequence of definition 19. calls on void targets are prohibited. The call validity rule in definition 19 replaces the validity rule in section 8.23.9 of the Eiffel ECMA standard [4]. With this approach some safe feature calls are rejected. Such a situation can occur if there is a feature call on a uncontrolled separate expression to which a non-separate object is attached. In section 11 we will refer to this object as a false traitor.

Example 2 (Valid targets). Listing 1.4 shows a feature *print_book*. This feature makes a copy of the book and notifies the author of the book.

Listing 1.4. printer class

```
   class PRINTER feature
2    print_book (a_book: separate BOOK)
          −− Print 'a_book'.
4      do
          a_book.copy
6         a_book.author.notify
       end
8 end


10 class BOOK feature
     author: AUTHOR −− The author of this book.
12   initial_price: INTEGER −− The price as initially recommended.
     is_clean: BOOLEAN −− Is this book clean?
14
     copy
16        −− Copy this book.
       do
18     ...
       ensure
20       this_book_is_not_clean: not is_clean
       end
22
     clean
24        −− Clean this book.
       require
26       this_book_is_not_clean: not is_clean
       do
28     ...
       ensure
30       this_book_is_clean: is_clean
       end
32 end
```

The author is accessible through a non-separate attribute in the book class. Therefore the author and its book are on the same processor. In this example we want to see whether the two calls *a_book.print* and *a_book.author.notify* are valid according to definition 19. For this, we have to apply definition 18 to the two expressions *a_book* and *a_book.author*. The expression *a_book* is an attached formal argument and therefore it is controlled. The explicit type of *a_book* is $(!, \top, BOOK)$. Judging from this, *a_book* is attached. In addition, *a_book* is non-writable because it is a formal argument. We can therefore use definition 11 to derive the implicit type $(!, a\_book.handler, BOOK)$. We will now use this implicit type to derive the type of the expression *a_book.author*. We noted that the author and the book must be on the same processor. This means that we can use the book's processor tag for the author. The result type combiner in definition 27 will state this more clearly. With the implicit type of *a_book* the type of the expression *a_book.author* becomes $(!, a\_book.handler, AUTHOR)$. In conclusion the expression *a_book.author* has a qualified explicit processor tag that is related to the attached formal argument *a_book*. Therefore the expression is controlled. We can conclude that all targets are valid.

We already argued that any execution of a SCOOP program is free of low-level data races. Next to low-level data races there are high-level data races. They occur if multiple processors access a set of objects in a non-atomic way, i.e. in an interleaved manner, and there is at least one write access. As a consequence of the synchronization step in the feature application rule in definition 17 and the valid call rule in definition 19, a SCOOP system is free of high-level data races by design as stated by proposition 2.

Proposition 2. *A SCOOP system is free of high-level data races.*

Postcondition evaluation. The postcondition of the feature must be executed and checked. Note that if f is a routine that was called in qualified way or if f was called as a creation procedure then the invariant is part of this postcondition, as described in section 8.9.26 of the Eiffel ECMA standard [4]. There is one obvious way to evaluate the postcondition. Every processor that handles one or more targets in the postcondition evaluates its share of the postcondition while processor p_x is waiting for the results to come back. Once all the results have been gathered, processor p_x can determine whether the postcondition holds or not. However, this approach introduces sequentiality because p_x must wait for the query evaluations to finish. It turns out that p_x does not need to wait if none of its objects is used as a target in the postcondition. Any involved processor will do.

In any case, processor p_x gets the guarantee that the postcondition will be satisfied eventually. More precisely, it will be satisfied when the execution of the features called within f terminated. The last set of feature requests on any postcondition target will be the ones coming from the postcondition evaluation. Thus the postcondition gets evaluated at the right time just after all the feature called within f have terminated. Further feature request on the postcondition targets, issued after the execution of f, will only be applied after the postcondition has been evaluated. The postcondition might not hold right after the execution of f; but it will will hold when it becomes relevant, just before other feature request can be issued on the postcondition targets.

A postcondition evaluation can result in a violated postcondition. Such a state will trigger an exception in the supplier processor.

Result returning. We consider a situation where f returns an expanded object. The copy semantics of expanded objects could mislead to return a shallow copy from p_x to p_c. This is not a good idea. If the result object on p_x has an attached non-separate entity then the copied object on p_c has a non-separate entity to which a separate object on p_x is attached. We would have introduced a traitor. We introduce the import operation as defined in definition 20 to return an expanded object without this issue.

Definition 20 (Import operation). *The import operation executed by a processor p and applied to an object o on a different processor q involves the following sequence of actions:*

1. *Make a copy of o called o'.*
2. *Make a copy of all the non-copied objects that are reachable from o through non-separate references.*
3. *For every non-separate once function f of every copied object the following actions must be done:*
   (a) *If f is fresh on p and non-fresh on q then f must be marked as non-fresh on p and the value of f on q must be used as the value of f on p.*
   (b) *If f is fresh on p and fresh on q then f remains fresh on p.*
   (c) *If f is non-fresh on p then f remains non-fresh on p and the result of f on p remains the same.*
4. *For every once procedure f of every copied object the following actions must be done:*
   (a) *If f is fresh on p and non-fresh on q then f must be marked as non-fresh on p.*
   (b) *If f is non-fresh on p then f remains non-fresh on p.*
5. *Rewire the copied object structure in such a way that it mirrors the original object structure. Separate entities do not need to be altered in the copied object structure as they can still point to the original separate objects.*
6. *Put the copied object structure on p.*

Objects reachable through separate references do not need to be copied as their entities are already equipped with the right type with respect to p. Once functions with a non-separate result type complicate the import operation a bit. As it will be formulated later in definition 37, such a function f must be evaluated at most once on a given processor p and all the objects on p with f must share the result. We need to be careful in a situation where we import an object with a function f that has already been evaluated on processor q and on processor p. We cannot have two different values for the same once function on the same processor. Definition 20 takes care of issues of this kind. Similarly, it takes care of once procedures; they have a once per processor semantics as well. The terminology on freshness has been taken from section 8.23.20 of the ECMA standard [4]. A once routine is called fresh on a particular processor if and only if it has never been executed on any object handled by this processor. Otherwise the once routine is called non-fresh.

Example 3 (Import operation). Figure 1 shows the objects o, a, b and c forming an object structure. The objects o and a are on the same processor. The objects b and c are on separate processors. The result of the import operation applied to the object o by a processor p different than the handler of o is shown in the lower half of figure 1. Objects o results in a copied object o' on p. Because object a is non-separate with respect to o, processor p receives a copied object a' as well. The objects b and c do not need to be copied. They can be shared by both object structures as they were separate.

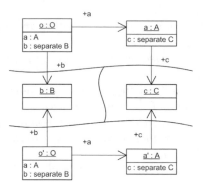

Fig. 1. Import operation example object diagram

The import operation computes the non-separate version of an object structure. It potentially results in a copied object structure that contains both copied and original objects. This can be an issue in case one of the copied objects has an invariant over the identities of objects as example 4 shows.

Example 4 (Invariant violation as a result of the import operation). Imagine two objects x and y on one processor and another object z on another processor. Object x has a separate reference a to z and a non-separate reference b to y.

Object z has a separate reference c to y. Object x has an invariant with a query $a.c = b$. An import operation on x executed by a third processor will result in two new objects x' and y' on the third processor. The reference a of object x' will point to the original z. The reference b of object x' will point to the new object y'. Now object x' is inconsistent, because $a.c$ and b identify different objects, namely y and y'.

The deep import operation is a variant of the import operation that does not mix the copied and the original objects. The drawback of the deep import operation is the increased overhead.

Definition 21 (Deep import operation). *The deep import operation executed by a processor p and applied to an object o on a different processor involves the following sequence of actions:*

1. *Make a copy of o called o'.*
2. *Make a copy ons' of all the non-copied objects that are reachable from o through non-separate references.*
3. *Make a copy os' of all the non-copied objects that are reachable from o through separate references.*
4. *For every non-separate once function f of every copied object the following actions must be done:*
   (a) *If f is fresh on p and non-fresh on q then f must be marked as non-fresh on p and the value of f on q must be used as the value of f on p.*
   (b) *If f is fresh on p and fresh on q then f remains fresh on p.*
   (c) *If f is non-fresh on p then f remains non-fresh on p and the result of f on p remains the same.*
5. *For every once procedure f of every copied object the following actions must be done:*
   (a) *If f is fresh on p and non-fresh on q then f must be marked as non-fresh on p.*
   (b) *If f is non-fresh on p then f remains non-fresh on p.*
6. *Rewire the copied object structure in such a way that it mirrors the original object structure.*
7. *Put the copied object o' and the non-separate copied object structure ons' on p.*
8. *Put each copied object in the separate copied object structure os' on the processor of the respective original object.*

Example 5 (Deep import operation). Figure 2 shows the objects o, a, b and c forming an object structure. The objects o and a are on the same processor. The objects b and c are on separate processors. The result of the deep import operation applied on the object o by a processor p different than the handler of o is shown on the lower half of the figure. All the objects involved in the object structure got copied.

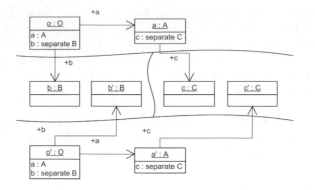

Fig. 2. Deep import operation example object diagram

Lock releasing. After the execution of f, processor p_x does not require the request queue locks anymore. At this point the request queue locks might still contain feature requests from p_x. However, there are no more new feature request because the execution of f is over. Therefore p_x can release the locks. For this, processor p_x does not wait until all the features requests triggered in the execution of f finished. Instead, it appends an unlock operation to each locked request queue. As a result, different request queues may become unlocked at different times after they are done with all the feature requests. Next to an increase in parallelism, asynchronous unlocking permits safe realization of certain synchronization scenarios that would lead to deadlocks otherwise.

5.2   Feature Call

So far we studied the context in which a feature call can occur. A feature call results in the generation of feature request by the client processor on a potentially different supplier processor. The feature request gets executed eventually by the supplier processor. Note the change of roles. A supplier processor becomes a client processor when the supplier processor makes a call.

The calling processor has a number of locks to ensure exclusive access. The client processor might be in possession of some locks that are necessary in the synchronization step of the resulting feature request on the supplier processor. In such a situation, the client processor can temporarily pass its locks to the supplier processor. This step is called lock passing and it happens right after argument passing. Once these two steps completed, the client processor can place its feature request. If the called feature is a query then the client processor must wait for the result. Before the feature call can be completed, the client processor must revoke the passed locks. Definition 22 explains these steps in more details.

Definition 22 (Feature call). *A feature call $x.f(\overline{a})$ results in the following sequence of actions performed by the client processor p_c:*

1. *Argument passing:*
   - *Attach the actual arguments $\bar{a}$ to the formal arguments of f.*
   - *Arguments of expanded type need to be imported by the supplier processor p_x.*
2. *Lock passing:*
   - *Full lock passing: If any controlled actual argument of a reference type gets attached to an attached formal argument of f then pass all the currently held request queue locks and call stack locks to p_x.*
   - *Call stack locks passing: In case there are no such arguments and there is a separate callback, i.e. p_x already had a request queue lock on p_c at the moment of the call then pass the call stack locks to p_x.*
3. *Feature request: Ask p_x to apply f to x.*
   - *Schedule f for an immediate execution by p_x using the call stack of p_x and wait until it terminates, if any of the following conditions hold:*
     - *The feature call is non-separate, i.e. $p_c = p_x$.*
     - *The feature call is a separate callback.*
   - *Otherwise, schedule f to execute after the previous calls on p_x using the request queue of p_x.*
4. *Wait by necessity: If f is a query then wait for its result.*
5. *Lock revocation: If lock passing happened then wait for f to terminate and revoke the locks.*

Lock passing, feature request, and lock revocation. Deadlock avoidance is the motivation behind lock passing. Without lock passing, it is very easy to get into a deadlock. Suppose that processor p_x needs a particular lock in the application of feature f. If this lock is in possession of processor p_c then p_x cannot proceed until p_c releases this lock. If f happens to be a query then p_c has to wait for the result of f while p_c is holding on to the lock. According to the conditions given by Coffman et al [3] a deadlock occurred. If the client processor p_c could temporarily pass on the lock to p_x then p_x would be able to apply the requested feature, return the result, and let p_c continue. We call this solution full lock passing.

Full lock passing includes passing the request queue locks and the call stack locks. It happens if any controlled actual argument of a reference type gets attached to an attached formal argument of f. An attached formal argument means that the request queue will be locked in the synchronization step of f's application. A controlled actual argument means that p_c has a request queue lock on the handler of the actual argument. In short, p_c has a lock required by p_x. Full lock passing is only relevant for arguments of a reference type. Arguments of expanded type will be copied using the import operation during argument passing.

If full lock passing happens then p_c passes all its locks to p_x and not only the locks that triggered the lock passing mechanism. This generous behavior eliminates more potential deadlocks compared to a solution where only a subset of the locks gets passed. As soon as at least one lock gets passed, processor p_c cannot proceed until it can revoke the locks after the feature f terminated. Otherwise the atomicity guarantees expressed by proposition 2 could be violated due to two processor who could potentially be working on the same set of objects. As p_c has to wait in any case that involves lock passing, it does not hurt to pass all the locks and not just a subset.

A feature call results in a feature request. The client processor p_c generates a feature request to be handled by the supplier processor p_x. The feature request could either go to the end of the request queue or on top of the call stack of processor p_x. If the two processors are the same then the call is non-separate and f must be applied immediately. This is the sequential case. The request queue is irrelevant for this and only the call stack is involved. There is another, more special case, where feature f must be applied immediately. A separate callback occurs when the supplier processor p_x already held a lock on the client processor p_c at the moment of the feature call to f. This can happen in the following situation: We assume p_x initiated a chain of feature calls involving full lock passing. At the end of this chain processor p_c executes the feature call $x.f(\overline{a})$. Processor p_x is responsible for the application of this call. At this point processor p_x is waiting until its feature call terminates to revoke the locks. We assume the feature call f involves lock passing as well. In this situation p_c will wait for the feature call f to terminate. If the feature call f gets added to the end of the request queue of p_x then the system ends up in a deadlock. Processor p_c would be waiting for processor p_x to finish the feature application $x.f(\overline{a})$. But processor p_x would never get to this point because it would still be waiting for its locks to come back. Immediate execution is the way out of this. The feature f must be applied immediately using the call stack of p_x. At the moment of a separate callback the processor p_c is in possession of the call stack lock on p_x, because p_x passed its locks. However, p_x will require this lock during its own execution. Therefore p_c must temporarily pass back its call stack locks to p_x and wait for the locks to return. Again, it does not hurt to pass back all call stack locks instead of just one. In the remaining case the call is a normal separate call. The feature request gets added to the end of the request queue of processor p_x. The processor loop described in definition 3 will put the feature request on top of the call stack as soon as all previous feature requests terminated.

Note that it is not possible to lock a request queue of a processor p that is not in possession of its own call stack lock. We assume p is not in possession of its own call stack lock. This is only possible if p passed its locks in a feature call. This means that p is currently applying a feature and waiting for the locks to return. While p is applying a feature, its request queue is locked. Therefore it is not possible to lock the request queue of p. If a processor q has a request queue lock on p then there are two options. Processor q could have acquired the request queue lock in the synchronization step and therefore p is in possession of its call stack lock. The request queue lock on p could also have been passed to q. This means that some processor must have acquired the request queue lock on p. The only way how p could have lost its call stack lock is a chain of lock passing operation where processor p is involved. In this case p would have passed on its call stack lock to processor q.

Wait by necessity. Next to lock passing, there is another situation where p_c has to wait for p_x to finish its feature application of f. If f is a query then the subsequent statements after the call to f potentially depend on the result of the query. Thus processor p_c needs to wait for the query to terminate before it can proceed. This scheme is called wait by necessity.

5.3 Lock Revocation

After the feature f terminated, the locks of p_x and p_c must be restored to the state before lock passing happened.

Valid assumptions after a feature call. Processor p_c can be assured that every future feature call on a target mentioned in the postcondition of f will be applied after all the feature requests resulting from the application of f. This includes the feature requests resulting from a postcondition evaluation. This is ensured by the synchronization step in the application of f.

Example 6 (Feature calls and feature applications). Consider the feature *sell_book* in listing 1.5.

Listing 1.5. seller class

```
   class SELLER feature
2    sell_book (a_book: separate BOOK; a_buyer: separate BUYER; a_valuer:
         separate VALUER)
           -- Sell 'a_book' to 'a_buyer' after asking 'a_valuer' for the price.
4       local
           l_estimated_price: INTEGER
6       do
           a_book.clean
8          l_estimated_price := a_valuer.estimate (a_book)
           a_buyer.buy (a_book, l_estimated_price)
10      end
   end
12
   class VALUER feature
14   estimate (a_book: separate BOOK): INTEGER
           -- The estimated price of 'a_book'.
16      do
           Result := f (a_book.initial_price)
```

18   **end**
  end

We use the following notation to describe a processor p with a request queue rq, request queue locks rql, and call stack locks csl: $p :: rq, rql, csl$. We start from a point where the request queue of the current processor p_c contains the feature *sell_book*.

$p_c ::$ (**Current**.*sell_book* (*a_book, a_buyer, a_valuer*)), (), (p_c)
$p_{book} ::$ (), (), (p_{book})
$p_{valuer} ::$ (), (), (p_{valuer})

As a first step, p_c removes the feature *sell_book* from its request queue and puts it on its call stack as described in definition 3. Next p_c starts with the feature application according to definition 17. As there is no precondition, processor p_c asks the scheduler to get the request queue locks on the handlers p_{book}, p_{buyer}, and p_{valuer}. We assume that each of these handlers are different from each other. Eventually these locks are available and p_c can execute the body of *sell_book*. Note that *sell_book* is now on the call stack and not in the request queue anymore.

$p_c ::$ (), $(p_{book}, p_{buyer}, p_{valuer})$, (p_c)
$p_{book} ::$ (), (), (p_{book})
$p_{valuer} ::$ (), (), (p_{valuer})

The body has three feature calls. Their semantics is described in definition 22. The treatment of *a_book.clean* is easy. There are no arguments to be passed. The feature request step results in the following situation:

$p_c ::$ (), $(p_{book}, p_{buyer}, p_{valuer})$, (p_c)
$p_{book} ::$ (*a_book.clean*), (), (p_{book})
$p_{valuer} ::$ (), (), (p_{valuer})

The remaining two steps of a feature call do not apply here. The treatment of *a_valuer.estimate* (*a_book*) is more complex as it involves lock passing. According to definition 18 the expression *a_book* is controlled in the feature *sell_book*. The expression is used as an actual argument of reference type in the call. The corresponding formal argument is attached. We just encountered a situation where the caller has a request queue lock which is necessary in the execution of the supplier. Lock passing and the addition of a feature request result in the following situation:

$p_c ::$ (), (), ()
$p_{book} ::$ (*a_book.clean*), (), (p_{book})
$p_{valuer} ::$ (*a_valuer.estimate* (*a_book*)), $(p_{book}, p_{buyer}, p_{valuer})$, (p_{valuer}, p_c)

Note that the call stack lock of p_c gets passed to give p_{valuer} a chance to handle a separate callback. In the current example we do not make use of this. At this point processor p_c has to wait until the locks can be revoked. While p_c is waiting, processors p_{book} and p_{valuer} proceed in parallel. They can dequeue a feature from the beginning of their request queues, put it on their call stacks, and apply the features.

$p_c :: (), (), ()$
$p_{book} :: (), (), (p_{book})$
$p_{valuer} :: (), (p_{book}, p_{buyer}, p_{valuer}), (p_{valuer}, p_c)$

At this point p_c can retrieve the result, revoke the locks and do the assignment.

$p_c :: (), (p_{book}, p_{buyer}, p_{valuer}), (p_c)$
$p_{book} :: (), (), (p_{book})$
$p_{valuer} :: (), (), (p_{valuer})$

The last instruction $a\_buyer.buy$ (a_book, $l\_estimated\_price$) triggers another passing of locks. Here, processor p_c will have to wait due to the passed locks, even though the instruction itself does not impose wait by necessity. Last but not least, p_c will add unlock operations to the end of the request queues of p_{book}, p_{buyer}, and p_{valuer}.

6 Object Creation

Constructing objects is more complicated in SCOOP than in Eiffel because an object needs to be created on a processor. Definition 23 refines the definitions in section 8.20 of the Eiffel ECMA standard [4].

Definition 23 (Object creation). *A creation call $x.cp(\overline{a})$ on the target x of type (d, p, C) and with the creation procedure cp results in the following sequence of actions performed by the client processor p_c:*

1. *Processor creation*
   - *If x is separate, i.e. $p = \top$, then create a new processor p_x.*
   - *If x has an explicit processor specification, i.e. $p = \alpha$, then*
     - *if the processor denoted by p already exists then take $p_x = p_p$.*
     - *if the processor denoted by p does not exist yet then create a new processor p_x.*
   - *If x is non-separate, i.e. $p = \bullet$, then take $p_x = p_c$.*
2. *Locking: If $p_x \neq p_c$ and p_c does not have a request queue lock on p_x yet then lock the request queue of p_x.*
3. *Object creation: Ask p_x to create a fresh instance of C using the creation procedure cp. Attach the newly created object to x.*

4. *Lock releasing: Add an unlock operation to the request queue of p_x if a lock has been obtained earlier.*

The type of an entity specifies the locality of the attached object. When an entity is used as the target of a creation routine then the new object must be handled by a compatible processor. In some cases such a processor might already exist in other cases a compatible processor must be created. If $p = \bullet$ then the new object must be created on the current processor. If $p = \top$ then any processor could be taken. To exploit parallelism, a new processor gets created. An explicit processor specification specifies a particular processor. If the explicit processor specification is qualified then the specified processor exist already because there is an attached entity whose object is handled by this processor. For an unqualified explicit processor specification it might be necessary to create a new processor if this did not happen already.

After the new object got created there needs to be a call to the creation routine. This call is handled like a feature call as described in definition 22. If the call to the creation routine is separate and p_c does not have the request queue lock on p_x then it is necessary to acquire a request queue lock on p_x before the call. The lock must be released after the call. The new object gets attached to the entity x as soon as the object is created but without waiting for the creation procedure to be applied. This means that x points to a potentially inconsistent object until the creation procedure terminates. However, this is not harmful because new feature requests will be added after the feature request for the creation routine.

Example 7 (Object creation). Feature *initialize* in listing 1.6 shows four creation instructions for four different books. In this example we will go through this list and explain what will happen at runtime.

Listing 1.6. book collection class

```
   class BOOK_COLLECTION feature
2    hamlet: HAMLET -- Hamlet.
     robinson: separate ROBINSON -- Robinson.
4    cinderella: separate <p> CINDERELLA - Cinderella.
     tarzan: separate <p> TARZAN -- Tarzan.
6
     p: PROCESSOR
8
     initialize
10       -- Initialize this book collection.
       do
12         create hamlet
           create robinson
14         create cinderella
           create tarzan
16     end
```

```
    end
18
    class HAMLET inherit BOOK end
20 class ROBINSON inherit BOOK end
    class CINDERELLA inherit BOOK end
22 class TARZAN inherit BOOK end
```

The first instruction creates a book and stores it in *hamlet*. The type of this entity is non-separate. Thus Hamlet will be created on the current processor. The second instruction creates the book called Robinson. The type of the entity is separate and thus a new processor must be created and used as the handler of the new book. The third instruction creates another classic called Cinderella. The type **separate** $<p>$ *CINDERELLA* has an unqualified explicit processor specification. We assume that the specified processor has not been created before. Under this assumption, the processor must be created and used as the handler of the new book. In the last instruction the book called Tarzan gets created. The type of the target **separate** $<p>$ *TARZAN* has an unqualified explicit processor specification that specifies the same processor as the entity *cinderella*. Based on the previous instruction it is clear that this processor already exists. Thus there is no need to create a new processor. The books Cinderella and Tarzan are handled by the same processor.

7   Contracts

Design by Contract [8] introduces a new paradigm in object-oriented programming. The use of contracts imposes a crucial reduction of complexities in object-oriented development, in particular when it comes to correctness reasoning. By enriching class interfaces with contracts each class implementation can be verified and proven correct separately. Contracts typically consist of preconditions and postconditions for features and invariants on a class level. These contracts result in mutual obligations of clients and suppliers. In the context of classes enriched with contracts, the principle called separation of concerns gains in importance because the client can rely on the interface of the supplier without the need to know its implementation details. Eiffel supports contracts in the form of assertions being checked at runtime. Sections 7.5 and 8.9 from the Eiffel standard [4] provide more details on contracts in Eiffel.

Unfortunately the traditional interpretation of contracts breaks down in the context of concurrency. In concurrent programs a client calling a feature of a class generally cannot establish the precondition of the feature any more. The reason is that in general feature calls are asynchronous and the point in time of the feature call and the moment of the actual execution of the feature body do not coincide, as it is the case in a sequential program. Thus the objects involved in the precondition may be changed in between by feature calls from other clients. This results in the situation where the precondition that was satisfied at the moment of the call is violated at the moment of execution. Similarly, postconditions cannot be interpreted as full guarantees any more.

SCOOP introduces a new approach to a uniform and clear semantics of contracts in a concurrent context. Thus SCOOP generalizes the principles of Design by Contract, and additionally fosters the use of modular proof techniques. The advantage of the proposed semantics of contracts is that it applies equally well in concurrent and sequential contexts. Following the idea of Eiffel, contracts in SCOOP are formulated as assertions directly written into the code and evaluated during runtime. If an assertion is evaluated and it is not satisfied, then an exception is raised. For preconditions this rule must be carefully revisited due to the observation made above that it may happen that a caller (from a different handler than the target object's handler) cannot be held responsible for establishing the whole assertion of the feature. These considerations result in a refined rule saying that a violated precondition clause that is not under the control of the caller does not lead to an exception - instead the feature call is queued for a later application. Similarly, the semantics of postconditions are adapted to the concurrent context.

7.1   Controlled and Uncontrolled Assertion Clauses

Following the new generalized semantics of contracts proposed by [11], the handling of a feature call strongly depends on the controllability of the involved assertion clauses. The notion of controlled and uncontrolled assertion clauses introduced in the following essentially captures the idea of controlled expressions (definition 18): An assertion clause is called controlled with respect to the current context if all involved objects are under the control and cannot be modified by other processors. Otherwise the assertion clause is called uncontrolled.

Definition 24 (Controlled assertion clause). *For a client performing the call $x.f(\overline{a})$ in the context of a routine r, a precondition clause or a postcondition clause of f is* controlled *if and only if, after the substitution of the actual arguments $\overline{a}$ for the formal arguments, it only involves calls on entities that are controlled in the context of r. Otherwise, it is* uncontrolled.

Example 8 (Controlled and uncontrolled precondition clauses). We illustrate the difference between controlled and uncontrolled precondition clauses by the example shown in listing 1.7.

Listing 1.7. cleaner class

```
    class CLEANER feature
2     manual: BOOK -- The cleaning manual.

4     clean (a_book: separate BOOK)
            -- Clean 'a_book'.
6        require
```

```
              a_book_is_not_clean: not a_book.is_clean
  8      do
              a_book.clean
 10      end
      end
 12
      class CLEAN_BOOK_COLLECTION inherit BOOK_COLLECTION
              feature
 14    clean_all (a_cleaner: separate CLEANER; a_extra_book: separate BOOK
              )
              -- Clean all available books.
 16      require
              ...
 18      do
              -- Clean all books in the collection.
 20          a_cleaner.clean (robinson) -- a_book_is_not_clean uncontrolled
             a_cleaner.clean (hamlet) -- a_book_is_not_clean controlled
 22          ...
             -- Clean additional books.
 24          a_cleaner.clean (a_extra_book) -- a_book_is_not_clean controlled
             a_cleaner.clean (a_cleaner.manual) -- a_book_is_not_clean controlled
 26      end
      end
```

We consider a client calling the feature *clean_all*. In the body of *clean_all*, the precondition *a_book_is_not_clean* of the feature call *a_cleaner.clean (robinson)* is uncontrolled since *robinson* is not controlled in the context of *clean_all*; *robinson* is declared as a potentially separate object whose processor's request queue is not locked in *clean_all*. On the other hand, *a_book_is_not_clean* is controlled in the three remaining calls to *clean* because the targets of the call to *is_clean* in the precondition are controlled in *clean_all*. The expression *hamlet* is non-separate hence controlled. The expression *a_extra_book* is separate but it is a formal argument of *clean_all*. Therefore it also controlled. Finally, *a_cleaner.manual* is separate in the context of *clean_all*, but it is non-separate from *a_cleaner* and *a_cleaner* is controlled hence *a_cleaner.manual* is controlled too.

Remark 1. The notion of an assertion clause originates in section 8.9 of the Eiffel ECMA standard [4].

7.2   Semantics of Contracts

In the following we will precisely describe how contracts given by invariants, preconditions and postconditions are interpreted during runtime of a SCOOP program.

Semantics of preconditions. In concurrent programs the usual correctness semantics of preconditions does not fit anymore because in general the client cannot guarantee that the precondition will hold at the moment of the feature application. This inconsistency in the standard interpretation of preconditions in the concurrent context is called *separate precondition paradox* in [11]. This suggests the *wait semantics* for preconditions involving separate clauses. If the precondition is violated only due to violated uncontrolled precondition clauses, the feature application has to be delayed until the precondition clauses holds. On the other hand, a violated controlled precondition clause has to be blamed on the client because no other processor than the client's processor could have accessed the objects occurring in a controlled precondition clause. For such a case an exception needs to be raised in the client. Asynchronous Exceptions raise some problems; this is discussed in section 14.

Example 9 (Precondition semantics). We consider class *READING_LIST* in listing 1.8. It used a bounded buffer to maintain books to be read.

Listing 1.8. reading list class

```
   class READING_LIST inherit BOOK_COLLECTION feature
2    bestsellers: separate BUFFER[separate BOOK] -- The bestsellers.
     favorites: BUFFER[separate BOOK] -- The favorites.
4
     store (a_book_list: separate BUFFER[separate BOOK]; a_book: BOOK)
6       -- Store 'a_book' in 'a_book_list'.
     require
8       a_book_list_is_not_full: not a_book_list.is_full
        a_book_is_clean: a_book.is_clean
10   do
        a_book_list.put (a_book)
12   ensure
        a_book_list_is_not_empty: not a_book_list.is_empty
14   end

16 get (a_book_list: separate BUFFER[separate BOOK]): separate BOOK
        -- Remove a book from 'a_book_list'.
18   require
        a_book_list_is_not_empty: not a_book_list.is_empty
20   do
        Result := a_book_list.get
22   end

24 add_hamlet_to_all (a_extra_book_list: separate BUFFER[separate BOOK])
        -- Add Hamlet to all book lists including 'a_extra_book_list'.
26   require
        ...
28   do
        store (a_extra_book_list, hamlet)
30   store (bestsellers, hamlet)
```

    store (*favorites*, *hamlet*)
32   end
    end

The feature *store* has as formal arguments a book list and a book; when applied it puts the book into the book list. The precondition of that feature requires that the book list is not full and moreover, that the book is clean. The latter is always a correctness condition since waiting is meaningless if the book is not clean. However, the semantics of the former precondition depends on the locality of the actual arguments. This is illustrated by the feature *add_hamlet_to_all*, where there are three feature calls to *store*. For the first call the precondition *a_book_list_is_not_full* is a correctness condition since *a_extra_book_list* is controlled and hence the precondition clause is controlled. For the second call the precondition is a waiting condition since *bestsellers* is uncontrolled. Finally, for the third call the precondition is a correctness condition since *favorites* is a non-separate attribute of the class and hence *a_book_list_is_not_full* is controlled as well.

Definition 25 (Precondition semantics). *A precondition expresses the necessary requirements for a correct application of the feature. The execution of the feature's body is delayed until the uncontrolled precondition clauses are satisfied. A violated controlled precondition clause immediately marks the precondition as violated.*

The generalized semantics proposed in [11,12] comprises both interpretations of precondition clauses. As seen in the example, they can be correctness conditions or wait conditions. Correctness conditions only apply to those clauses that are controlled by the client: the client can ensure that the precondition clause hold at the moment of the feature application. The uncontrolled precondition clauses cannot be established by the client, i.e., the client cannot take the responsibility for satisfying them at the moment of the feature application. For this reason wait semantics are applied in this case. Note that waiting always happens at the supplier side. Wait conditions can be used to synchronize processors with each other. A supplier processor only proceeds when the wait condition is established.

Semantics of postconditions. Similar to the previously mentioned separate precondition paradox, we can constitute a *separate postcondition paradox* for postconditions. On return from a separate call, the client cannot be sure that the postcondition still holds. After the termination of the call and *before* returning from the call another object may have modified the state of an object occurring in an uncontrolled postcondition clause. However, the client knows that the postcondition was fulfilled on termination of the call. Thus after returning from the call the client can only assume the controlled postcondition clauses since no other client can invalidate these. The interpretation of postconditions is symmetric to the treatment of preconditions. Controlled postcondition clauses are a guarantee given to the client and an obligation on the supplier.

In order to avoid blocking semantics of postconditions and to increase parallelism, postconditions are evaluated individually and asynchronously by the object's handler. This means that the client can continue its own activity after returning from a feature call without waiting for the evaluation of a postcondition. The client gets the guarantee that the postcondition will hold eventually.

Example 10 (Postcondition semantics). Listing 1.9 shows a testable version of class *READING_LIST*.

Listing 1.9. reading list test class

```
   class TESTABLE_READING_LIST inherit READING_LIST feature
2    test (a_extra_book_list: separate BUFFER[separate BOOK])
             -- Run a test on all book lists including 'a_extra_book_list'.
4      require
            ...
6      local
            l_book: separate BOOK
8      do
            store (a_extra_book_list, hamlet)
10           store (bestsellers, hamlet)
            store (favorites, hamlet)
12
            l_book := get (a_extra_book_list)
14           l_book := get (bestsellers)
            l_book := get (favorites)
16     end
   end
```

The feature call *store* (*a_extra_book_list*, *hamlet*) in feature *test* has a controlled postcondition. The postcondition involves an asynchronous call to the separate entity *a_extra_book_list*. However, the postcondition can be assumed immediately, because it will hold eventually. The second (again asynchronous) call *store* (*bestsellers*, *hamlet*) ensures the uncontrolled postcondition. The caller gets the guarantee that the postcondition holds after termination but the postcondition cannot be assumed at a later point in time since the current processor does not have a request queue lock on *bestsellers*. For the call *get* (*a_extra_book_list*), the precondition is controlled, hence it is a correctness condition and it holds since the postcondition of *store* (*a_extra_book_list*, *hamlet*) can be assumed. For the second call *get* (*bestsellers*), the precondition is uncontrolled, hence it is a waiting condition. The postcondition of *store* (*bestsellers*, *hamlet*) can be assumed to hold on termination of that feature, but not at the time of the call *get* (*bestsellers*).

Definition 26 (Postcondition semantics). *A postcondition describes the result of a feature's application. Postconditions are evaluated asynchronously; wait by necessity (i.e. the need to wait for a result of the feature application) does not apply. Postcondition clauses that do not involve calls on objects handled by the same processors are evaluated independently.*

A violation of a postcondition clause raises an exception in the processor that has evaluated this clause.

Semantics of invariants. Invariants express class level consistency conditions on objects that must be satisfied in every observable state (see sections 7.5 and 8.9.16 of the ECMA standard [4]). This means that invariants must be satisfied before and after every generally or selectively exported routine that is not used as a creation procedure. In case of a routine used as a creation procedure the invariant must be satisfied after the execution. On the evaluation side invariants get evaluated on both start and termination of a qualified call to a routine that is not used as a creation procedure. It is also evaluated after every call to a creation procedure (see 8.9.26 of the ECMA standard [4]). Invariants are allowed to have non-separate calls only - separate calls are prohibited. This is a direct consequence of the target validity rule 19. Therefore they can be evaluated without the acquisition of further locks. Note that a feature used in an invariant can have separate formal arguments.

Semantics of loop assertions and check instructions. There are further types of assertions namely loop variants, loop invariants, and check instructions. Similar to the semantics of postconditions they are evaluated asynchronously, hence wait by necessity does not apply here. Because the assertions cannot be split up in individual clauses (see remark above) the assertion is evaluated at once. Formal reasoning is again not affected since they can (like postconditions) be assumed immediately. Notice that all such assertions are controlled since all call targets must be controlled. If a loop assertion or a check fails, an exception is raised in the supplier.

7.3 Proof Rule

The new generalized semantics of contracts in a concurrent context suggest the following mutual obligations between clients and suppliers. The supplier may assume all the controlled and uncontrolled precondition clauses and must ensure - after the execution of the routine's body - all controlled and uncontrolled postcondition clauses. These obligations are exactly the same as in a sequential context, thus from the contract point of view, the same implementation is suitable for both sequential and concurrent contexts. However, in the concurrent context the obligations and the guarantees of the client differ. The client must establish all *controlled* precondition clauses. The uncontrolled precondition clauses will possibly delay the execution of the feature due to the wait semantics, but nevertheless they will hold when the execution of the feature's body takes place. Conversely, the client can only assume the *controlled* post-condition clauses, because - even though the supplier must establish all post-condition clauses - in the meantime uncontrolled objects involved in an un-controlled postcondition clause may have changed. Hence the client has fewer obligations but it gets fewer guarantees. This is expressed in the following proof rule.

$$\frac{\{INV \wedge Pre_r\}body_r\{INV \wedge Post_r\}}{\{Pre_r^{ctr}[\overline{a}/\overline{f}]\}x.r(\overline{a})\{Post_r^{ctr}[\overline{a}/\overline{f}]\}} \tag{1}$$

$Pre_r^{ctr}[\overline{a}/\overline{f}]$ denotes the controlled clauses of the precondition of the routine r with the formal arguments $\overline{f}$ substituted simultaneously by $\overline{a}$, similarly for $Post_r^{ctr}[\overline{a}/\overline{f}]$. With this proof rule we can prove partial correctness of routines. Given that under the assumption $INV \wedge Pre_r$ the executing of $body_r$ results in a state where $INV \wedge Post_r$ holds, we can deduce that in a given context the call $x.r(\overline{a})$ in a state where $Pre_r^{ctr}[\overline{a}/\overline{f}]$ is satisfied leads to a state where $Post_r^{ctr}[\overline{a}/\overline{f}]$ holds. This proof rule is parametrized by the context. The resulting precondition and postcondition clauses depend on the context, which is expressed in the conclusion by adding ctr to the precondition and postcondition.

With the new proof rule we cannot prove total correctness, what we can prove however is partial correctness. Uncontrolled preconditions and postconditions can lead to deadlocks and infinite waiting on non-satisfied preconditions. In its current state the programming model of SCOOP cannot rule out deadlocks completely. However, the likelihood of a deadlock is decreased significantly by introducing selective locking and lock passing. See the outlook section 14 for future work and work that has been done to improve that fact. As pointed out in [11], a fully modular proof system for SCOOP would require much more expressive contracts.

The new proof rule looks very similar to the sequential Hoare rule [6]. The difference between the Hoare rule and the new proof rule resides in the conclusion. The new proof rule limits the assertion clauses to controlled assertion clauses. There is however a case where the Hoare rule becomes a special case of the new proof rule. In a sequential program every assertion clause that involves only attached entities is controlled. Therefore if all assertion clauses only involve attached entities then every assertion clause becomes controlled, i.e. $Pre_r[\overline{a}/\overline{f}] = Pre_r^{ctr}[\overline{a}/\overline{f}]$ and $Post_r[\overline{a}/\overline{f}] = Post_r^{ctr}[\overline{a}/\overline{f}]$.

8   Type Combiners

An entity e declared as non-separate is seen as such by the current object o. However, separate clients of o should see e as separate because from their point of view the object attached to e is handled by a different processor. Following this thought, there is a need to determine how a particular type is perceived from the point of view of an object different than the current object. Type combiners are the answer to this question.

8.1   Result Type Combiner

The result type combiner shown in definition 27 determines the type T_e of a query call $x.f$ based on the type T_{target} of x and the type T_{result} of f. The result type combiner gives the result type of a query from the perspective of the client. The type T_{result} is relative to the target x and the result type combiner determines how this type should be seen by the client.

Definition 27 (Result type combiner). $* : Type \times Type \mapsto Type$

$$(d_1, p_1, C_1) * (d_2, p_2, C_2) = \begin{cases} (!, \bullet, C_2) & \text{if } isExpanded(C_2) \\ (d_2, p_1, C_2) & \text{if } \neg isExpanded(C_2) \wedge p_2 = \bullet \\ (d_2, \top, C_2) & \text{otherwise} \end{cases}$$

The result type combiner is a function of two arguments. The first argument is the type of the target T_{target} and the second argument is the type of the result T_{result}.

The first case handles the situation where the result class type is expanded. Results of expanded types are passed back to the client using the import operation described in definition 20. Doing so the result becomes non-separate from the perspective of the client. Thus the result type combiner yields non-separateness as the combined type. The result stays expanded and thus the combined type must be attached. The remaining cases handle the situations where the class of the return type is not expanded.

If the result type is non-separate with respect to the target, i.e. $p_2 = \bullet$, then we conclude that the result must be handled by the same processor as the target. Therefore the combined type has the processor tag of the target type. This situation is handled by the second case.

If the result type is separate with respect to the target, i.e. $p_2 = \top$, then the result can be considered separate from the point of view of the client. This works because $p = \top$ means potentially separate. Thus the combined type can be separate as well. This is reflected in case number three.

If the result type explicitly denotes a processor, i.e. $p_2 = \alpha$, then one could think that the processor tag of the combined type must be p_2 because it is an exact specification of a processor. This is not true. The explicit processor tag p_2 only makes sense in the context of class C_2 for the target x. A processor tag is not a global identification. However, the client can conclude that the result will be potentially separate. This is shown in the third case.

Example 11 (Basic usage of the result type combiner). In combination with genericity the result type combiner can get complicated. Consider listing 1.10.

Listing 1.10. simple library class

```
  class LIST[G −> separate ANY] feature
2   last: G
        −− The last element of the list.
4
    put (a_element: G)
6        −− Add 'a_element' to the list.
      do
8      ...
      end
10 end

12 class SIMPLE_LIBRARY feature
      books: LIST[separate BOOK] −− The books.
14 end
```

The class $SIMPLE\_LIBRARY$ declares a feature *books* of type $LIST[$**separate** $BOOK]$. The actual generic parameter **separate** $BOOK$ is relative to the object attached to *books*. The result type combiner determines the type of *books.last* from the perspective of the library. The type of the target *books* is $(!, \bullet, LIST[(!, \top, BOOK)])$. The result type of *last* is $(!, \top, BOOK)$. As a result one gets $(!, \bullet, LIST[(!, \top, BOOK)]) * (!, \top, BOOK) = (!, \top, BOOK)$.

Example 12 (Iterative usage of the result type combiner). The result type combiner can be applied iteratively to multi-dot expressions. Consider listing 1.11.

Listing 1.11. stacked library class

```
  class STACK[G] feature
2   top: G −− The top element.
   end
4
  class STACKED_LIBRARY feature
6   books: LIST[STACK[separate BOOK]] −− The books.
   end
```

The class $STACKED\_LIBRARY$ defines a feature *books* of type $LIST[STACK$ $[$**separate** $BOOK]]$. In this example we will determine the combined type of *books.last.top* from the perspective of an instance of $STACKED\_LIBRARY$. The result type combiner must be applied from left to right because the targets are determined from left to right. The target type of *books* together with the result type of *last* result in the first combined type. This first combined type is the target type for the call to *top*. This target type and the result type of *top* result in the final combined type.

$$(!, \bullet, LIST[B]) * \overbrace{(!, \bullet, STACK[A])}^{B} * \overbrace{(!, \top, BOOK)}^{A} =$$

$$(!, \bullet, STACK[A]) * \overbrace{(!, \top, BOOK)}^{A} = (!, \top, BOOK)$$

8.2   Argument Type Combiner

The argument type combiner determines the admissible type T_{actual} of an actual argument a in a call $x.f(a)$. It is based on the target type T_{target} and the type T_{formal} of the formal argument. In other words the argument type combiner determines how the client perceives the type of an argument.

Definition 28 (Argument type combiner). $\otimes : Type \times Type \mapsto Type$

$$(d_1, p_1, C_1) \otimes (d_2, p_2, C_2) = \begin{cases} (!, \bullet, C_2) & \text{if } isExpanded(C_2) \\ (d_2, p_1, C_2) & \text{if } \neg isExpanded(C_2) \wedge p_1 \neq \top \wedge p_2 = \bullet \\ (d_2, \top, C_2) & \text{if } \neg isExpanded(C_2) \wedge p_2 = \top \\ (d_2, \bot, C_2) & \text{otherwise} \end{cases}$$

The argument type combiner is a function of two arguments. The first argument T_{target} is the type of the target and the second argument T_{formal} is the type of the formal argument.

The first case handles formal arguments of expanded type. Actual arguments of expanded types are passed to the supplier using the import operation described in definition 20. Doing so, the actual argument becomes non-separate from the perspective of the supplier. The client can assume the argument is non-separate. Therefore the argument type combiner yields non-separateness as the combined type. The actual argument is expanded and thus the combined type needs to be attached. The remaining cases handle the situations where the class of the actual argument type is not expanded.

If the formal argument type is non-separate with respect to the target, i.e. $p_2 = \bullet$, then we know that the actual argument must be handled by the same processor as the target. This processor is specified by the target type. If the target type is separate, i.e. $p_1 = \top$, then there is no chance of knowing which processor it is. In the remaining cases we know with certainty which processor to use for the actual argument: when the target type explicitly denotes a processor, i.e. $p_1 = \alpha$, when the target type is non-separate, i.e. $p_1 = \bullet$, or when $p_1 = \bot$. The situation where $p_1 = \bot$ cannot occur because this processor tag is only used to type the void reference. In conclusion, we can only know which processor is expected if $p_1 \neq \top$. If this condition is satisfied then the combined type can have the processor tag of the target type. This scenario is described in the second case.

If the formal argument type is separate relative to the target, i.e. $p_2 = \top$ then the client can provide an actual argument on any processor. Therefore the actual argument can be considered as potentially separate from the perspective of the client. This scenario is handled by the third case.

If the formal argument type explicitly names a processor, i.e. $p_2 = \alpha$, then one could think that the processor tag of the combined type must be the processor tag of the formal argument type because we can exactly determine the processor of the actual argument. This is not true. The processor tag is not a global identification. It only makes sense in the context of class C_2 for the target x. In this situation we know that f is expecting an actual argument on a particular processor, but we do not know which one. Therefore this situation is illegal. This is indicated in the forth case where the processor tag of the combined type is set to $\perp$. The forth case also handles the situation where the formal argument is non-separate with respect to the target, i.e. $p_2 = \bullet$ but the target type is separate, i.e. $p_1 = \top$. As explained earlier this situation is illegal as well.

9   Type Conformance

In this section we will refine the existing type conformance rules described in sections 8.14.6 and 8.14.8 of the Eiffel ECMA standard [4] for the new type system to ensure soundness. We define the conformance of one type to another type over the conformance of the type components. Definition 29 states this more clearly. We use the symbol $\sqsubseteq$ for class type conformance and we use the symbol $\preceq$ for type conformance. The typing environment Γ contains the class hierarchy of the program enriched with ANY and $NONE$ along with the type declaration for all features, local variables, and formal arguments as defined by Nienaltowski [11].

Definition 29 (Type conformance)

$$
\frac{
\begin{array}{l}
\Gamma \vdash E_1 \sqsubseteq E_2 \\
\Gamma \vdash \forall j \in \{1, \ldots, m\}, (d_t, p_t, C_t) = relatedActualGenericParameter(b_j) : (\\
\quad (d_t, p_t, C_t) \preceq (d_{b_j}, p_{b_j}, C_{b_j}) \wedge \\
\quad ((d_t = d_{b_j} = ?) \vee (d_t = d_{b_j} \wedge p_t = p_{b_j} \wedge C_t = C_{b_j})) \\
)
\end{array}
}{
\Gamma \vdash E_1[a_1, \ldots, a_n] \sqsubseteq E_2[b_1, \ldots, b_m = (d_{b_m}, p_{b_m}, C_{b_m})]
} \tag{2}
$$

The related actual generic parameter of an actual generic parameter b_j is the actual generic parameter a_i whose formal generic parameter is used in the inheritance declaration of E_1 as an actual generic parameter for the formal generic parameter of b_j, provided such an a_i exists. Otherwise it is the actual generic parameter for the formal generic parameter of b_j as defined in the inheritance declaration of E_1 or one of its ancestors.

$$
\frac{
\begin{array}{l}
\Gamma \vdash C_1 \sqsubseteq C_2 \\
\Gamma \vdash isExpanded(C_2) \rightarrow (C_1 = C_2)
\end{array}
}{
\Gamma \vdash (d, p, C_1) \preceq (d, p, C_2)
} \tag{3}
$$

$$
\frac{\Gamma \vdash (d, p, C_1) \preceq (d, p, C_2)}{\Gamma \vdash (d, p_1, C_1) \preceq (d, \top, C_2)}
\qquad
\frac{\Gamma \vdash (d, p, C_1) \preceq (d, p, C_2)}{\Gamma \vdash (d, \perp, C_1) \preceq (d, p_2, C_2)}
\tag{4}
$$

$$\frac{\Gamma \vdash (d, p_1, C_1) \preceq (d, p_2, C_2)}{\Gamma \vdash (!, p_1, C_1) \preceq (?, p_2, C_2)} \tag{5}$$

Example 13 (Related actual generic parameters). Listing 1.12 shows a class *ARRAY*. This class inherits from class *INDEXABLE*.

Listing 1.12. array and indexable classes

```
  class ARRAY[F] inherit INDEXABLE[INTEGER, F] ... end
2
  class INDEXABLE[G, H] ... end
```

We use E_1 to identify the type *ARRAY*[separate *BOOK*] and we use E_2 to identify the type *INDEXABLE*[*INTEGER*, separate *BOOK*]. We use a_1 for the single actual generic parameter in E_1 and we use b_1 and b_2 to denote the first and the second actual generic parameters in E_2. The goal of this example is to find the related actual generic parameters of b_1 and b_2. The formal generic parameter of a_1 is F. In the inheritance declaration of class *ARRAY* the formal generic parameter F is used as an actual generic parameter for the formal generic parameter H of class *INDEXABLE*. As b_2 belongs to H, a_1 is the related actual generic parameter of b_2. For b_1 there are no more actual generic parameter in E_1 that could serve as the related actual generic parameter. However, class *ARRAY* uses $(!, \bullet, INTEGER)$ as the actual generic parameter for the formal generic parameter G of class *INDEXABLE*. As b_1 belongs to G, $(!, \bullet, INTEGER)$ is the related actual generic parameter of b_1.

Equations 2 and 3 deal with class type conformance. Equation 2 deals with generically derived class types and equation 3 handles class types that are not generically derived. In principle, equation 2 is the covariant Eiffel rule with a restriction that prevents traitors as a special form of cat calls. Such a cat call is shown in example 14. To prevent catcalls, the definition requires equality between two related actual generic parameters. This requirement can only be ignored if the actual generic parameter in the sub type is detachable. This implies that the corresponding formal generic parameter has a detachable constraint. As a consequence, every feature that has a formal argument of a type equal to such a detachable formal generic parameter must ensure that the formal argument is non-void prior to a safe call. The object test is a mechanism to test whether an expression is non-void. In addition, an object test ensures that the attached object has a certain dynamic type. Note that the dynamic type includes the processor tag. In conclusion, a detachable actual generic parameter implies the necessity of a check of the processor tag. A detachable actual generic parameter in the sub type implies a detachable actual generic parameter in the super type because the sub type must conform to the super type. More information on object tests can be taken from the Eiffel ECMA standard [4]. Equation 3 shows that expanded classes cannot serve as ancestors and thus a class type conforms to an expanded class type only if the two class types are actually the same.

The processor tag conformance rule in equation 4 states that every processor tag conforms to the $\top$ processor tag. Furthermore it defines that the $\bot$ processor tag conforms to every other processor tag. As a result, processor tags can be arranged in a lattice with the $\top$ processor tag on the top and the $\bot$ processor tag at the bottom. Every other processor tag is in the middle, conforming to the top element. The bottom element conforms directly to the middle elements and indirectly to the top element. The $\top$ processor tag denotes a potentially separate processor. An object on any processor can be attached to an entity of such a type. Therefore the explicit processor tag and the non-separate processor tag conform to the $\top$ processor tag. The $\bot$ processor tag symbolizes no processor and it is used to type the void reference. A void reference can be assigned to any writable entity of detachable type, regardless of the processor tag of the entity. As a consequence, the $\bot$ processor tag conforms to any other processor tag. Note that the explicit processor tag does not conform to the non-separate processor tag, even though one can denote the current processor with the explicit processor tag.

An entity of detachable type potentially has an object attached to it. Equation 5 states that the ! detachable tag conforms to the ? detachable tag. The reverse argument is not true. An entity of attached type cannot store a void reference. Note that this definition is compatible with the self-initialization rule for generic parameters as described in section 8.12.6 of the Eiffel ECMA standard [4].

Example 14 (Traitor cat calls). In listing 1.13 the class *ILLEGAL_LIBRARY* declares an attribute *books* of type *LIST*[separate *BOOK*].

Listing 1.13. illegal library class

```
   class ILLEGAL_LIBRARY feature
2    initialize
         -- Initialize this library.
4      do
         create {LIST[BOOK]} books
6        books.put (create {separate BOOK})
       end
8
     books: LIST[separate BOOK]  -- The books.
10 end
```

The type of the formal argument in *books.put* is **separate** *BOOK*. Therefore the feature *books.put* can be called with **create** {**separate** *BOOK*} as an actual argument. If equation 2 would permit covariant actual generic parameters without restrictions then it would be possible to attach an object of type *LIST*[*BOOK*] to the entity *books*. However, a call to the feature *books.put* would then result in a traitor, because the object stored in *books* expects a non-separate formal argument whereas the call provides a separate actual argument. For this reason definition 29 does not allow the attachment of an object of type *LIST*[*BOOK*] to an entity of type *LIST*[separate *BOOK*].

Definition 29 implies that there must be a root type in the type system. Any object can be attached to an entity of this type. In the Eiffel type system, the class *ANY* is at the top of the type hierarchy. Thus *ANY* is suitable as the class type component of the root type. To be most general, the root type must be detachable and separate.

Definition 30 (Root type). *The root type is* $(?, \top, ANY)$.

Example 15 (Valid and invalid subtypes). Listing 1.14 shows a number of entities. In this example we will explore whether these entities can be assigned to each other.

Listing 1.14. entities to demonstrate valid and invalid subtypes

```
  a: HAMLET
2 b: detachable separate BOOK
  c: separate <p> BOOK
4 d: separate <q> BOOK
  e: ARRAY[detachable HAMLET]
6 f: ARRAY[HAMLET]
  g: INDEXABLE[INTEGER, detachable separate BOOK]
8
  p: PROCESSOR
10 q: PROCESSOR
```

We will start with the entities a and b. We will use definition 29 to determine whether $(!, \bullet, HAMLET)$ conforms to $(?, \top, BOOK)$. We omit premises that do not apply and we omit premises that are satisfied trivially.

$$\frac{\dfrac{\dfrac{\Gamma \vdash HAMLET \sqsubseteq BOOK}{\Gamma \vdash (d, p, HAMLET) \preceq (d, p, BOOK)}}{\Gamma \vdash (d, \bullet, HAMLET) \preceq (d, \top, BOOK)}}{\Gamma \vdash (!, \bullet, HAMLET) \preceq (?, \top, BOOK)}$$

We read the derivation bottom-up. In the first step we use the detachable tag conformance rule from equation 5. In the second step we use the processor tag conformance rule from equation 4. The class type conformance rule from equation 3 leads us to the last premise, which can be derived from the typing environment. The details on the typing environments can be taken from section 6.11.4 in Nienaltowski's dissertation [11]. The derivation shows that a can be assigned to b. In a similar way, one can derive that c and d can be assigned to b. It is however not possible to do any other assignments among a, b, c, and d. In particular, c cannot be assigned to d because the types specify different processors.

So far we only looked at types that are not generically derived. In a next step we will take a look at generically derived types to see whether e can be assigned to g. We use the class type conformance rule for generically derived class types from equation 2.

$$\cfrac{\Gamma \vdash ARRAY \sqsubseteq INDEXABLE \quad \cfrac{\Gamma \vdash HAMLET \sqsubseteq BOOK}{\cfrac{\Gamma \vdash (d,p,HAMLET) \preceq (d,p,BOOK)}{\Gamma \vdash (?,\bullet,HAMLET) \preceq (?,\top,BOOK)}}}{\Gamma \vdash ARRAY[(?,\bullet,HAMLET)] \sqsubseteq INDEXABLE[(!,\bullet,INTEGER),(?,\top,BOOK)]}$$

We do not show the premise $(!,\bullet,INTEGER) \preceq (!,\bullet,INTEGER)$, because it is satisfied trivially. In the same spirit we do not show the premise $(d_t = d_{b_j} = ?) \vee (d_t = d_{b_j} \wedge p_t = p_{b_j} \wedge C_t = C_{b_j})$. The derivation shows that indeed e can be assigned to g. The entity f cannot be assigned to g. This is due to the attached actual generic parameter of f, which is not compatible with the detachable generic parameter in g.

10 Feature Redeclaration

A child class inherits features from a parent class. An inherited feature can either be reused, undefined, or redeclared. In a redeclaration, the child class provides a new implementation. The redeclaration can have a weaker precondition and it can have a stronger postcondition. Any feature redeclaration must ensure that the redeclared version of the feature can be called whenever the parent feature can be called. In particular, the contracts and the signatures must be compatible. Sections 8.10.26, 8.14.4, and 8.14.5 of the Eiffel ECMA standard [4] define rules to take care of this for Eiffel. In this section we will refine these rules for SCOOP. Definition 31 defines valid result type redeclarations and definition 32 does the same for formal arguments.

Definition 31 (Valid result type redeclaration). *The result type of a feature can be redeclared from T_1 to T_2 if and only if T_2 conforms to T_1, i.e. $T_2 \preceq T_1$.*

Just like in Eiffel, the result type can be redeclared covariantly. For all three components of a SCOOP type it is always possible to return something more specific than what the client of a feature expects.

Definition 32 (Valid formal argument redeclaration). *The type of a formal argument x can be redeclared from $T_1 = (d_1, p_1, C_1)$ to $T_2 = (d_2, p_2, C_2)$ if and only if all of the following conditions are true:*

- *If T_1 is detachable then T_2 is detachable, i.e. $d_1 = ? \rightarrow d_2 = ?$. T_2 can only be detachable if x is not a target in the inherited postcondition.*
- *Types T_2 and T_1 have identical processor tags, i.e. $p_2 = p_1$, or T_2 is separate, i.e. $p_2 = \top$.*

- *Class type C_2 conforms to C_1, i.e. $C_2 \sqsubseteq C_1$. If C_2 and C_1 are not the same then T_2 is detachable, i.e. $C_2 \neq C_1 \rightarrow d_2 = ?$.*

In Eiffel, formal arguments can be redeclared in a covariant way. However, if the class type changes then the redeclared formal argument must be detachable. A detachable formal argument can contain the void reference. This forces the redeclared feature to use an object test to ensure that the formal argument is non-void. Next to the non-void check the object test ensures that the formal argument has a certain dynamic type. Therefore the redeclared feature is required to check the dynamic type of the formal argument. This makes it possible for the redeclared feature to receive an actual argument whose type is a super type of the redeclared formal argument type, as it is possible in a covariant redeclaration. Definition 32 goes along this line for the class type. A class type of a formal argument can be redeclared covariantly as long as the redeclared formal argument becomes detachable. The processor tag of a formal argument can be redeclared contravariantly. The covariant redeclaration is not allowed for processor tags because it would lead to traitors. If the processor tag of a formal argument can be redeclared covariantly then it would be possible to redeclare a separate formal argument to non-separate. The contravariant redeclaration is not a problem because the redeclared feature can always use a more general processor tag.

Detachable tags encode selective locking. Assuming a formal argument could be redeclared covariantly from detachable to attached then the application of the redeclared feature would lock the request queue of the formal argument. However, the parent feature specifies a non-locking formal argument. The redeclared feature could not be called whenever the parent feature is called. On the other hand a formal argument can be redeclared contravariantly from attached to detachable because this would alleviate the locking requirements. Furthermore it is always safe to assume a detachable formal argument when the actual argument is non-void.

A redeclaration of a formal argument from attached to detachable imposes a risk on the validity of the inherited postcondition. Assuming a parent feature has a postcondition clause that contains a query on a formal argument. According to the valid target rule in definition 19 this formal argument must be attached. A redeclaration of the formal argument from attached to detachable renders the inherited postcondition clause invalid. An invalid postcondition clause is equivalent to a weaker postcondition and thus this situation is not acceptable. Therefore a formal argument can only be redeclared from attached to detachable if the formal argument is not a target in the inherited postcondition clause.

There is a similar issue for inherited precondition clauses. A redeclaration of a formal argument from attached to detachable renders the precondition clause invalid. An invalid precondition clause is equivalent to a weaker precondition. This situation is accepted because this is only a problem for the redeclaring feature and not for the client of the feature. The redeclared feature can assume a weaker precondition as it ignores the invalid precondition clause. As a consequence, such a precondition clause can be assumed to hold vacuously. This is expressed in definition 33.

Definition 33 (Inherited precondition rule). *Inherited precondition clauses with calls on a detachable formal argument hold vacuously.*

Example 16 (Valid feature redeclaration). Listing 1.15 shows a valid redeclaration of the feature *cheaper_alternative*.

Listing 1.15. finder class

```
   class LOCAL_FINDER feature
2    cheaper_alternative (a_book: BOOK): BOOK
           -- A cheaper alternative to 'a_book'.
4      do
          ...
6      ensure
           Result.initial_price < a_book.initial_price
8      end
   end
10
   class WORLDWIDE_FINDER
12
   inherit LOCAL_FINDER
14   redefine
         cheaper_alternative
16   end

18 feature
      cheaper_alternative (a_book: separate BOOK): BOOK
20         -- A cheaper alternative to 'a_book'.
         do
22       ...
         end
24 end
```

The formal argument gets redeclared from $FT_1 = (!, \bullet, BOOK)$ to $FT_2 = (!, \top, BOOK)$. This is valid according to definition 32. Note that FT_2 cannot be detachable because the formal argument is a target in the inherited postcondition. A detachable type would make the inherited postcondition invalid. The processor tag changes from non-separate to separate. It is allowed to accept a non-separate object in a separate entity.

11   False Traitors

At runtime a non-separate object can get attached to a separate entity. The type system permits this. The downside of such an action is a loss of information in the type system. We know that the entity points to a non-separate object, but the type system cannot make this assumption. For example it is not possible to assign the separate entity to a non-separate entity. The type system would complain about a traitor, even though the attached object is in fact non-separate. We call such an object a false traitor.

Definition 34 (False traitor). *A false traitor is a non-separate object accessible through to a separate expression.*

This is not a SCOOP specific problem. The same issue occurs when an object gets attached to an entity whose static type is a proper parent of the object's dynamic type. The solution is the same as in Eiffel. An object test can be used to ensure that the dynamic type of the expression is non-separate.

12   Agents

Agent objects wrap feature calls. An agent can be passed around and the wrapper feature can be called at a later time. When the agent gets created any of the actual arguments can be predefined. An agent call must only provide the remaining actual arguments. These remaining actual arguments are called open and the predefined ones are called closed. Similarly, it is possible to have an open or a closed target. An open target specifies the type of the future target instead of the target itself. In this section we will discuss the location of a new agent. We consider two options. The agent could be handled by the current processor or the agent could be handled by the processor of the target.

The creation of a new agent on the current processor causes problems. Such an agent would be non-separate from the current object. Therefore the agent would always be a valid target on the current processor. If the agent encapsulates a feature call on a separate target then the current processor could call the encapsulated feature on the separate object without having acquired a request queue lock. The agent would be a non-separate object that encapsulates a separate object and we would have a traitor situation.

If the new agent is handled by the same processor as the target then this problem does not occur. This way, the agent represents its target properly in terms of location. Agent calls can be freely mixed with other feature calls. A lock on the request queue of the handler of encapsulated target is ensured through a lock on the request queue of the handler of the agent. There is however a price for this scheme with respect to open targets. At construction time, the handler of the agent must be known and it must be equal to the handler of the future target. If the target type is non-separate then this is not a problem because the exact processor is know. If the target type has an explicit processor specification then the exact processor is known at creation time. However, the explicit processor specification is only valid in the context where the agent gets created. If the agent gets called in a different context then the exact processor of the target is unknown at call time. If the target type is separate then there is no way of knowing the exact handler when the agent gets created. In conclusion, the type of an open target must be non-separate. As a further restriction, the open target type must be attached because it is not possible to invoke a method on a non existing target. Definition 35 captures these requirements.

Definition 35 (Agent creation). *A new agent is handled by the same processor as its target. An open target agent must have an attached and non-separate type.*

The type of an agent must show that the agent is on the same processor as the target. Definition 36 redefines section 8.27.17 of the Eiffel ECMA standard [4].

Definition 36 (Agent expression type). *Consider an agent expression with target type $T_x = (!, p, X)$ and feature f. Let $i_1, \ldots, i_m$ be the open argument positions and let $T_1, \ldots, T_m$ be the types of f's formal arguments at positions $i_1, \ldots, i_m$ (taking T_{i_1} to be T_x if the target is open, e.g. $i_1 = 0$). The agent expression has the following type:*

- *The type is $(!, p, PROCEDURE[(!, \bullet, X), (!, \bullet, TUPLE[T_1, \ldots, T_m])])$ if f is a procedure.*
- *The type is $(!, p, FUNCTION[(!, \bullet, X), (!, \bullet, TUPLE[T_1, \ldots, T_m]), T_R])$ if f is a function of result type T_R other than $(!, \bullet, BOOLEAN)$.*
- *The type is $(!, p, PREDICATE[(!, \bullet, X), (!, \bullet, TUPLE[T_1, \ldots, T_m])])$ if f is a function of result type $(!, \bullet, BOOLEAN)$.*

Example 17 (Agents). Listing 1.16 shows a class representing book traders.

Listing 1.16. trader class

```
  class TRADER feature
2   option: separate PROCEDURE[SELLER, TUPLE[separate BUYER]]

4   prepare_option (a_seller: separate SELLER; a_book: separate BOOK;
          a_valuer: separate VALUER)
        do
6           option := agent a_seller.sell_book (a_book, ?, a_valuer)
        end
8 end
```

The feature *prepare_option* creates an option to sell a particular book through a particular seller using a particular valuer at a later time. Profit can be generated if a book has been bought at a low price through the estimate of one valuer and if the book can be sold later at a higher price through the estimate of another valuer. In this example the option is represented by an agent for the feature *sell_book* with the seller as the target. The book and the valuer are closed arguments. The buyer is left as an open argument. The open argument is indicated with the question mark. The type of the agent is the type of the attribute *option*. The agent has the same processor tag as the target.

13   Once Routines

A once routine gets executed at most once in a specified context. In Eiffel, a once routine either has a once per object, a once per thread, or a once per system semantics. If the once routine is a once function then the result gets shared within the specified context. Sections 8.23.20, 8.23.21, and 8.23.22 of the Eiffel ECMA standard [4] describe this in more details. In SCOOP, processors replace the notion of threads. In this section we will refine the existing Eiffel rules. Instead of the original options we consider a once per system or a once per processor semantics.

The result of a once function with a separate result type is supposed to be shared by different processors. Otherwise it makes no sense to declare the result as separate. Therefore such a function must have the once per system semantics. Once functions with a non-separate result type on the other hand must have a once per processor semantics. Otherwise there would be one object for multiple non-separate once functions on multiple processors. Clearly, the object can only be non-separate with respect to one processor. For all other processors the object would be a traitor. Once procedures do not come with these complications as they do not have a result. We assign a once per processor semantics to once procedures to give each processor the chance to make a fresh call to the procedure.

Definition 37 (Once routines semantics). *A once routine either has a once per system or a once per processor semantics.*

- *Once functions with a separate result type have the once per system semantics.*
- *Once functions with a non-separate result type have the once per processor semantics.*
- *Once procedures have the once per processor semantics.*

Example 18 (Once functions). Listing 1.17 shows a class representing phone directories of a country.

Listing 1.17. phone directory class

```
   class PHONE_DIRECTORY feature
2    national_directory: separate BOOK
        once
4        ...
        end
6
     local_directory: BOOK
8    once
         ...
10    end
   end
```

The country is divided into several states. Each state has a set of phone numbers. In addition there are some national phone numbers that are valid in every state. The phone directory takes this into account with two once functions: *national_directory* is a book containing all the national numbers and *local_directory* is a book with the local numbers. We imagine that each state is handled by a different processor and that the phone directory is on yet another processor. The feature *national_directory* is a separate once function. It has a once per system semantics. This takes into account that there is one directory for the whole nation. The feature *local_directory* is a non-separate once function and thus it has a once per processor semantics. This reflects the fact that there is one local directory per state.

14   Limitations and Future Work

At the beginning of this article we emphasized SCOOP's simplicity in comparison to semaphore based concurrent programming models. There are some threats to the validity of this claim. Our claim is not supported by any systematic study. Furthermore there has been progress on other concurrent programming models that make it easier to write correct and reusable concurrent programs. In particular there exist powerful concurrency libraries that can be used by developers, e.g. the concurrency libraries of Java (see e.g. [5]). A full support of our claim requires a study that compares SCOOP to the state-of-the art of concurrent programming models.

We do not claim that SCOOP programs run faster than other concurrent programs. However, performance is a key objective in any concurrent program. Performance of SCOOP programs is negatively affected if a centralized scheduling algorithm is used. A decentralized scheduling algorithm solves this issue and makes the system scalable. Performance can also be negatively influenced if the program under execution applies locking too coarsely. The differentiation between read- and write locks could improve the situation together with other refinements of the model. One refinement concerns wait by necessity. The SCOOP model can be optimized by only waiting when the result of the query is about to be accessed. As long as the result is not being accessed, it does not need to be available. A profiler for SCOOP specific metrics could help to find bottlenecks in SCOOP programs.

Currently SCOOP does not solve the asynchronous exception problem. Consider a situation where the execution of a procedure on a separate object results in an exception. It is possible that the client processor left the context of the feature call. In such a case the client processor is no longer able to handle the exception. The problem is tackled by Arslan and Meyer [1] as well as Brooke and Paige [2]. Arslan and Meyer define the guilty processor as the one who called the feature that triggered the exception. In their approach the target processor is considered busy by non-guilty processors. Only the guilty processor can resolve the situation by handling the exception as soon as the guilty processor locks the request queue of the busy processor once again. Brooke and Paige propose another mechanism to handle asynchronous exceptions. Their approach includes the notion of failed or dead objects.

Deadlocks are still an open problem in SCOOP. The selective locking mechanism is a useful technique to reduce the potential for deadlocks. However, this is not a method for ensure absence of deadlocks. It is necessary to conduct a comprehensive study on how deadlocks can occur in SCOOP programs. Such a study would facilitate an approach to avoid deadlocks in SCOOP programs. One approach in this direction is presented by Ostroff et al. [13]. They describe a virtual machine for SCOOP. The goal is to use model-checking and theorem proving methods to check global temporal logic properties of SCOOP programs.

The operational semantics used by Ostroff et al. may be extended to cover more of SCOOP. A complete definition could serve as a precise description of the model. At the moment SCOOP's complexity and the intrinsic details are hidden behind informal descriptions. The formalization could be the basis for formal proofs of properties promised by the model as well as for formal proofs of SCOOP programs. Interesting properties of the model include the absence of data races and the soundness of the type system.

Even though SCOOP naturally embraces distribution right from its start there are still open issues to be solved. In particular, it is unclear how distributed scheduling or mapping of processors to resources should be devised and implemented. Furthermore there is a fixed association of one object to a particular processor. It unclear whether this processor must be constant over time. Object migration would be especially beneficial for distribution because the latency of separate feature calls becomes significant in distributed programs.

The execution of a concurrent program can be different from one execution to the other. Hence, some bugs only show in some scheduling scenarios. This makes testing of concurrent applications very cumbersome. By design, SCOOP already rules out a number of scheduling related bugs such as high-level and low-level data races. Other potential bugs remain. It would be interesting to extend a testing framework to make scheduling a factor in test cases. Along the same line, it would be interesting to develop a debugger for SCOOP programs.

It would be interesting to have a design tool where one can graphically specify the dynamic and the static view of a SCOOP program. The dynamic view includes processors, the objects, and the interactions. The dynamic view uses concepts introduced in the static view. The static view shows the classes and existing SCOOP components. The graphical design is linked to the SCOOP code. Hence the designer can produce a SCOOP program out of the diagrams.

As part of the ETH Verification Environment (EVE) there is an implementation of SCOOP in progress. The implementation is available on our project website http://scoop.origo.ethz.ch.

References

1. Arslan, V., Meyer, B.: Asynchronous exceptions in concurrent object-oriented programming. In: Symposium on Concurrency, Real-Time and Distribution in Eiffel-like Languages Proceedings, pp. 62–70 (2006)
2. Brooke, P.J., Paige, R.F.: Exceptions in concurrent eiffel. Journal of Object Technology 6(10) (2007)
3. Coffman, E.G., Elphick, M.J., Shoshani, A.: System deadlocks. ACM Computing Surveys 3(2), 67–78 (1971)

4. ECMA. Ecma-367 eiffel: Analysis, design and programming language 2nd edition. Technical report, ECMA International (2006)
5. Goetz, B., Bloch, J., Bowbeer, J., Lea, D., Holmes, D., Peierls, T.: Java Concurrency in Practice. Addison-Wesley, Reading (2006)
6. Hoare, C.A.R.: Procedures and parameters: An axiomatic approach. In: Symposium on Semantics of Algorithmic Languages, pp. 102–116 (1971)
7. Meyer, B.: Sequential and concurrent object-oriented programming. In: Technology of Object-Oriented Languages and Systems, pp. 17–28 (1990)
8. Meyer, B.: Applying design by contract. IEEE Computer 25(10), 40–51 (1992)
9. Meyer, B.: Systematic concurrent object-oriented programming. Communications of the ACM 36(9), 56–80 (1993)
10. Meyer, B.: Object-Oriented Software Construction, 2nd edn. Prentice Hall, Englewood Cliffs (1997)
11. Nienaltowski, P.: Practical framework for contract-based concurrent object-oriented programming. PhD thesis, Swiss Federal Institute of Technology Zurich (2007)
12. Nienaltowski, P., Meyer, B.: Contracts for concurrency. In: First International Symposium on Concurrency, Real-Time and Distribution in Eiffel-like Languages, pp. 27–49 (2006)
13. Ostroff, J.S., Torshizi, F.A., Huang, H.F., Schoeller, B.: Beyond contracts for concurrency. Formal Aspects of Computing 21(4), 319–346 (2008)

Using the Spec# Language, Methodology, and Tools to Write Bug-Free Programs

K. Rustan M. Leino[0] and Peter Müller[1]

[0] Microsoft Research, Redmond, WA, USA
leino@microsoft.com
[1] ETH Zurich, Switzerland
peter.mueller@inf.ethz.ch

Abstract. Spec# is a programming system for the development of correct programs. It consists of a programming language, a verification methodology, and tools. The Spec# language extends C# with contracts, which allow programmers to document their design decisions in the code. The verification methodology provides rules and guidelines for how to use the Spec# features to express and check properties of interesting implementations. Finally, the tool support consists of a compiler that emits run-time checks for many contracts and a static program verifier that attempts to prove automatically that an implementation satisfies its specification. These lecture notes teach the use of the Spec# system, focusing on specification and static verification.

0 Introduction: What Is Spec#

The Spec# programming system was built as a research effort to gain experience in programming with specifications, focusing on how one can specify object-oriented programs and how the specifications can be enforced dynamically and statically [2]. These lecture notes give a tutorial account of how to write and specify programs in Spec#. The aim here is for the specifications to be detailed enough that programs can be verified statically, using the Spec# static program verifier. The verifier checks that programs satisfy their specifications and that they do not lead to run-time errors. It assumes sequential execution; that is, it does not check for concurrency errors such as data races and deadlocks, and it might miss errors caused by insufficient synchronization of threads.

The verifier is run like the compiler—in fact, it can be turned on to run at "design time", in the background as the programmer types in the program [0]. Akin to the way a compiler performs separate compilation, the Spec# program verifier performs *modular verification*, which means that it can be applied to pieces of a program separately. A programmer interacts with the program verifier only by supplying program text and specifications and by receiving error messages, analogously to how a programmer interacts with the compiler. The goal of this tutorial is to provide the user with an understanding of the concepts that underlie the Spec# specifications, which will also help in deciphering the error messages.

The specifications of a program must describe the steady state of data structures and must account for the changes that such data structures undergo. This can be done in various ways. The way Spec# does this is to impose a programming discipline, a

P. Müller (Ed.): LASER Summer School 2007/2008, LNCS 6029, pp. 91–139, 2010.

methodology, that guides how specifications and programs are written. This methodology is closely tied to the specification constructs provided by the language, for example the **invariant** declaration. Through our experience, we have found that programming problems that fit the methodology can be specified and verified with ease; however, we have also found that it is too easy to fall outside the boundaries of what the methodology permits. For this reason, it is much easier to verify programs when they are designed with specification in mind from the start.

In the literature, the methodology used by Spec# has been called the *Boogie methodology*, since the Spec# programs are verified using a tool called Boogie. In retrospect, this is a bit confusing, because the Boogie language and tool are also used in applications that are unrelated to Spec#. To reduce confusion in this tutorial, we will use the words *Spec# methodology* and *program verifier*.

It is specifically not a goal of this tutorial to justify the Spec# methodology, only to explain how it is used. Also, this tutorial is not a reference manual; it is more of a cookbook for how to handle common situations. We conclude many sections in this tutorial with notes on advanced features that we cannot describe in detail here and with suggestions for further reading. These notes are marked with a "steep ascent" sign. We focus on static verification of programs, but occasionally add remarks that pertain to the dynamic checks that the Spec# compiler emits. Finally, we have done our best to explain what Spec# is today, which in many small ways differs from what is described in research papers that we and our colleagues have written; for example, the research papers use many variations of syntax, describe solutions to specification problems that have not been implemented in the Spec# programming system, spend many words and theorems justifying the soundness of the approach, sometimes show specifications in full detail whereas Spec# uses a host of defaults, and do not mention additional features and automation that is available in Spec#.

Installing and Using Spec#. The Spec# binaries (and sources) and installation instructions are available from `http://specsharp.codeplex.com/`. We recommend using Z3 [5] as the theorem prover for the Spec# program verifier; it can be installed from `http://research.microsoft.com/projects/z3/`. The Spec# installation requires Visual Studio. Once installed, Spec# can be used within Visual Studio or from the command line.

All examples presented in this tutorial are available online [11]. They compile and verify with the latest Spec# version (v1.0.21125), which requires Visual Studio .NET 2008. To try an example `File.ssc` from the command line, first compile the program to a library:

```
ssc /t:library /debug /nn File.ssc
```

and then run the program verifier

```
SscBoogie File.dll
```

The compiler option `/debug` produces a file `File.pdb` with debug information, which is needed by the program verifier. The `/nn` switch makes non-null types the default (see Section 1.0) and is used for all examples in this tutorial. Rather than running the verifier separately, it is also possible to invoke it from the compiler by adding the `/verify` switch (which in some cases has the side effect of giving more detailed source locations in error messages). The `/help` option of the compiler and the verifier displays a list of all available options.

To run the examples inside Visual Studio, create a new Spec# project (from File → New → Project) and edit its project properties (by right-clicking on the name of the project in the Solution Explorer and then choosing Properties) as follows. In the section "Configuration Properties", set "ReferenceTypesAreNonNullByDefault", "RunProgramVerifier", and "RunProgramVerifierWhileEditing" to true. The compiler's parser and type checker and the program verifier will now run automatically in the background while you are editing your code. The compiler and verifier show any errors they detect using red or green squigglies at the location of each error. Hoving with the mouse over such a squiggly displays the error message. All error messages are also shown in the Error List (whose pane is made visible by View → Error List). To compile your program into executable code, build the project (using Build → Build Solution).

1 Basics

In this section, we go through a number of small examples that illustrate the syntax of some familiar specification constructs, as well as the use of some less familiar constructs. It also serves as an incomplete summary of features that Spec# adds to its basis, C#. We assume a basic familiarity with C-like syntax, like that found in Spec#, C#, Java, or C++. We also assume a basic familiarity with object-oriented concepts (for example, classes, instances, fields) and how these are represented in Java-like languages.

1.0 Non-null Types

One of the most frequent errors in object-oriented programs is to dereference the null reference. To eradicate this error, Spec#'s type system distinguishes between *non-null types* and *possibly-null types*. In this tutorial, we assume non-null types to be the default. In this mode, the type **string** is the type of all proper string objects, whereas the type **string**? includes the string objects plus **null**.

The class NonNull in Fig. 0 declares three string fields, two with a non-null type and one with a possibly-null type. On entry to a constructor, fields have zero-equivalent values, in particular, fields of reference type initially hold the null reference. Each constructor of a class is responsible for initializing non-null fields with non-null values.[0] If the class does not explicitly declare a constructor, a default constructor is implicitly added by the compiler. In that case, non-null fields have to be initialized using a field initializer in the declaration of the field. The constructor of class NonNull initializes aString through a field initializer and anotherString through an assignment inside the constructor body. It leaves maybeAString un-initialized.

---

[0] There are actually two kinds of constructors in the language, those that, explicitly or implicitly, call a constructor of the superclass and those that instead call another constructor of the same class (using **this**(...)). Here and throughout, we only discuss the first kind of constructor; in several ways, the other kind operates more like a method than a constructor.

```
class NonNull {
  string aString = "Hello";
  string anotherString;
  string? maybeAString;

  public NonNull() {
    anotherString = "World";
  }

  public int GetCharCount() {
    return aString.Length + maybeAString.Length;   // type error
  }
}
```

Fig. 0. An example using non-null and possibly-null types. The body of GetCharCount does not type check because it dereferences a possibly-null reference, maybeAString.

The Spec# type checker does not allow possibly-null references to be dereferenced. For instance, without further information, it flags the call maybeAString.Length in Fig. 0 as a type error. There are several ways to make this code type check. First, we could guard the call by a conditional statement (**if**) or expression. For instance, we could write the second summand as

```
(maybeAString != null ? maybeAString.Length : 0)
```

Second, we could add a specification (for instance, an inline assertion, see below) that expresses that maybeAString holds a non-null value. Third, we could convey the information to the type checker through a type cast. For example, we could have written

```
((string)maybeAString).Length
```

which casts maybeAString from the possibly-null type **string**? to the non-null type **string**. Here, since the type of the target is **string**, the dereference is permitted. The correctness of the cast is checked by the program verifier.[1]

A synonym for the non-null type **string** is **string**![2] The type cast can therefore also be expressed as (**string**!). In cases where the programmer only intends to cast the nullity aspect of the type, Spec# allows the cast to be written simply as (!). Thus, the call could also have been written as ((!)maybeAString).Length.

---

[1] As for other type casts, the compiler emits a run-time check for the cast. For this type cast, the run-time check will include a comparison with **null**.

[2] If the compiler is run in the mode where class names by default stand for the corresponding possibly-null type, then one routinely uses **string**! to denote the non-null type. Also, regardless of the compiler mode used, both inflections ? and ! are useful in the implementations of generic classes: if T is a type parameter constrained to be a reference type, then the naked name T stands for the actual type parameter (which might be a possibly-null type or a non-null type), T? stands for the possibly-null version of the type, and T! stands for the non-null version of the type.

1.1 Method Contracts

One of the basic units of specification in Spec# is the method. Each method can include a *precondition*, which describes the circumstances under which the method is allowed to be invoked, and a *postcondition*, which describes the circumstances under which the method is allowed to return. Consequently, an implementation of the method can assume the precondition to hold on entry, and a caller of the method can assume the postcondition to hold upon return. This agreement between callers and implementations is often known as a method *contract* [16].

```
int ISqrt(int x)
  requires 0 <= x;
  ensures result*result <= x && x < (result+1)*(result+1);
{
  int r = 0;
  while ((r+1)*(r+1) <= x)
    invariant r*r <= x;
  {
    r++;
  }
  return r;
}
```

Fig. 1. A Spec# program that computes the positive integer square root of a given number. To try this example in Spec#, include this method in a class declaration like "**class** Example { ... }".

Consider the method ISqrt in Fig. 1, which computes the integer square root of a given integer x. It is possible to implement the method only if x is non-negative, so the method uses a **requires** clause to declare an appropriate precondition. The method also uses an **ensures** clause to declare a postcondition. This postcondition uses the keyword **result**, which refers to the value returned by the method.[3] The program verifier enforces preconditions at call sites and postconditions at all normal (that is, non-exceptional) exit points.[4] Note that a non-terminating method execution does not reach an exit point and, therefore, trivially satisfies its postcondition. The Spec# verifier does not check for termination.

Syntactically, a method can use any number of **requires** and **ensures** clauses, in any order. The effective precondition is the conjunction of the **requires** clauses and the

---

[3] Like **value** in C# (and Spec#), **result** is a context-sensitive keyword. In particular, **result** is reserved only in postconditions; elsewhere, result is just an ordinary identifier.

[4] Pre- and postconditions are also enforced dynamically by compiler-emitted checks. Through these dynamic checks, a Spec# programmer benefits from contracts even if the program verifier is never applied. If an entire program is successfully verified by the program verifier, then the dynamic checks are guaranteed never to fail and could therefore, in principle, be removed. With one exception—the **assume** statement, which we explain in Section 1.2—the dynamic checks form a subset of the checks performed by the program verifier.

effective postcondition is the conjunction of the **ensures** clauses. Other specification constructs in Spec# can be used cumulatively in a similar way. As Fig. 1 suggests, method contracts are declared between the method type signature and the method body; if the method has no body, as for abstract methods and interface methods, the contract follows the semicolon that for such methods ends the method type signature.

```
class Counter {
  int x;

  public void Inc()
    ensures old(x) < x;
  {
    x = 2*x;   // error
  }
}
```

Fig. 2. A simple class with an instance field that is modified by a method. The method implementation fails to establish the postcondition in the case that x was initially less than or equal to zero; thus, the program verifier reports an "unsatisfied postcondition" error.

A postcondition is a *two-state predicate*: it relates the method's pre-state (the state on entry to the method) and the method's post-state (the state on exit from the method). To refer to the pre-state, one uses the **old** construct: **old**(E) refers to the value of expression E on entry to the method.[5] For example, consider the Counter class in Fig. 2. The postcondition of method Inc uses **old** to say that the final value of x is to be strictly greater than its initial value.[6] Regardless of **old**, an in-parameter mentioned in a method contract always refers to the value of the parameter on entry (in other words, the fact that the language allows in-parameters to be used as local variables inside the method body has no effect on the meaning of the contract), and an **out** parameter always refers to the value of the parameter on exit; **ref** parameters, which are treated as copy-in copy-out, are sensitive to the use of **old**.

The Counter example in Fig. 2 also shows that contracts operate at a level of abstraction that is not available directly in the code: the contract promises that x will be

---

[5] The **old** construct can be mentioned only in postconditions, not in, for example, inline assertions or loop invariants, see below. When those specifications need to refer to the pre-state value of an expression, one has to save it in an auxiliary local variable and use that variable in the specification.

[6] As a matter of consistent style, we prefer the operators < and <= over > and >=. This lets inequalities be read (by a human) from left to right, as if they were placed in order along a number line. For example, 0 <= x && x < N "shows" x to lie between 0 and less than N; compare this to the form x >= 0 && x < N, which does not give the same visual queue. A common mistake is to write the negation of this condition as 0 < x || x >= N. If all inequalities are turned the same way, the correct negation, x < 0 || N <= x, shows x as lying "left" of 0 or "right" of N. Though we use and advocate this style, it has no effect on the operation of the program verifier.

incremented, but does not let callers know by how much; the method body is thus free to make the amount of increment a private implementation decision. Note that the implementation in Fig. 2 does not live up to the postcondition; this could be fixed by adding a precondition such as 0 < x.

With one major exception, expressions that are given as part of contracts (like the condition given in a **requires** clause) are like any other expressions of the language. For example, they must type check and be of an appropriate type (**bool** in the case of **requires**). The major exception is that expressions in contracts are restricted to be *side effect free* (*pure*). For example, the declaration **requires** x++ is not allowed. The reason for this restriction is that contracts are supposed to describe the behavior of the program, not to change it. In particular, whether run-time contract checking is enabled (during testing) or disabled (in production code to increase performance) must not influence the behavior of the program.

1.2 Inline Assertions

While method contracts indicate conditions that are expected to hold on method boundaries, the **assert** statement can be used in code to indicate a condition that is expected to hold at that program point. Unlike a method contract, which spells out a contract between a caller and an implementation, the **assert** statement only provides a form of redundancy in the code—after all, the asserted condition is supposed to be a logical consequence of the surrounding code. This redundancy can be useful, because it gives a programmer a way to check his understanding of the code. In particular, the program verifier will attempt to prove that the assert does indeed always hold. We shall see several uses for this familiar statement throughout this tutorial.

For example, adding the statement

```
assert r <= x;
```

---

anywhere between the declaration of r and the **return** statement in Fig. 1 will cause the program verifier to check that r is bounded by x.

Sometimes a programmer expects a condition to hold somewhere in the code, but the condition cannot be proved as a logical consequence of the surrounding code and specifications. For example, it may be that the condition follows from a pattern of calls to methods that have not been given strong enough formal specifications. In such cases, using an **assert** would cause the program verifier to issue a complaint. More appropriate in such a case is to use an **assume** statement, which (like the **assert**) generates a run-time check but (unlike the **assert**) is taken on faith by the program verifier. There are good uses of **assume**, but one needs to be aware that it trades static checking for dynamic checking. Hence, by writing down a condition that does not hold—an extreme example would be **assume false**—the program verifier will be satisfied and the incorrect assumption will not be revealed until the condition fails at run-time. Good engineering will pay special attention to **assume** statements during testing and manual code inspections.

The compiler and type checker also pay some attention to **assert** and **assume** statements. For example, the type checker considers inline assertions for its non-null analysis. For instance, the type error in method GetCharCount (Fig. 0) can be prevented by adding **assume** maybeAString != **null** before the **return** statement.

1.3   Loop Invariants

A loop may prescribe an infinite number of different iteration sequences. Clearly, it is not feasible to reason about every one of these individually. Instead, the loop's iterations are reasoned about collectively via a *loop invariant*. The loop invariant describes the set of states that the program may be in at the beginning of any loop iteration.

The program verifier treats loops as if the only thing known at the beginning of an iteration is that the loop invariant holds. This means that loop invariants must be sufficiently strong to rule out unreachable states that otherwise would cause the program verifier to generate an error message. For example, the condition r <= x holds on every loop iteration in Fig. 1, but this loop invariant by itself would not be strong enough to prove that the method establishes its postcondition. The program verifier enforces the loop invariant by checking that it holds on entry to the loop (that is, before the first iteration) and that it holds at every *back edge* of the loop, that is, at every program point where control flow branches back to the beginning of a new iteration.

The loop in method ISqrt in Fig. 1 is a bit of a special case and coincides with the form of the simple loops usually employed in teaching material. What's special is that the loop has only one exit point, namely the one controlled by the loop guard, which is checked at the beginning of each loop iteration. In this special case, one can conclude that the loop invariant and the negation of the loop guard hold immediately after the loop. (In the case of ISqrt, this condition is exactly what is needed to prove the method postcondition. In many other cases, this condition is stronger than needed for the proof obligations that follow the loop, in the same way that an inductive hypothesis in mathematics is usually stronger than the theorem proved.) In the general case of a loop with multiple exits, one cannot conclude that the loop invariant holds immediately following the loop, but it is still true that the loop invariant holds at the beginning of every iteration, including at the beginning of the last iteration, the (partial) iteration in which control flow exits the loop.

For example, consider the method in Fig. 3, which performs a linear search, backwards. Note that the loop invariant 0 <= n holds at the beginning of every loop iteration, but it does not always hold after the loop, and ditto for the loop invariant with a quantifier. The program verifier explores all possible ways through the loop body to determine what may be assumed to hold after the loop.

Speaking of quantifiers, the example shows both an existential quantifier (**exists**) and a universal quantifier (**forall**). Each bound variable in a quantifier must be given a range with an **in** clause. Here, the range is a half-open integer range; for example, the range (0: a.Length) designates the integers from 0 to, but not including, a.Length. The program verifier currently supports only integer ranges in quantifiers, as well as ranges over array elements that can be converted into quantifiers over integer ranges. For example, the postcondition can equivalently be written as

```
ensures result == exists{int x in a; x == key};
```

```
bool LinearSearch(int[] a, int key)
  ensures result == exists{int i in (0: a.Length); a[i] == key};
{
  int n = a.Length;
  do
    invariant 0 <= n && n <= a.Length;
    invariant forall{int i in (n: a.Length); a[i] != key};
  {
    n--;
    if (n < 0) {
      break;
    }
  } while (a[n] != key);
  return 0 <= n;
}
```

Fig. 3. A linear search that goes through the given array backwards. The example illustrates a loop with multiple exit points. In addition, the example illustrates the use of several **invariant** declarations, which are equivalent to conjoining the conditions into just one **invariant** declaration, and the use of quantifier expressions. Note that the interval (x: y) is half open, that is, i **in** (x: y) says that i satisfies x <= i && i < y.

Quantified expressions are not confined to use in contracts, but can also be used in code. For example, one could implement the linear-search method with a single line:

```
return exists{int x in a; x == key};
```

However, the program verifier currently does not understand quantifiers in code, so it complains that it cannot prove the postcondition for this single-line implementation.[7]

Not all loop invariants need to be supplied explicitly. The program verifier contributes to the loop invariant in two ways beyond what is declared. First, it performs a simple interval analysis, which amounts to that inequality relations between a variable and a constant often do not need to be supplied explicitly. For example, for a basic loop like

```
s = 0;
for (int i = 0; i < a.Length; i++) {
  s += a[i];
}
```

the program verifier infers the loop invariant 0 <= i; together with the loop guard i < a.Length, the program verifier thus automatically verifies that this loop body

---

[7] As an implementation detail, the program verifier does not work directly on the source code, but on the bytecode emitted by the compiler. For contracts, the compiler also spills out some meta-data that helps the program verifier. But to the program verifier, a quantifier in code just looks like the loop that the compiler emits for it, and that loop does not have a loop invariant that would permit verification.

always accesses the array within its bounds. As another example, the program verifier infers the loop invariant 0 <= r for ISqrt in Fig. 1, though that condition is not needed to verify the method. The simple interval analysis does not understand values derived from the heap, for example, so it is not able to infer the loop invariant 0 <= n in Fig. 3.[8] Second, the program verifier infers and limits what the loop modifies. For instance, it performs a simple syntactic analysis to infer that ISqrt does not modify x. We will have more to say about modifications in Section 1.4.

Recall that the program verifier does not check that programs terminate. If a programmer wants help in checking that a loop terminates, it is possible to manually insert such checks. For example, the program in Fig. 4 computes the value of a *variant function* (see, *e.g.*, [15]) at the beginning of the loop body and then checks, just before the end of the body, that the variant function is bounded and that the iteration has strictly decreased the variant function. The responsibility for that the manually inserted code actually does imply termination (for example, that all paths to the next loop iteration are considered) lies with the user.

The current version of the Spec# program verifier does not check for arithmetic overflow. Hence, for example, the error of computing mid in Fig. 4 as:

```
int mid = (low + high) / 2;   // potential overflow
```

is not checked. Similarly, any overflow in the multiplication in Fig. 2 is not detected.

1.4   Accounting for Modifications

It is important that a caller can tell which variables a method may modify. For illustration, consider class Rectangle in Fig. 5.

To inform its callers that only X and Y are modified, method MoveToOrigin uses a postcondition that specifies the values of Dx and Dy to be unchanged. Another way of accomplishing this is to use a **modifies** clause, like in the contract of method Transpose. If a method's **modifies** clause does not explicitly list some field of **this**, then the **modifies** clause implicitly includes **this**.*, which means that the method is allowed to modify any field of **this**. More precisely, unless the method has a **modifies** clause that designates a field of **this** or explicitly lists **this**.*, **this**.** (explained in Section 3.1), or **this**.0 (explained below), then the method contracts gets an implicit **modifies this**.*. The default **this**.* is why the previous examples we have shown do not complain about illegal modifications.

There are subtle differences between using a postcondition to exclude some modifications (from the default **this**.*), like MoveToOrigin does, and using a **modifies** clause to allow certain modifications, like method Transpose does. The former allows temporary modifications inside the method body, whereas the latter does not. For instance, the code f++; f-- is considered a side effect that needs to be accounted for in the **modifies** clause. Moreover, the former allows fields in superclasses and subclasses

---

[8] The program verifier also implements some more powerful domains for its abstract-interpretation inference [3], including the polyhedra abstract domain [4]. These can be selected with the program verifier's /infer option.

```
int BinarySearch(int[] a, int key)
  requires forall{int i in (0:a.Length), int j in (i:a.Length); a[i]<=a[j]};
  ensures -1 <= result && result < a.Length;
  ensures 0 <= result ==> a[result] == key;
  ensures result == -1 ==> forall{int i in (0: a.Length); a[i] != key};
{
  int low = 0;
  int high = a.Length;

  while (low < high)
    invariant 0 <= low && high <= a.Length;
    invariant forall{int i in (0: low); a[i] < key};
    invariant forall{int i in (high: a.Length); key < a[i]};
  {
    int variant = high - low;  // record value of variant function
    int mid = low + (high - low) / 2;
    int midVal = a[mid];

    if (midVal < key) {
      low = mid + 1;
    } else if (key < midVal) {
      high = mid;
    } else {
      return mid; // key found
    }
    assert 0 <= variant;  // check boundedness of variant function
    assert high - low < variant;  // check that variant has decreased
  }
  return -1;  // key not present
}
```

Fig. 4. A method that performs a binary search in array a. The precondition says the array is sorted, and the postconditions say that a negative result value indicates the key is not present and that any other result value is an index into the array where the key can be found. The example also illustrates a hand-coded termination check, which uses a variant function. Finally, the example uses the short-circuit implication operator ==>, which is often useful in specifications, but may also be used in code. As is suggested by the textual width of the operator, ==> has lower precedence than && and ||, and the if-and-only-if operator <==> has even lower precedence.

```
public class Rectangle {
  public int X, Y;
  public int Dx, Dy;

  public void MoveToOrigin()
    ensures X == 0 && Y == 0;
    ensures Dx == old(Dx) && Dy == old(Dy);
  {
    X = 0;   Y = 0;
  }

  public void Transpose()
    modifies Dx, Dy;
    ensures Dx == old(Dy) && Dy == old(Dx);
  {
    int tmp = Dx;   Dx = Dy;   Dy = tmp;
  }

  public void Disturb(Rectangle r)
    modifies r.*;
  {
    X = r.Y;   r.X = Y;
    Dx = min{Dx, r.Dx};
    r.Dy = max{X, Dy + r.Dy, 100};
  }

  public void CopyPositionTo(Rectangle r)
    modifies this.0, r.X, r.Y;
  {
    r.X = X;   r.Y = Y;
  }

  public Rectangle Clone()
  {
    Rectangle res = new Rectangle();
    res.X = X;
    res.Y = Y;
    res.Dx = Dx;
    res.Dy = Dy;
    return res;
  }
}
```

Fig. 5. An example that shows several ways of specifying modifications. Method `Disturb`, which performs some arbitrary changes to the rectangles **this** and r, includes uses of Spec#'s built-in **min** and **max**, here applied to lists of 2 and 3 elements, respectively.

to be modified, whereas the latter does not. We defer further discussion of subclass and virtual-method issues until Section 1.5.

Method Disturb in Fig. 5 obtains the license to modify fields of parameter r by including r.* in the **modifies** clause. In addition, it is allowed modifications of **this**.* by default, as usual.

Method CopyPositionTo modifies two fields of its parameter r, but does not modify any field of **this** (unless **this** and r happen to be the same). To specify that behavior, the method explicitly lists in its **modifies** clause the special form **this**.0. By itself, **this**.0 does not refer to any field, but has the effect that the default **this**.* is not added. So if **this** and r happen to be the same object, CopyPositionTo may modify fields of **this** because it may modify fields of r. If **this** and r are different, the method may modify r.*, but not fields of **this**.

Method Clone illustrates that new objects may be modified without declaring these modifications in the **modifies** clause. In other words, a **modifies** clause constrains the modification only of those objects that were allocated in the pre-state of the method. Besides newly allocated objects, there are other objects whose modification is implicitly permitted. We discuss those in Section 2.0.

Spec# does not feature conditional **modifies** clauses (like in JML [8]), which would allow a method to include a modification term only in certain situations. Instead, the method must include all possible modifications in the **modifies** clause and then use **ensures** clauses to say when certain fields are not modified.

Array elements can also be listed in **modifies** clauses. In Fig. 6, method Swap affects only elements i and j of the given array. Method Reverse can change any and all elements of b, but must leave array a unchanged. The figure also shows a method Caller, which calls the other two methods and demonstrates some of the properties that the specifications of those methods allow the caller to conclude. Note how the **assert** statements let us confirm our understanding of what the program verifier does with the specifications.

To reason about the behavior of a loop, it is also important to have modifies information. In Spec#, loops do not have explicit **modifies** clauses; instead, they inherit the **modifies** clause of the enclosing method. For example, consider the following method:

```
void ContrivedModifications()
  requires 8 <= Dx;
  modifies X, Y;
{
  Y = 125;
  while (X < 27) {
    X += Dx;
  }
  assert 8 <= Dx;
  assert Y == 125;  // error reported here
}
```

The method's **modifies** clause grants the loop license to modify X and Y, but not Dx. Therefore, the program verifier knows that 8 <= Dx remains true throughout the

```
public void Swap(int[] a, int i, int j)
  requires 0 <= i && i < a.Length;
  requires 0 <= j && j < a.Length;
  modifies a[i], a[j];
  ensures a[i] == old(a[j]) && a[j] == old(a[i]);
{
  int tmp = a[i];  a[i] = a[j];  a[j] = tmp;
}

public void Reverse(int[] a, int[] b)
  requires a.Length == b.Length && a != b;
  modifies b[*];
  ensures forall{int i in (0: a.Length); b[i] == a[a.Length-1-i]};
{
  int low = 0;
  int high = a.Length;
  while (low < high)
    invariant high + low == a.Length;
    invariant forall{int i in (0: a.Length), i < low || high <= i;
                      b[i] == a[a.Length-1-i]};
  {
    high--;
    b[low] = a[high];
    b[high] = a[low];
    low++;
  }
}

public void Caller(int[] a)
  requires 100 <= a.Length;
{
  int[] b = new int[a.Length];
  int x = a[57];
  int last = a.Length - 1;
  Reverse(a, b);
  assert x == a[57];          // Reverse leaves a unchanged
  assert b[last - 57] == x;   // this is where a[57] ends up
  Swap(b, 20, 33);
  assert b[20] == a[last - 33];   // b[20] and b[33] were swapped
  assert b[last - 57] == x;       // Swap leaves b[last-57] unchanged
}
```

Fig. 6. Examples that show the **modifies** clause syntax for array elements. The quantifier in the loop invariant of Reverse uses a filter expression, i < low || high <= i. Alternatively, for this universal quantifier, the filter could have been written as an antecedent of an implication ==> in the quantifier's body.

method. Note, however, that no analysis is done to determine that this loop does not make use of its license to modify Y; hence, the program verifier assumes nothing about the value of Y after the loop, and an explicit loop invariant about Y is required in order to prove the last assertion in the example.

1.5 Virtual Methods

Calls to virtual methods are dynamically bound. That is, the method implementation to be executed is selected at run time based on the type of the receiver object. Which implementation will be selected is in general not known at compile (verification) time. Therefore, Spec# verifies a call to a virtual method M against the specification of M in the *static* type of the receiver and enforces that all overrides of M in subclasses live up to that specification [16,14]. This is achieved through specification inheritance [6]: an overriding method inherits the precondition, postcondition, and **modifies** clause from the methods it overrides. It may declare additional postconditions, but not additional preconditions or **modifies** clauses because a stronger precondition or a more permissive **modifies** clause would come as a surprise to a caller of the superclass method.

Class Cell in Fig. 7 declares a virtual setter method for the val field. The override in subclass BackupCell is allowed to declare an additional postcondition. It also has to satisfy the inherited specification. In particular, method BackupCell.Set has to live up to the implicit **modifies** clause of Cell.Set. This example shows that for virtual methods, the default **this**.* is preferable over a more specific **modifies** clause such as **this**.val because the former allows subclass methods to modify additional fields declared in subclasses. Class GrowingCell attempts to implement a cell whose value can never decrease. Since callers of Cell.Set cannot anticipate the extra precondition, it is rejected by the Spec# compiler.

1.6 Object Invariants

The data associated with an object usually takes on many fewer values than the types of the fields would allow. For example, the implementation Rectangle in Fig. 5 may keep the width and height fields Dx and Dy as non-negative integers, even though their types would also admit negative values. Furthermore, the designer of the class may decide to set both Dx and Dy to 0 whenever the area of a rectangle is 0. Such properties can be captured as *object invariants*. For example, class Rectangle may declare

```
invariant 0 <= Dx && 0 <= Dy;
invariant Dx == 0 || Dy == 0 ==> Dx == 0 && Dy == 0;
```

The object invariant is checked to hold at the end of each constructor of the class. The program verifier also checks that every update to a field maintains the object invariant. For example, with the invariants above, the program verifier checks that any value assigned to Dx is non-negative. However, it is not always possible to maintain object invariants with every assignment. For example, if Dx is changed from a positive value to 0 (or vice versa), then the second invariant above requires Dy to undergo a similar change; this means that there will be some point in the program when one of Dx and Dy

```
using Microsoft.Contracts;

public class Cell {
  [SpecPublic] protected int val;

  public virtual void Set(int v)
    ensures val == v;
  { val = v; }
}

public class BackupCell : Cell {
  [SpecPublic] protected int backup;

  public override void Set(int v)
    ensures backup == old(val);
  {
    backup = val;
    val = v;
  }
}

public class GrowingCell: Cell {
  public override void Set(int v)
    requires val <= v;   // error
  { base.Set(v); }
}
```

Fig. 7. An example illustrating specification inheritance. The precondition in GrowingCell.Set is rejected by the compiler. The custom attribute [SpecPublic] (declared in the Microsoft.Contracts namespace, which is conveniently included with a **using** declaration) allows a non-public field to be mentioned in public specifications. We discuss better ways to support information hiding in Section 7.

has been updated but the other has not yet been updated accordingly. To allow object invariants to be broken temporarily, Spec# includes a block statement **expose**. While an object is exposed, its invariants need not hold; instead, they are checked at the end of the **expose** block.

For example, if a Rectangle method wants to increase both the width and height by 10, it would do the following:

```
expose (this) {
  Dx += 10;
  Dy += 10;
}
```

Without the **expose** statement, the program verifier would complain with the somewhat cryptic message "Assignment to field Rectangle.Dx of non-exposed target object may break invariant: ...". The **expose** statement is not always needed, however. For example, if instead of adding 10 to Dx and Dy, the method were to double each of the fields:

```
Dx *= 2;
Dy *= 2;
```

then no **expose** is needed, since each statement maintains the class invariants.

To explain what is going on, we say that an object is in one of two states: *mutable* or *valid*. When an object is in the mutable state, its object invariants need not hold and its fields can freely be updated. When an object is in the valid state, its object invariant is known to hold. Fields of a valid object are allowed to be updated only if the update maintains all invariants. An object starts off as mutable and remains mutable until the end of the constructor. After its construction, **expose** statements are used to temporarily change an object from valid to mutable.

We will have much more to say about object invariants in the rest of the tutorial. While things will get more complicated, the following basic intuitions will remain the same: object invariants describe the steady state of the data of an object and there are times when object invariants may be temporarily violated. An additional issue that we will encounter is that an object invariant can be enforced only if it is known to the program verifier, so in the modular setting where only some of the program's classes are visible, not all expressions are admissible as object invariants and more machinery is needed to check those object invariants that are admissible.

2   Working with Object Invariants

In this section, we take a deeper look at working with objects and their invariants.

2.0   Aggregate Objects and Ownership

Abstractly, objects provide certain state and functionality, but the implementation is rarely limited to the fields and methods of a single object. Instead, the fields of the object reference other objects, often of different classes, and those objects reference further objects, and so on. In other words, the implementation of a class usually builds on other classes. We say that the joint functionality provided by these objects combine into providing one *aggregate object*, and we say that the sub-objects or sub aggregate objects are *components* of the larger aggregate object.

In Spec#, fields that reference a component of the aggregate are declared with the [Rep] attribute, where "rep" stands for "representation". This makes it possible for the program text to distinguish between component references and other object references that a class may have.

To keep track of which objects are components of which aggregates, Spec# uses the notion of *object ownership*. We say that an aggregate object *owns* its component objects. For example, for an object b of type Band in Fig. 8, b is the owner of b.gt, as indicated by the [Rep] attribute.[9]

---

[9] Ownership describes the structure of objects and is used by the program verifier. However, no ownership information is kept at run time, so there are no dynamic checks that correspond to the static checks performed by the program verifier. Consequently, the only way to detect ownership-related errors is to apply the program verifier; at run time, such errors go undetected.

```
using Microsoft.Contracts;

class Band {
  int gigs;
  [Rep] Guitar gt;
  Accountant accnt;

  public void Play() {
    expose (this) {
      gigs++;
      gt.Strum();
    }
  }

  public Band() {
    gt = new Guitar(10);   // ...
  }

  // ...
}
```

Fig. 8. A simple example that shows a representation field gt, that is, a field that references a component of the enclosing aggregate object. Notice that the **using** declaration is needed in order to use Microsoft.Contracts.Rep unqualified. The example also shows another field, accnt, which references an object that is not a component of the aggregate. Finally, the example shows a typical method that operates on the aggregate object by calling methods on its components.

We explained before that an object is either in the mutable state (where its invariants need not hold) or in the valid state (where its invariants are known to hold), and that the **expose** statement is used to temporarily bring a valid object into the mutable state. To take ownership into account, we subdivide the valid state. If a valid object has no owner object or its owner is mutable, then we say that the object is *consistent*. This is the typical state in which one applies methods to the object, for there is no owner that currently places any constraints on the object. If the valid object does have an owner and that owner is in the valid state, then we say the object is *committed*. Intuitively, this means that any operation on the object must first consult with the owner. Figure 9 illustrates a typical heap configuration.

An implicit precondition of a method is that the target be consistent. This implies that all components of the target are committed. Thus, to operate on a component, the method body must first change the target into the mutable state, which implies that all of its component change from committed to consistent.

For example, method Play in Fig. 8 wants to invoke the Strum method on **this**.gt. Doing so without the **expose** statement would result in an error:[10]

---

[10] The line and column numbers in the error messages refer to the files on the tutorial web page [11], but we abbreviate the file names here.

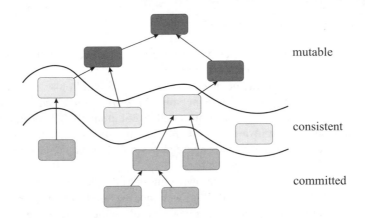

mutable

consistent

committed

Fig. 9. A typical heap configuration. Objects are denoted by boxes; arrows point to an object's owner. Every heap has a thin layer of consistent objects that separate the mutable objects from the committed. The **expose** statement temporarily shifts this layer downward by making a consistent object mutable (and the objects it owns consistent).

```
Fig8.ssc(14,7): The call to Guitar.Strum() requires target object to be peer
consistent (owner must not be valid)
```

Most often when the program verifier produces this error, the program is either missing an **expose** statement or is trying to operate on an object whose owner is unknown. Sometimes, the latter is due to a missing [Rep] declaration.

Components of aggregate objects are implementation details that are not relevant to clients of the aggregate. Therefore, whenever a method may modify the state of an aggregate object, it is also allowed to modify its components, without mentioning those components in the **modifies** clause. For instance, since method Play may modify the state of its receiver (by its default **modifies** clause **this.***), it may implicitly also modify the state of the Guitar object gt, which is a component of the Band aggregate. So, in summary, there are three cases in which a method has the permission to modify a field o.f: when o.f is listed (implicitly or explicitly) in the **modifies** clause, when o has been allocated during the execution of the method, and when o is a committed component of an object that may be modified by the method. To make use of the second option, postconditions sometimes contain o.IsNew, which expresses that an object o has been allocated by the method.

2.1   Ownership-Based Invariants

An object invariant of an aggregate is allowed to constrain the state of its components. For example, the Band class in Fig. 8 may expect its guitarist to be reasonably good:

```
invariant 7 <= gt.Level;
```

Or perhaps it wants to relate the guitarist's participation with the band's number of gigs:

```
invariant gigs <= gt.PerformanceCount;
```

Not all expressions are admissible as object invariants. For example, there are restrictions on which subexpressions can be dereferenced. Spec# permits an object invariant if the program verifier has a way of checking that the invariant holds whenever the object is valid. One such way is to use ownership: An *ownership-based* invariant of an object may depend on the state of that object and its components. The program verifier can check ownership-based invariants by enforcing that the components of an aggregate object are changed only while the aggregate is mutable. So, "consulting with the owner" is done by exposing the aggregate.

The invariants above are admissible ownership-based invariants, because the field they dereference (gt) is a [Rep] field. If gt were not declared as [Rep], then trying to include the invariants above in class Band would result in the following error, pointing to the dereference of gt:

```
Fig8.ssc(8,18): Expression is not admissible: it is not visibility-based[11],
and first access 'gt' is non-rep thus further field access is not admitted.
```

Suppose Band includes the invariant about gt.PerformanceCount above, and suppose the Strum method is specified to increment PerformanceCount by 1. Then the **expose** statement in Fig. 8 correctly maintains the invariant, even though the update gigs++ by itself may cause the invariant to be temporarily violated. On the other hand, if gigs were incremented *before* the **expose** statement, then the program verifier would flag an error, because invariants of valid objects must be maintained with every assignment.

We have explained that mutable objects are not subject to invariant checking, whereas each field update of a valid object must maintain the object's invariants. But because of the principle that updates of component objects must first consult the owner, field updates are disallowed on committed objects. For example, if the body of method Play started with the update

```
gt.Level++;
```

then the program verifier would complain:

```
Fig8.ssc(12,5): Target object of assignment is not allowed to be committed
```

We mentioned that an implicit precondition of a method is that its target be consistent. This is important for modular verification: Knowing that the target's owner is already exposed allows the body of Guitar.Strum to update PerformanceCount even if it is not aware of the Band invariant about gt.PerformanceCount. Moreover, it means that method Play can make any change to the fields of the Band, as long as it maintains the Band invariant, and it does not need to be concerned about the invariants declared in classes that may (directly or transitively) own the Band object.

From what we have seen so far, public methods might as well wrap their entire body inside an **expose** (**this**) statement. While that might be a good rule of thumb, it is not

---

[11] We discuss visibility-based invariants at the end of this subsection.

always appropriate. First, one might argue that trying to make **expose** blocks as small as possible is a good idea, because that makes it more clear where invariants might be temporarily violated. Second, changing **this** to mutable disables certain operations, in particular those that require **this** to be consistent. An example of that situation arises if a public method calls another public method on **this**.

 Spec# also supports so-called *visibility-based* invariants, which allow the invariant expression to dereference fields that are not declared with [Rep]. However, there is another admissibility condition: A visibility-based invariant may dereference a field only if the declaration of the invariant is visible where the field is declared. This allows the static verifier to check for every field update that all objects whose visibility-based invariants depend on that field are exposed. Visibility-based invariants are useful to specify invariants of object structures that are not aggregates. The web site for this tutorial [11] contains an example of visibility-based invariants. Further details can be found in our research paper on object invariants [9].

 In addition to ownership-based and visibility-based invariants, a dereference of a field f in an invariant is admissible on the grounds that the value of f does not change. For example, if f is a **readonly** field or is declared in an [Immutable] class, then any invariant can depend on f. More generally, the invariant is admissible if the f field belongs to a *frozen* object, one whose fields will never change again. Spec# already has a notion of immutable types, but we omit details here, because we are working on replacing it with an implementation of the more flexible notion of frozen objects [12].

2.2 Subclasses

A central facility provided by a subclass mechanism is the ability to extend a class with more state. This has an effect on invariants and ownership, so we now refine the notions we have introduced earlier.

A *class frame* is that portion of an object that is declared in one particular class, not its superclasses or subclasses. For example, an object of type ResettingController, see Fig. 10, has three class frames: one for ResettingController, one for Controller, and one for the root of the class hierarchy, **object**.

Each class frame can contain its own object invariants, which constrain the fields in that class frame. For example, class Controller declares an invariant that constrains rate, but the subclass ResettingController does not mention the superclass fields.

We refine the notions of mutable and valid to apply individually to each class frame of an object. For example, an object of type ResettingController can be in a state that is valid for class frames ResettingController and **object** and mutable for class frame Controller. We say an object is consistent or committed only when all its class frames are valid. In other words, our terms "consistent" and "committed" apply to the object as a whole, whereas "mutable" and "valid" apply to each class frame individually.

The **expose** statement changes one class frame of an object from valid to mutable. The class frame to be changed is indicated by the static type of the (expression denoting the) object. For example, in class ResettingController, **expose** ((Controller)**this**) exposes the Controller class frame of the target, whereas the statement **expose** (**this**) exposes the ResettingController class frame of the same object. Omitting the first of these **expose** statements leads to the following complaint:

```
using Microsoft.Contracts;
using System;

public class Controller {
  [Rep] protected Sensor s0;
  [Rep] protected Sensor s1;
  protected bool alarm;
  protected int rate;

  invariant s0.measurement != s1.measurement ==> alarm;
  invariant rate == (alarm ? 10: 2);

  public Controller() {
    s0 = new Sensor();
    s1 = new Sensor();
    rate = 2;
  }

  // ...
}

public class ResettingController : Controller {
  DateTime alarmTriggered;
  int clearedAlarms;
  invariant 0 <= clearedAlarms;

  public void CheckAlarm()  // call periodically
  {
    if (alarmTriggered.AddSeconds(5) <= DateTime.UtcNow &&
        s0.measurement == s1.measurement) {
      expose ((Controller)this) {
        alarm = false;
        rate = 2;
      }
      expose (this) {  // optional
        clearedAlarms++;
      }
    }
  }
}
```

Fig. 10. An example that shows a superclass and a subclass (we omitted the declaration of class Sensor). The invariant declared in each class is treated independently of the other. The invariants of Controller express that an alarm is triggered when the measurements from the two duplicate sensors are different. When an alarm has been signaled, the sampling rate of the sensor goes up. Class ResettingController clears an alarm in case the last divergence between the measurements was at least five seconds ago.

```
Fig10.ssc(32,9): Error: Assignment to field Controller.alarm of non-exposed
target object may break invariant: rate == (alarm ? 10: 2)
```

Fields of valid class frames can be updated (without an **expose** statement) provided the update maintains the invariant; for example, the second **expose** statement in Fig. 10 is not needed. As before, however, field updates are not allowed on committed objects.

Once an object has been fully constructed, only one class frame of an object is allowed to be mutable at a time. For example, if one tried to nest the two **expose** statements in Fig. 10, the program verifier would issue an error:

```
Fig10.ssc(34,17): Object might not be locally exposable
```

As a final adjustment to working with subclasses, we refine the notion of ownership: an owner is an (object, class) pair. As with **expose** statements, static types and enclosing contexts are used to indicate the class-component of this pair. For example, for an object o with a [Rep] field f, the owner of o.f is (o,C), where C is the class that declares f.

 In the discussion above, an object invariant constrains the fields declared in the same class. Sometimes it is necessary to specify object invariants that relate fields from different class frames. For instance, class ResettingController might contain an invariant that requires alarmTriggered to have some default value whenever alarm is false. An invariant is allowed to mention a field from a superclass if that field is declared with attribute [Additive]. To update an additive field, one has to expose the object for the class declaring that field and all of its subclasses, which is done one class at a time with a special **additive expose** statement. This ensures that the class frame with the invariant is mutable when the field is updated. The tutorial web site contains an example with a additive fields. Additive fields are the default in many of our papers [1,9,10]. The difference between additive and non-additive fields is discussed in another publication [13].

2.3   Establishing Object Invariants

Each constructor of a class is responsible for initializing the fields of the class in accordance with the object invariant. A constructor starts off mutable for the object being constructed and the enclosing class. Therefore, fields of **this** declared in that class can be assigned to without exposing the receiver, as illustrated by the assignments in the constructor of Controller (Fig. 10). The class frame is changed to valid at the end of the constructor, which is therefore where the invariant is checked.[12]

[Rep] attributes on fields can be seen as special object invariants that constrain the owner of the object stored in the field. Any assignment to a [Rep] field must preserve that special invariant, even when the class frame containing the field is mutable. In the Controller example, the [Rep] fields s0 and s1 do not admit the value **null**, so the constructor must assign to them. In Spec#, typical constructors produce objects that are un-owned, so the right-hand sides of the assignments to s0 and s1 are un-owned Sensor objects. So how is the ownership relation instituted? Any assignment to a [Rep] field also has the effect of setting the owner of the right-hand side of the

---

[12] If the program verifier has occasion to report an error for the default constructor, the source location it uses is that of the name of the class.

assignment. Thus, Spec# automatically institutes the ownership relation when a [Rep] field is being assigned to. Such an assignment requires the right-hand side to have no owner or to already have the desired owner. That is, the assignment might set an owner of a previously un-owned object, but it won't automatically *change* an existing owner.

Until an object has been initialized for all of its class frames, it is not consistent (it has mutable class frames) and, thus, cannot be used as receiver or argument to methods that expect consistent arguments. We discuss how to work with partially-initialized objects in the following advanced remark.

> Non-null types express a special kind of invariant that needs to be established by each constructor. The virtual machine initially sets all fields of a new object to zero-equivalent values, in particular, fields of reference types to **null**. So before the new object has been fully initialized, it would be unjustified to assume that non-null fields actually contain non-null values.
>
> Until the initialization of an object is completed, we say that the object is *delayed*, meaning that it is in a raw state where we can rely neither on the non-nullness of its fields nor on its object invariants. Moreover, field values of delayed objects are themselves allowed to be delayed. By default, the **this** object is delayed inside constructors.
>
> A delayed object is in general not allowed to escape from its constructor. However, sometimes it is useful to call methods on delayed objects or to pass a delayed object as an argument to a method call. This is permitted if the callee method or its parameter is marked with the attribute [Delayed]. The consequence of this choice is that the method is then not allowed to assume fields of non-null types to have non-null values, let alone assume the object invariant to hold.[a]
>
> An alternative is to mark the constructor with the attribute [NotDelayed]. This requires that all non-null fields of the class be initialized before an explicit call of the superclass (aka *base class*) constructor, **base**. A constructor can make a **base** call to a [NotDelayed] superclass constructor only if it itself is marked as [NotDelayed]. A consequence of this design is that after the **base** call, the **this** object is fully initialized and no longer delayed. Therefore, it can be passed to methods without the [Delayed] attribute.
>
> Fähndrich and Xia [7] describe the details of delayed objects. Examples for delayed objects and explicit **base** calls can be found on the tutorial web page.
>
> ---
> [a] Any reference-valued parameter of a method, not just the receiver, can be marked with [Delayed]. However, there is a bug in the current version of the program verifier that makes the verification of methods with more than one [Delayed] parameter unsound.

3   Owners and Peer Groups

In this section, we explore more dimensions of ownership, especially sets of objects with the same owner, so-called *peers*.

3.0   Peers

The ownership model introduced so far allows aggregate objects to maintain invariants and to assume consistency of their components, for instance, when calling a method of a component. However, not all interacting objects are in an aggregate-component relationship. For example, a linked-list node n interacts with its successor node n.next, but n.next is usually not thought of as a component of n. Rather, n and n.next have a more equal relationship, and both nodes may be part of the same enclosing aggregate object. Therefore, both nodes are more appropriately declared as *peers*, that is, objects with the same owner. This is accomplished by the attribute [Peer].

A general guideline is to use [Rep] wherever possible, because it strengthens encapsulation and simplifies verification. [Peer] is appropriate when two objects are part of the same aggregate (that is, the aggregate object has direct access to both objects) or when the objects are part of a recursive data structure (such as the nodes of a linked list).

Another guideline is to use [Rep] when the field references an object whose type or mere existence is an implementation detail of the enclosing class, and to use [Peer] when the field references an object that can also be accessed by clients of the enclosing class. For example, in a typical collection-iterator pattern, the iterator has a field that references the collection. This field is best marked as [Peer], because the collection is not an implementation detail of the iterator and clients of the iterator may also access the collection directly.

As another example illustrating the use of peer objects, consider the two classes in Fig. 11. The Dictionary class makes use of some unspecified number of Node objects, which by the [Peer] declaration on the next field are all peers. The Dictionary class maintains a reference to the first and last of the Node objects, and declares the head and tail fields as [Rep]. Note that, in general, a Dictionary object owns many more objects than the two that are referenced directly by its fields.

Let us consider how the peer relation is instituted. The situation is analogous to [Rep] attributes: if pr is a [Peer] field, then assignment o.pr = x automatically institutes a peer relation between o and x. Essentially, the assignment sets the owner of x to be the same as the owner of o. But, as for [Rep] fields, Spec# won't change an owner, so the operation requires the right-hand side to start off having no owner or already having the desired owner. Moreover, an assignment to a [Peer] field requires that the target object not be committed—one is allowed to add peers to an object o only at times when the invariant of o's owner need not be maintained. We will illustrate these rules with the two versions of an Insert method shown in Fig. 11.

The body of method InsertA first records the value of head in local variable h, and then sets head to a newly allocated Node. Since head is declared with [Rep], the assignment to **this**.head also sets the owner of the new Node to **this**. Then, since next is a [Peer] field, the assignment head.next = h sets the owner of h to be the same as the owner of head, which is **this**; in this case, the owner of h was already **this**, so the assignment to the [Peer] field is allowed and has no net effect on the ownership of h.

The **expose** statement in InsertA is required. First, the class invariant in Dictionary would be broken by the assignment to head if head were initially **null**. By using the **expose** statement, the code is allowed to temporarily violate the invariant; the assignment to tail restores the invariant. Second, the assignment of a [Peer] field requires the target object not to be committed; without the **expose** statement in InsertA, the program verifier would issue a complaint:

```
Fig11.ssc(23,7): Target object of assignment is not allowed to be committed
```

```
public class Dictionary {
  [Rep] Node? head = null;
  [Rep] Node? tail = null;
  invariant head == null <==> tail == null;

  public bool Find(string key, out int val) {
    for (Node? n = head; n != null; n = n.next) {
      if (n.key == key) { val = n.val;  return true; }
    }
    val = 0;  return false;
  }

  public void InsertA(string key, int val) {
    expose (this) {
      Node? h = head;
      head = new Node(key, val);  // new.owner = this;
      head.next = h;              // h.owner = head.owner;
      if (tail == null) {
        tail = head;              // head.owner = this;
      }
    }
  }

  public void InsertB(string key, int val) {
    expose (this) {
      Node n = new Node(key, val);
      if (head != null) {
        Owner.AssignSame(n, head);  // n.owner = head.owner;
        n.next = head;              // head.owner = n.owner;
      }
      head = n;                     // n.owner = this;
      if (tail == null) {
        tail = head;                // head.owner = this;
      }
    }
  }
}

class Node {
  public string key;
  public int val;
  [Peer] public Node? next;
  public Node(string key, int val) { this.key = key;  this.val = val; }
}
```

Fig. 11. An example showing a linked list of key-value pairs. A Dictionary object owns all the Node objects it reaches from head. The two variations of an Insert method illustrate two different ways to accomplish the same result. The comments in the code show the automatic and manual ownership assignments.

Method InsertA first updates head and then sets the next field of the new object. An alternative would be to first set the next field and then update head, as in:

```
Node n = new Node(key, val);
n.next = head;
head = n;
```

But this code fragment poses a problem: when the [Peer] field n.next is assigned to, Spec# will want to change the owner of the right-hand side, head, to the owner of n, but since head already has an owner (and it is not the owner of n, for n has no owner at this point), Spec# would have to do an ownership change, which it won't do. In cases like this, when one wants to change the owner of the target object, not of the right-hand side, one has to resort to a manual ownership assignment. This is illustrated in method InsertB, which uses the method Microsoft.Contracts.Owner.AssignSame. While the automatic ownership assignments take care of the case when the right-hand side is **null**, the manual ownership assignments do not; hence, the **if** statement in InsertB. The remaining automatic ownership assignments in InsertB, see the comments in the figure, have no net effect.

It is worth noting the direction of ownership assignments. Automatic ownership assignments always affect the right-hand side of the field assignment. In contrast, the Owner methods that can be used to manually change ownership change the owner of the first parameter. For illustration, see the first two comments in method InsertB.

3.1 Peer Consistency

In the Dictionary example above, the peer objects, of type Node, are designed together with the owner class, Dictionary. This need not always be the case. Sometimes, objects may naturally occur as related abstractions, but without a specific client context in mind. For example, a collection object may have a number of iterator objects. The collection and its iterators are programmed together, but they can be used in any client context, just like a collection by itself could be.

We show a simple collection and iterator example in Fig. 12. Each iterator holds a reference to the collection it is iterating over. The iterator does not own the collection— clients that use collections need the ability to acquire ownership; besides, a collection may have several iterators, and they cannot all own the collection. Instead, the field c is declared as [Peer]. Let us first explore why the field is declared [Peer] at all (as opposed to having no ownership attribute) and then, in the next subsection, explore how the peers are instituted.

Consider the GetCurrent method of the iterator. To determine if it has gone through all the elements in the collection, it compares its index, i, with the number of elements in the collection, Count. Then, it accesses the collection's array, which requires the index to be less than the length of that array. The correctness of this operation relies on the invariant Count <= a.Length, which holds of valid collection objects. But how do we know the collection to be valid?

One could add a precondition to GetCurrent, using the property IsConsistent, which is available in all objects and which yields whether an object is consistent:

```
public class Collection {
  [Rep] internal int[] a;
  public int Count;
  invariant 0 <= Count && Count <= a.Length;

  public int Get(int i)
    requires 0 <= i && i < Count;
    modifies this.0;
  { return a[i]; }

  public Iterator GetIterator() {
    Iterator iter = new Iterator();
    Owner.AssignSame(iter, this);
    iter.c = this;
    return iter;
  }

  // ...
}

public class Iterator {
  [Peer] internal Collection? c;
  int i = 0;
  invariant 0 <= i;
  public bool MoveNext() {
    i++;
    return c != null && i < c.Count;
  }
  public int GetCurrent() {
    if (c != null && i < c.Count) return c.a[i];
    else return 0;
  }
  public void RemoveCurrent()
    modifies this.**;
  {
    if (c != null && i < c.Count) {
      for (int j = i+1; j < c.Count; j++)
        invariant 0 < j && c != null && 0 < c.Count;
      {
        expose (c) { c.a[j-1] = c.a[j]; }
      }
      expose (c) { c.Count--; }
    }
  }
}
```

Fig. 12. A rudimentary collection and iterator example, illustrating the use of peer objects independent of any owning context. The example leaves out many common features of collections and iterators that are not the focus here. The access mode **internal** indicates that the field can be accessed by other classes in the same *assembly* (which is .NET speak for "module").

```
public int GetCurrent()
  requires c != null && c.IsConsistent;
```

However, such a precondition reveals implementation details (one would have to declare field c as [SpecPublic], change its access level, or use abstraction mechanisms).

Since it is quite common for objects to rely on the consistency of some of their peers, Spec# uses another approach. It adds an implicit precondition to every method that requires all in-bound parameters, including the target parameter, *and all their peers* to be consistent. When an object and all its peers are consistent, we say the object (and each of its peers) is *peer consistent*. Peer consistency is also an implicit postcondition of all out-bound parameters and return values.

Requiring peer consistency as the precondition of GetCurrent is more than we need for the example, but it has the advantage that GetCurrent does not explicitly need to name the associated collection in its precondition.

To summarize, because of the implicit precondition of peer consistency, all we need to do to verify method GetCurrent is to declare the field c as [Peer]. The peer consistency of **this** then implies the (peer) consistency of c, and thus the invariant of c can be assumed to hold and the array access c.a[i] can be verified to be within bounds.

The peer-consistency precondition makes it very easy to call methods of peer objects. Suppose the direct array access c.a[i] in method GetCurrent were replaced by a call c.Get(i). The implicit precondition of Get is that the receiver, c, be peer consistent. Since the iterator **this** and its collection c are peers, the peer consistency of **this** (which is the implicit precondition of GetCurrent) implies the peer consistency of c. Note that it is not necessary (nor possible) to enclose a call to c.Get(i) in an **expose (this)** statement, whereas if c had been declared a [Rep], it would have been necessary (and possible) to do so.

The peer-consistency precondition also allows a method to expose peer objects. For instance, method RemoveCurrent exposes the collection c to remove an element. Its **modifies** clause uses the wild-card **this.****, which denotes all fields of all peers of **this**. A more usable example would add a postcondition to recover information about the state of the collection and the iterator.

Any time a method invokes a method on some object, say x, it needs to live up to the precondition of the callee, which includes establishing the peer consistency of x. If x is a parameter of the enclosing method or has been obtained from a **new** call or as the return value of some other method, then x is typically already known to be peer consistent. When x is obtained from a field of an object, say o.f, then peer consistency typically follows from the [Rep] or [Peer] attribute on the declaration of field f. Omitting such an attribute often causes the program verifier to issue a complaint like:

```
Sec3.1.ssc(12,5): The call to Demo.M() requires target object to be peer
consistent
```

because it cannot prove x and its peers to be valid. Peer consistency also includes not being committed. Therefore, if f is a [Rep] field, one needs to expose o before calling a method on o.f. Otherwise, the verifier reports an error such as:

```
Sec3.1.ssc(13,5): The call to Demo.M() requires target object to be peer
consistent (owner must not be valid)
```

Occasionally, it is useful to call methods on a receiver or with arguments that are not peer consistent. For instance, a method might want to expose its receiver and then, from inside an **expose** statement, call an auxiliary method on the receiver (see the tutorial web site for an example). Spec# provides two ways of avoiding the implicit precondition of peer consistency.

All implicit specifications can be turned off by marking a method with [NoDefaultContract]. However, often one would like to turn off implicit specifications more selectively.

Methods parameters can also be declared with the attribute [Inside]. The implicit precondition for an [Inside] parameter p of static type C says that p is exposed for C, and it says nothing about the peers of **this**. To mark **this** as [Inside], place the attribute on the method.

A consequence of using [Inside] is that the method cannot assume the object invariant of the [Inside] receiver or parameter, and the caller of the method cannot assume the object invariant to hold upon return. Instead, an [Inside] method must write explicit pre- and postconditions that explain which conditions are to hold on entry and exit.

3.2 Peer Groups

In the previous subsection, we motivated the notion of peer consistency and the use of that condition as an implicit method precondition. Let us now explore what peers and peer consistency mean when an object has no owner.

An object always has some (possibly empty) set of peers, regardless of whether or not the object has an owner. We say that an object always belongs to a *peer group*. When an owner is assigned, the entire peer group is assigned that owner, so the peer relation among the objects of the peer group is preserved. For example, for a [Rep] field rp, an assignment o.rp = x transfers the entire peer group of x into ownership by o. For a [Peer] field pr, an assignment a.pr = x merges the entire peer group of x into the peer group of a. (As we mentioned before, both of these kinds of ownership assignments require x to be un-owned or to already have the desired owner.) The use of peer groups and the implicit precondition of peer consistency mean that an object does not need to reveal to its clients what its peers are, which provides information hiding.

Peer groups may be enlarged and may be merged, but Spec# does not currently provide any way to break up a peer group.

The treatment of peer groups and ownership in Spec# also means that the order in which objects are made peers or assigned owners does not matter. For example, if one wants to establish a situation where o owns both a and b, one can first merge the peer groups of a and b and then set object o as the owner of the resulting peer group, or one can first set o as the owner of a and then merge the peer group of b into that of a. As an analogy, consider the process of going to dinner with some friends. One can either first gather a group of friends (analogy: peers) and then decide which restaurant (analogy: owner) to go to, or one can first decide which restaurant to go to and then find friends to come along.

4   Arrays

In this section, we explain how Spec# handles arrays, especially how non-null types and ownership work for array elements.

4.0   Covariant Array Types

C#, and therefore also Spec#, has covariant array types. That means that a variable of static type T[] can hold an array whose allocated type is U[], where U is any subtype of T. The property that the elements of an array are indeed of the array's element type cannot be ensured by the static type system. Instead, it is enforced dynamically by the .NET virtual machine and also checked statically by the program verifier.[13]

For example, without further information, the method

```
void SetArrayElement(Controller[] a, int i)
  requires 0 <= i && i < a.Length;
  modifies a[i];
{
  a[i] = new Controller();  // possible error
}
```

will cause the program verifier to complain:

```
Sec4.0.ssc(6,5): RHS might not be a subtype of the element type of the array
being assigned
```

This warns about the possibility that a has allocated type, say, ResettingController[], in which case it is not allowed to assign a Controller object into a.

To prevent this complaint, one has to convince the program verifier that array-element updates are correct, which usually boils down to showing that the allocated type of the array equals its static type, say T[]. In some cases, this can be determined without additional specifications, in particular if T is a **sealed** class or if T is a class that is internal to the assembly (*e.g.*, non-**public**) and the assembly does not define any subclasses of T. In other cases, one needs to write a specification that constrains the allocated type of the array.

For instance, in the example above, the following precondition takes care of the problem:

```
requires a.GetType() == typeof(Controller[]);
```

---

[13] However, Spec# currently ignores co-variance errors that occur when an array with non-null element type is cast to an array of possibly-null elements. The compiler does not emit the necessary run-time check, and the verifier also ignores this issue.

The GetType method (which is defined for all references) returns an object (of type System.Type) that represents the allocated type of a, and the expression **typeof**(T), where T denotes a type, returns a System.Type object that represents the type T. GetType may also be used in object invariants, which is useful when arrays are stored in fields.

4.1   Arrays of Non-null Elements

Array types typically have the form T?[]!, meaning that the array itself is non-null, whereas the array elements are possibly-null instances of T. Either the ? or the ! can be omitted, depending on the defaults used by the compiler. Besides this common form, Spec# supports all other combinations of non-null and possibly-null, in particular, non-null element types as in T![]!.

Unlike fields of non-null types, whose initialization in the constructors of the class can be assured by syntactic definite-assignment rules, arrays of non-null elements are initialized by arbitrary code that follows the **new** allocation of the arrays. Until that

```
public void ExampleArrays() {
  string[] food = { "black-eyed peas", "red hot chili peppers", "cream" };
  WriteAll(food);

  string[] series = new string[3];
  series[0] = "The prime numbers start with 2, 3, 5, 7, 11, 13, 17";
  series[1] = "The Fibonacci numbers start with 0, 1, 1, 2, 3, 5, 8";
  series[2] = "The perfect numbers start with 6, 28, 496, 8128";
  NonNullType.AssertInitialized(series);
  WriteAll(series);

  string[] facts = new string[10];
  for (int n = 0; n < facts.Length; n++)
    invariant n <= facts.Length;
    invariant forall{int i in (0: n); facts[i] != null};
  {
    facts[n] = (n+1) + " ants is more than " + n + " elephants";
  }
  NonNullType.AssertInitialized(facts);
  WriteAll(facts);
}
public void WriteAll(string[] ss)
{
  foreach (string s in ss) {
    Console.WriteLine(s);
  }
}
```

Fig. 13. The WriteAll method takes a non-null array of non-null strings. Method ExampleArrays shows several ways of initializing arrays with non-null elements. Method NonNullType.AssertInitialized is declared in Microsoft.Contracts.

initialization is completed, one cannot rely on the type of the array to accurately reflect the non-nullness of the array elements. For this reason, the Spec# type checker provides a special marker, in the form of a method `NonNullType.AssertInitialized`, which is used to indicate a program point where the initialization code has completed. The type checker will not give the array its declared non-null type until that point.

For illustration, Fig. 13 shows the initialization of three arrays. Array food is initialized in the same statement that allocates it, so the type checker can treat it as having type **string**[] immediately. Arrays series and facts are initialized by code sequences. Thus, before these arrays can be used as having type **string**[], the code must call `AssertInitialized`. At that call site, the program verifier checks that every array element is non-null.[14]

If a program tries to use the array element before the array has been given its declared type, the compiler will complain. For example, if the assignment to series[2] in Fig. 13 is replaced by series[2] = series[1], the following type error results:

```
Fig13.ssc(13,17): Cannot store delayed value into non(or incompatibly)-
delayed location
```

despite the fact that the right-hand side of the assignment actually does have a non-null value at that time.

Also, if the code does not include a call to `AssertInitialized` for an array of non-null elements, the type checker complains:

```
Fig13.ssc(10,14): Variable 'series', a non-null element array, may not have
been initialized. Did you forget to call NonNullType.AssertInitialized()?
```

Perhaps confusingly, the source location mentioned in the error message points to where the array is declared, but this does not mean that `AssertInitialized` has to be called there.

4.2   Ownership of Arrays and Array Elements

Just like nullness, Spec# allows one to specify ownership independently for an array and its elements.

In Fig. 14, we show a class that uses an array of (possibly-null) Step objects. Method AddStep of the class queues up drawing steps and method Apply performs the work associated with these steps.

Ownership of Arrays. The last object invariant dereferences the array: steps[i]. To make this invariant admissible, the class declares the field steps to be [Rep]. Without the [Rep] attribute, the compiler's admissibility checker would report an error:

```
Fig14.ssc(11,39): Expression is not admissible: first access on array or
binding member must be rep.
```

---

[14] At run time, `AssertInitialized` performs a dynamic check that the array elements are not **null**. The time needed to do so is proportional to the length of the array, but that is no worse than the time required to initialize the array in the first place.

```
using System;
using Microsoft.Contracts;

public class DrawingEngine {
  [Rep] [ElementsRep] Step?[] steps = new Step?[100];
  invariant 1 <= steps.Length;
  int cnt;
  invariant 0 <= cnt && cnt <= steps.Length;
  invariant forall{int i in (0: cnt); steps[i] != null};

  public void AddStep(byte op, int argX, int argY) {
    if (cnt == steps.Length) { EnlargeArray(); }
    expose (this) {
      Step s = new Step(op, argX, argY);
      steps[cnt] = s;
      cnt++;
    }
  }
  void EnlargeArray()
    ensures cnt < steps.Length;
  {
    expose (this) {
      Step?[] more = new Step?[2*steps.Length];
      Array.Copy(steps, 0, more, 0, steps.Length);
      steps = more;
    }
  }
  public void Apply() {
    for (int i = 0; i < cnt; i++) {
      Step? s = steps[i];
      assert s != null;
      expose (this) { s.DoWork(); }
    }
    cnt = 0;
  }
}

class Step {
  public byte op;
  public int argX, argY;
  public Step(byte op, int x, int y) {
    this.op = op;   argX = x;   argY = y;
  }
  public void DoWork() { /* ... */ }
}
```

Fig. 14. This example class uses an array of owned Step objects. The call to DoWork in method Apply requires s to be peer consistent. This information follows from the [ElementsRep] attribute on steps, which says that the array elements are owned by the DrawingEngine object. Note that we use an **assert** statement in method Apply to convince the type checker that s is non-null. The verifier can prove this assertion using the third object invariant, but the type checker does not consider object invariants.

Note that this invariant constrains the state of the array object, but not of the array elements. Therefore, this invariant does not require the array elements to be owned by the DrawingEngine object.

Arrays do not have object invariants. Therefore, they need not be exposed before an array element is updated. However, since an owning object might have an invariant that constrains the state of the array, array-element updates, like steps[cnt] = s in AddStep, require the array not to be committed (that is, require the owner to be mutable). The enclosing **expose** statement temporarily changes **this** from valid to mutable and thus, since steps is a [Rep] field, changes the array steps from committed to peer consistent. Without the **expose** statement, the program verifier would complain:

```
Fig14.ssc(17,7): Target array of assignment is not allowed to be committed
```

The **expose** statement could be wrapped around just the array-element update, but wrapping it as shown in Fig. 14 also works.

Similarly, by its implicit precondition, the call to Array.Copy in EnlargeArray requires its parameters to be peer consistent. The **expose** statement puts steps into the required state. As in AddStep, this particular **expose** statement is shown wrapped around several statements, not just the call statement that needs it.

Ownership of Array Elements.   The call s.DoWork() in method Apply requires the Step object s to be peer consistent. As we have discussed in Section 3.1, for objects stored in fields, peer consistency typically follows from ownership attributes on the fields. Here, s is stored in an array, and we use the [ElementsRep] attribute on the field steps to express that every non-null element of the array is owned by the enclosing DrawingEngine object.

Without [ElementsRep] on steps, the program verifier would produce several error messages for method Apply, complaining about the effects of DoWork and about the lack of peer consistency at the call to DoWork:

```
Fig14.ssc(34,23): method invocation may violate the modifies clause of the
enclosing method
Fig14.ssc(34,23): The call to Step.DoWork() requires target object to be
peer consistent
Fig14.ssc(34,23): The call to Step.DoWork() requires target object to be
peer consistent (owner must not be valid)
```

With the [ElementsRep] attribute, the code exposes **this**, which makes steps[i] peer consistent. Moreover, Apply is then allowed to modify the elements of steps because they are components of the DrawingEngine aggregate.

Spec# also provides an attribute [ElementsPeer], which expresses that the array elements are peers of the object containing the [ElementsPeer] field.

Spec# requires all elements of an array to have the same owner, even if that owner is not specified by an [ElementsRep] or [ElementsPeer] attribute. For an array arr, the call Owner.ElementProxy(arr) yields an artificial object that is a peer of the elements of arr. This artificial object exists even if arr contains all **null** elements. The element proxy of a new array is initially un-owned. It is set when the array is assigned to an [ElementsRep] or [ElementsPeer] field. The element proxy can be used to query and modify ownership information for arr's elements. For instance, the call Owner.AssignSame(Owner.ElementProxy(arr), **this**) makes the element proxy of arr—and thus all current and future elements of arr—a peer of **this**. Like all ownership assignments, this call requires the element proxy to be un-owned or to already have the desired owner. Analogously to updates of [Rep] or [Peer] fields, assignments to array elements, like steps[cnt] = s in AddStep, make the right-hand side of the assignment a peer of the array's element proxy.

5   Generics Classes

Instead of using arrays, it is often more convenient to use generic collection classes. In this section, we illustrate how to write clients of generic classes. We do not discuss how to implement generic classes, because the implementation of generic classes in the Spec# compiler and verifier still needs improvement.

Figure 15 shows another version of class DrawingEngine from Fig. 14, this time using the generic class List. The implementation based on List is significantly simpler. One reason for this is that we can use a list of non-null Step objects, which simplifies the specifications. The details of dealing with a partially-filled array are hidden inside the List class.

Ownership for generics is very similar to arrays, with two differences. First, for instances of generics, one can specify the owner individually for each generic type argument. This is done by passing the number of the type argument to the attributes [ElementsRep] and [ElementsPeer] (starting with 0, of course). For instance, declaring a field

```
[ElementsPeer(0)] Dictionary<K,V> dict;
```

adds implicit checks and assumptions to all operations on dict that values of type K are peers of **this**. When the number is omitted, like in the declaration of steps in Fig. 15, the attribute refers to all type arguments.

Second, there are no automatic owner assignments when objects are passed to operations of generic classes. For instance, method AddStep has to assign an owner to the new object s before passing it to List's Add method. Omitting this assignment leads to the following complaint from the verifier:

```
Fig15.ssc(13,7): Error: The call to System.····.List<Step!>.Add(Step! item)
requires item to be a peer of the expected elements of the generic object
```

6   Capturing Parameters

A standard way to construct an aggregate object is to construct the components inside the constructor of the aggregate. For example, the constructor of the Band class in Fig. 8

```
using System.Collections.Generic;
using Microsoft.Contracts;

public class DrawingEngine {
  [Rep] [ElementsRep] List<Step> steps = new List<Step>();

  public void AddStep(byte op, int argX, int argY) {
    expose (this) {
      Step s = new Step(op, argX, argY);
      Owner.AssignSame(s, steps);
      steps.Add(s);
    }
  }

  public void Apply() {
    foreach (Step s in steps) {
      expose (this) { s.DoWork(); }
    }
    steps = new List<Step>();
  }
}
```

Fig. 15. The DrawingEngine from Fig. 14, this time using the generic class List. The Step class is unchanged. Like for arrays, attribute [ElementsRep] indicates ownership for the elements of the collection. However, the owner has to be set explicitly before an object is stored in the list.

initializes its gt field to a Guitar object that it allocates. Sometimes, a component is provided by a client of the aggregate, either during construction or via a method. This is useful, because it allows the client to customize the component, for example by allocating it to be of a particular subclass.

6.0 Customizing Rep Fields

Consider again the Band class, this time with a constructor and a method that accept a Guitar that is to become a component of the Band, see Fig. 16. Since gt is declared as [Rep], the assignment gt = g will set the owner of g to **this**, and the operation requires g to be un-owned. This precondition and license to modify an owner are obtained by declaring the parameter with [Captured]. Intuitively, the [Captured] attribute says that the parameter is passed in but does not "come back out". More precisely, [Captured] says that the callee has the right to take ownership of the object referenced by the parameter, and that a caller should not expect to be able to directly use the object after the call.[15]

---

[15] Spec# currently does not support an [ElementsCaptured] attribute that would allow a method to capture the elements of an array or a generic collection.

```
class Band {
  [Rep] Guitar gt;

  public Band([Captured] Guitar g)
  {
    gt = g;
  }

  public void ReplaceGuitar([Captured] Guitar g)
    requires Owner.Different(this, g);
    ensures Owner.Is(g, this, typeof(Band));
  {
    gt = g;
  }

  // ...
}
```

Fig. 16. An example that shows how clients can, via either a constructor or a method, supply an object that is to become a component of the Band aggregate. This allows a client to supply an appropriate Guitar object. The [Captured] attribute allows the callee to assign ownership to a parameter. The method Owner.Is yields whether its first argument is owned by the class frame specified by its second and third argument—here, (**this**,Band).

The [Captured] attribute affects a method's (or constructor's) precondition and modifies clause[16], but it has no effect on the postcondition. So, without further specification, the caller does not get to find out how the parameter is captured. This is usually satisfactory when captured into a [Rep] field, since the [Rep] field is usually an implementation detail of the class. Nevertheless, it is possible to write an explicit postcondition. For example, a postcondition gt == g will do. Another way to do it is to use the Owner.Is predicate as shown for method ReplaceGuitar in Fig. 16.[17]

Here is a possible client of the Band:

```
Guitar g = new BumperGuitar();
Band r = new Band(g);
r.Play();
g.Strum();   // error
```

---

[16] In fact, there is no explicit way of listing an owner "field" in a **modifies** clause. Even the **modifies** clause term p.* does not give the right to modify the owner of p. So, the only way to obtain the license to modify the owner of a parameter object is to use the [Captured] attribute.

[17] Using Owner.Is in the postcondition of the constructor is more involved because of its actual parameter **this**, which may not have been fully constructed yet—a Band subclass constructor may have more work to do and, thus, the object is delayed (see Section 2.3).

This client decides to use a particular `Guitar` subclass, `BumperGuitar`, for the `Band` it constructs. Note that after calling the `Band` constructor, the caller still has a reference to the captured object g. However, the caller is not able to invoke a method on g, because the caller cannot be sure that g is peer consistent (in fact, it will be committed).

Here is another client, somewhat contrived:

```
Band r = new Band();
Guitar g = new BumperGuitar();
r.ReplaceGuitar(g);
r.Play();
expose (r) {
  g.Strum();
}
```

From the information in `ReplaceGuitar`'s postcondition, one can conclude that the **expose** statement makes g peer consistent. Therefore, this client's call to g.`Strum()` verifies.[18]

One more thing remains to be explained about the example in Fig. 16, namely the reason for the precondition of method `ReplaceGuitar`. Without this precondition, the program verifier would complain about the assignment in the method:

```
Fig16.ssc(21,5): when target object is valid, it is not allowed to have the
same owner as RHS, because that would cause a cycle in the ownership relation
```

Or, if the assignment to gt occurred inside an **expose** statement, the program verifier would issue a complaint at the end of that **expose** statement:

```
Fig16.ssc(23,5): All of the object's owned components must be fully valid
```

The reason for these errors is the following scenario: The [Captured] attribute on parameter g entails the precondition of g having no owner. But this precondition still allows g to have peers. Suppose that, on entry to the method, g and **this** were peers. Then, the implicit ownership assignment that takes place when assigning to the [Rep] field **this**.gt would create the incestuous situation that **this** owns g and yet **this** and g are peers! This is disallowed and is the reason for these errors.

The predicate `Owner.Different` says that its two arguments are not peers. By using it in the precondition of `ReplaceGuitar`, one avoids the errors above.

---

[18] One can draw the same conclusion had the method's postcondition been gt == g. However, it is not possible to prove, after the call to r.Play(), that r.gt == g. This is because the implicit modifies clause of r.Play() is r.*, which allows r.gt to be modified. But the modifies clause does not permit modifying an owner, which is why one can conclude that g is still owned by r at the time of the **expose**.

In addition to Different, the Owner class has a method Same. For static program verification, these two predicates are each other's negation. However, there is an important and
subtle difference in their run-time behavior. In principle, all contracts could be checked
at run time, but to keep the overhead reasonable, Spec# omits certain run-time information and run-time checks, for example, ownership information. Consequently, predicates
like Owner.Same, Owner.Different, and Owner.Is cannot be computed at run time. Instead, these predicates all return **true** at run time. As long as these predicates are used
in positive positions (that is, not negated) in contracts, the program verifier will enforce
stronger conditions than are enforced at run time. So, to make a choice between Same and
Different, use the one that you can use in a positive position. It would be good if Spec#
enforced this "positive position rule" for the predicates concerned, but the current version
of Spec# does not implement any such check.

6.1   Customizing Peer Fields

It is also possible to capture parameters into [Peer] fields. Consider the example in
Fig. 17, which shows two constructors that establish a peer relationship between the
object being constructed and the object given as a parameter.

```
public class Iterator {
  [Peer] public Collection Coll;

  public Iterator([Captured] Collection c)  // captures 'c'
    ensures Owner.Same(this, c);
  {
    Coll = c;  // c.owner = this.owner;
  }

  [Captured]
  public Iterator(Collection c, int x)  // captures 'this'
    ensures Owner.Same(this, c);
  {
    Owner.AssignSame(this, c);  // this.owner = c.owner;
    Coll = c;                   // c.owner = this.owner;
  }

  // ...
}
```

Fig. 17. An example that shows two ways of setting up a peer relationship in a constructor. The
first constructor captures the parameter into the peer group of the Iterator being constructed;
the second constructs an Iterator in the same peer group as the parameter. Alternatively, either
postcondition could have been written as (the stronger) **ensures** Coll == c.

Both constructors take a parameter c and ensure that, upon return, **this** and c are in the same peer group. A newly allocated object—that is, **this** on entry to a constructor—starts off in a new, un-owned peer group. Like any other method, unless its specification says otherwise, the constructor is not allowed to change this ownership information for **this**, or for any other parameter. Therefore, a **new** expression typically returns a new object in a new, un-owned (but not necessarily singleton) peer group.

The first constructor in Fig. 17 declares that it will capture the parameter, c. The ownership relation (or, rather, the peer-group relation) is instituted automatically when the [Peer] field Coll is assigned, as we have described in Section 3.0 and as suggested by the comments in Fig. 17. This solution is not always the best, because it requires the caller to pass in an un-owned collection c. A caller may be in a situation where the collection already has an owner and the caller wants to create a new iterator for that collection.

For these reasons, the second constructor in Fig. 17 shows the more common way to set up a peer relationship in a constructor. The [Captured] attribute on the constructor, which is to be construed as applying to the implicit **this** parameter, says that the instigating **new** expression may return with the new object being placed in a previously existing peer group (with or without an assigned owner). Thus "capturing" **this** instead of c is usually a good idea, since ownership relations previously known to the caller are unaffected. Moreover, since the object being constructed starts off with no owner, the body of the constructor can easily live up to the precondition of the ownership assignment it will effect. However, the automatic ownership assignment that is performed with peer-field updates goes the wrong direction, so the body needs to use a manual ownership assignment as shown in Fig. 17.

In the example, each of the two constructors declares a postcondition that tells callers about the ownership of the new object, namely that it will be a peer of the parameter c. This kind of postcondition is common when a peer relationship is established, but uncommon when a parameter is captured into a [Rep] field. The reason is the same as the reason for choosing between [Rep] and [Peer]: [Rep] denotes something of an implementation detail, promoting information hiding and letting the class write invariants that dereference the [Rep] field, whereas [Peer] is used when clients have an interest in the object referenced.

7 Abstraction

When specifying the methods of a class, it is desirable to write the method contract in terms of entities (fields, methods, or properties) that can be understood by clients without violating good principles of information hiding. The compiler enforces the following rules: Entities mentioned in the precondition of a method must be accessible to all callers; this means that they must be at least as accessible as the method itself. Entities mentioned in the postcondition of a method must be accessible to all implementations of the method; this means that contracts of virtual methods (which can be overridden in subclasses) cannot mention private entities and can mention internal entities only if the method or its enclosing class is internal. These rules ensure that callers

```
public class Counter {
  int inc;
  int dec;

  [Pure][Delayed]
  public int GetX()
  { return inc - dec; }

  public Counter()
    ensures GetX() == 0;
  {}

  public void Inc()
    ensures GetX() == old(GetX()) + 1;
  { inc++; }

  public void Dec()
    ensures GetX() == old(GetX()) - 1;
  { dec++; }
}
```

Fig. 18. A simple example that uses pure methods as a form of abstraction. Abstractly, a Counter is a value that can be retrieved by GetX(). Concretely, the value is represented as the difference between the number of increment and decrement operations performed. All method contracts are written in terms of the pure method GetX(), not the private fields inc and dec.

understand the preconditions they are to establish and implementations understand the postconditions they are to establish.[19]

But then, what can be used in contracts when most fields of the class are private implementation details? The solution lies in *abstracting* over those details. For that purpose, Spec# provides pure methods, property getters, and model fields, which we explain in this section.

7.0 Pure Methods

A method that returns a value without changing the program state can provide a form of abstraction. Such methods are called *pure* and are declared as such by the attribute [Pure]. Pure methods are not allowed to have side effects.

The program in Fig. 18 represents a counter that can be incremented and decremented. The current value of the counter is retrieved by the method GetX(), which is declared as [Pure]. The specifications of the constructor and methods are given in terms

---

[19] Spec# does not enforce similar restrictions on object invariants. So when a client exposes an object, it might not understand the condition that has to hold at the end of the **expose** block. However, since clients typically do not modify inaccessible fields, the program verifier can nevertheless often prove that the invariant is preserved.

of GetX(), which means that clients are separated from the implementation decision of storing the counter as the difference between the private fields inc and dec.

The way that the program verifier reasons about a pure method is via the specification of the method: if the (implicit and explicit) precondition holds, then the result will be a value that satisfies the postcondition.[20] In the common special case that the implementation of a pure method consists of a single statement **return** E, the compiler implicitly adds a postcondition **ensures result** == E to the pure method if that would make a legal postcondition, there is no explicit postcondition, and the method is not virtual.[21] In the example, it is this implicit postcondition of GetX() that lets the Counter constructor and the Inc and Dec methods be verified. Experience shows that this "postcondition inference" is usually desired. If one does not want the postcondition inference, the workaround is simply to provide an explicit postcondition, like **ensures true**, or to introduce a second statement in the body of the pure method, like:

```
[Pure] T MyPureMethod() { T t = E; return t; }
```

The implicit precondition for pure methods is different from the peer-consistency precondition of ordinary methods. To see why, consider the following possible method of the Band class (*cf.* Fig. 8):

```
[Pure]
public int MagicNumber() {
  return 3 + gt.StringCount();
}
```

where gt is a [Rep] field and StringCount is a pure method of the Guitar class. To compute its result, the implementation of this pure method makes use of values computed by components of the aggregate—here, the number of guitar strings. Such pure methods are common and of good form. However, if pure methods required peer consistency, then MagicNumber would have to expose **this** before calling gt.StringCount(). For side-effect-free methods, which can never break any invariants, exposing objects is unnecessary overhead. So, instead of requiring the receiver and its peers to be consistent (which implies that the owner is mutable), pure methods only require the receiver and its peers to be valid (saying nothing about the state of the owner). We call this condition *peer validity*. Note that if an object, like a Band object, is peer valid, then so are all its components, like the object gt.

---

[20] If a contract calls a pure method, then the contract itself must make sure that the pure method is called only when its precondition holds. In other words, a contract must always be well defined. However, the current version of the program verifier does not check all contracts to be defined. It does so for object invariants, but not for pre- and postconditions, for example. This current omission in the program verifier can sometimes lead to some confusion. In particular, if a pure method's precondition is violated in a contract, then the effect will be that the program verifier does not know anything about the result of the pure method.

[21] Since Spec# encourages the use of specifications, it would be natural if the compiler did the reverse: add an implicit implementation whenever the postcondition of a pure method has the simple form **ensures result** == E. However, this is currently not supported by the compiler.

The example in Fig. 18 uses the pure method GetX in the postcondition of the Counter constructor. Such usage is common but regrettably tricky. We explain it in the following advanced remark.

 Since the constructor is by default delayed (see advanced remark in Section 2.3), the type checker enforces that any method it calls (on **this**) is also delayed, including any call that occurs in the postcondition. Therefore, the example declares GetX to be [Delayed]. A consequence of that declaration is that method GetX cannot rely on the non-null properties of the receiver or the object invariant, but that does not present any problem in the example.

If the pure method GetX had to rely on the object invariant, things would get more complicated. Consider a variation of class Counter that represents a non-negative integer and includes a precondition 0 < GetX() for method Dec. Then, the class could be proved to maintain the invariant dec <= inc, and one may want to add the postcondition 0 <= **result** to the pure method GetX(). To prove such a postcondition, the method would require the invariant to hold, which is at odds with GetX() being [Delayed]. Note that it is not an option to require the invariant through a precondition **requires** dec <= inc, because this precondition would reveal hidden implementation details.

To specify this variation of class Counter, it is necessary for the constructor and GetX both to be non-delayed, which is achieved by removing [Delayed] from GetX and adding [NotDelayed] to the constructor. Furthermore, the constructor must live up to the implicit precondition of GetX, which is peer validity. This is a problem, because at the end of the Counter constructor, **this** is valid only for Counter and its superclasses—any subclass constructors have not yet finished, so the object is not yet valid for those class frames. A simple, but sometimes untenable, way to address that problem is to declare Counter as a **sealed** class, which forbids it from having subclasses. The resulting variation of Fig. 18 is available on the tutorial web page.

An alternative to making Counter sealed is to use the [Additive] mechanism mentioned in an advanced remark in Section 2.2. This mechanism allows us to express that the receiver of GetX is valid for the class frames Counter and **object**, but mutable for all other class frames (if any). This is exactly the case after the body of Counter's constructor, at the time the call to GetX in the postcondition is evaluated. See the tutorial web page for an example.

7.1 Property Getters

In .NET, the usual way to write a GetX() method is to write a *property* X and to provide for it a *getter*. Similarly, a SetX(x) method is usually written as the *setter* for a property X. Properties are a facility that hides the underlying representation—X looks like a stored value, but its value may be computed in some way rather than being directly represented. Figure 19 shows the Counter class written in this more common way of using a property getter.

In common usage patterns, property getters tend to present abstractions to clients, and the implementations of property getters tend to have no side effects. Therefore, Spec# makes property getters [Pure] by default. What we said in Section 7.0, for example about inferred postconditions and about delayed type correctness and object invariants, also applies to property getters. Note in Fig. 19 that, syntactically, the attribute [Delayed] is placed on the getter itself, not on the enclosing property declaration.

```
public class Counter {
  int inc;
  int dec;

  public int X {
    [Delayed]
    get { return inc - dec; }
  }

  public Counter()
    ensures X == 0;
  {}

  public void Inc()
    ensures X == old(X) + 1;
  { inc++; }

  public void Dec()
    ensures X == old(X) - 1;
  { dec++; }
}
```

Fig. 19. The Counter class of Fig. 18 written with a property getter X instead of method GetX()

7.2   Purity: The Fine Print

Pure methods (including pure property getters) need to be side-effect free. Consequently, a pure method's implicit **modifies** clause is empty and the method must not
use any explicit **modifies** clause. But the handling of pure methods is more subtle
than simple side-effect freedom. Pure methods must also satisfy the following three
requirements:

- *Mathematical Consistency:* We reason about pure methods in terms of their specifications. For this reasoning to be sound, the specifications must be mathematically
  consistent. In particular, if pure methods are specified recursively, the recursion
  must be well founded. Spec# ensures well-foundedness by assigning a *recursion
  termination* level (a natural number) to each pure method. The specification of a
  pure method M may call a pure method p.N only if p is a [Rep] field (or a sequence
  of [Rep] and [Peer] fields, starting with a [Rep] field) or if p is **this** and N's recursion termination level is strictly less than M's. Consequently, for each such call, the
  height of the receiver in the ownership hierarchy decreases or the height remains
  constant, but the level decreases, which ensures well-foundedness. For most pure
  methods, Spec# infers a recursion termination level automatically; it can also be
  specified using the [RecursionTermination(r)] attribute.
- *Determinism:* Pure methods are usually used as if they had all the properties of
  mathematical functions. In particular, pure methods are generally expected to be
  deterministic. However, this is not the case when a pure method returns a newly

allocated object. The compiler performs some conservative, syntactic checks to ensure that this non-determinism is benevolent. These checks may instruct the user to apply the attribute [ResultNotNewlyAllocated] to the pure method (in which case the program verifier checks that the result value is not newly allocated) or apply the attribute [NoReferenceComparison] to a pure method that may potentially get two newly allocated references as parameters.

– *Dependencies:* It is important to know what state changes may interfere with the value returned by a pure method. This is achieved by specifying the *read effect* of each pure method using the [Reads] attribute. Typical values for this attribute are:

  • [Reads(ReadsAttribute.Reads.Owned)] (the default for pure instance methods), which allows the contract and body of the pure method to read the fields of **this** and any object that is transitively owned by **this**
  • [Reads(ReadsAttribute.Reads.Nothing)] (the default for static pure methods), which allows a pure method to depend only on **readonly** fields.
  • [Reads(ReadsAttribute.Reads.Everything)], which allows a pure method to depend on all objects.

The compiler uses various syntactic rules to enforce that the contracts of pure methods stay within their allowed read effects. However, neither the compiler nor the program verifier in the current version of Spec# checks the body of a pure method against its specified read effects. Hence, any violation of the read effects in the body goes undetected.

Further details and examples of all three requirements are available online.

7.3   Model Fields

Besides pure methods and property getters, Spec# provides yet another abstraction mechanism. In contrast to regular fields, a *model field* cannot be assigned to; the model fields of an object o get updated automatically at the end of each **expose** (o) block [10]. The automatic update assigns a value that satisfies a constraint specified for the model field.

Figure 20 shows another version of the Counter class. The model field X is declared with a **satisfies** clause whose constraint holds whenever the object is valid.

A model field is simpler to reason about than a pure method. First, its value changes only at the end of **expose** blocks, whereas the value of a pure method may change whenever a location in the read effect of the pure method is modified. Second, a model field can be read even for mutable objects, whereas a pure method typically requires its receiver to be valid. This makes it much easier to use model fields in constructors (note that the code in Fig. 20 does not require a [Delayed] attribute) and object invariants.

However, model fields are more restrictive than pure methods. First, they have no parameters. Second, a **satisfies** clause may depend only on the fields of **this** and objects transitively owned by **this** (like a pure method marked with the attribute [Reads(ReadsAttribute.Reads.Owned)]). So, a general guideline is to use pure methods or property getters when model fields are too restrictive; otherwise, model fields are the better choice.

```
public class Counter {
  protected int inc;
  protected int dec;

  model int X {
    satisfies X == inc - dec;
  }

  public Counter()
    ensures X == 0;
  {}

  public void Inc()
    ensures X == old(X) + 1;
  {
    expose (this) { inc++; }
  }

  public void Dec()
    ensures X == old(X) - 1;
  {
    expose (this) { dec++; }
  }
}
```

Fig. 20. Class Counter of Fig. 18 with a model field X instead of method GetX(). The updates of inc and dec must be done inside an **expose** block to ensure that X is being updated accordingly.

A **satisfies** clause does not have to specify a single value for the model field. Especially in abstract classes, it is often useful to give a weak **satisfies** clause and then declare additional **satisfies** clauses in subclasses. The value of a model field o.f satisfies the **satisfies** clauses of those classes for which o is valid. The program verifier checks that the **satisfies** clauses are feasible, that is, that there is a value that satisfies them. This check fails for the following model field, because there is no odd number that can be divided by 6:

```
model int Y {
  satisfies Y % 2 == 1 && Y % 6 == 0;
}
```

Like for pure methods, the verifier applies heuristics to find an appropriate value. When the heuristics are too weak, it is also possible to convince the verifier of the feasibility by providing a suitable value using a **witness** clause in the declaration of a model field:

```
model int Z {
  satisfies Z % 2 == 1 && Z % 5 == 0;
  witness 5;
}
```

8   Conclusions

Learning to use a program verifier requires a different kind of thinking than is applied in some other programming contexts today. It is harder than making sure that the program sometimes works—it forces the programmer to think about all possible inputs, data-structure configurations, and paths. The programmer does not need to imagine all cases up front, because the program verifier will do this exhaustively. But the programmer constantly needs to face the question "How am I going to convince the program verifier that this part of my program design is correct?". This process, by itself, has side benefits. For example, it can encourage simpler designs and better use of information hiding. Also, the specifications that are written while interacting with the verifier record design decisions that programmers otherwise have to reconstruct manually from the code. Knowing what is involved in program verification can also improve one's programming practices in other languages, since it raises one's awareness of correctness issues and teaches the use of contracts at module interfaces.

Spec# is a state-of-the-art programming system for programming with specifications and applying program verification. Nevertheless, the system is not nearly as simple to use as we wish it were. For example, it is impossible to go very far without understanding what it means for an object to be "consistent". Therefore, learning how to use the system takes patience, and experience will show how best to handle certain situations.

We hope this Spec# tutorial provides a basis for understanding the many features of the system and understanding the error messages that the verifier produces. We also hope that the tutorial and the Spec# system itself will inspire others to improve the state of the art, in the open-source distribution of Spec# as well as in other programming systems yet to be designed.

Acknowledgments

We are grateful to Rosemary Monahan and Valentin Wüstholz for the extensive feedback on drafts of this tutorial.

References

0. Barnett, M., Chang, B.-Y.E., DeLine, R., Jacobs, B., Leino, K.R.M.: Boogie: A modular reusable verifier for object-oriented programs. In: de Boer, F.S., Bonsangue, M.M., Graf, S., de Roever, W.-P. (eds.) FMCO 2005. LNCS, vol. 4111, pp. 364–387. Springer, Heidelberg (2006)
1. Barnett, M., DeLine, R., Fähndrich, M., Leino, K.R.M., Schulte, W.: Verification of object-oriented programs with invariants. Journal of Object Technology 3(6), 27–56 (2004)
2. Barnett, M., Leino, K.R.M., Schulte, W.: The Spec# programming system: An overview. In: Barthe, G., Burdy, L., Huisman, M., Lanet, J.-L., Muntean, T. (eds.) CASSIS 2004. LNCS, vol. 3362, pp. 49–69. Springer, Heidelberg (2005)
3. Cousot, P., Cousot, R.: Abstract interpretation: a unified lattice model for static analysis of programs by construction or approximation of fixpoints. In: Conference Record of the Fourth Annual ACM Symposium on Principles of Programming Languages, pp. 238–252. ACM, New York (1977)

4. Cousot, P., Halbwachs, N.: Automatic discovery of linear restraints among variables of a program. In: Conference Record of the Fifth Annual ACM Symposium on Principles of Programming Languages, January 1978, pp. 84–96 (1978)
5. de Moura, L., Bjørner, N.S.: Z3: An efficient SMT solver. In: Ramakrishnan, C.R., Rehof, J. (eds.) TACAS 2008. LNCS, vol. 4963, pp. 337–340. Springer, Heidelberg (2008)
6. Dhara, K.K., Leavens, G.T.: Forcing behavioral subtyping through specification inheritance. In: 18th International Conference on Software Engineering, pp. 258–267. IEEE Computer Society Press, Los Alamitos (1996)
7. Fähndrich, M., Xia, S.: Establishing object invariants with delayed types. In: Gabriel, R.P., Bacon, D.F., Lopes, C.V., Steele Jr., G.L. (eds.) Proceedings of the 22nd Annual ACM SIG-PLAN Conference on Object-Oriented Programming, Systems, Languages, and Applications, OOPSLA 2007, pp. 337–350. ACM, New York (2007)
8. Leavens, G.T., Poll, E., Clifton, C., Cheon, Y., Ruby, C., Cok, D.R., Müller, P., Kiniry, J., Chalin, P., Zimmerman, D.M.: JML Reference Manual (May 2008), http://www.jmlspecs.org
9. Leino, K.R.M., Müller, P.: Object invariants in dynamic contexts. In: Odersky, M. (ed.) ECOOP 2004. LNCS, vol. 3086, pp. 491–515. Springer, Heidelberg (2004)
10. Leino, K.R.M., Müller, P.: A verification methodology for model fields. In: Sestoft, P. (ed.) ESOP 2006. LNCS, vol. 3924, pp. 115–130. Springer, Heidelberg (2006)
11. Leino, K.R.M., Müller, P.: Spec# tutorial web page (2009), http://specsharp.codeplex.com/Wiki/View.aspx?title=Tutorial
12. Leino, K.R.M., Müller, P., Wallenburg, A.: Flexible immutability with frozen objects. In: Shankar, N., Woodcock, J. (eds.) VSTTE 2008. LNCS, vol. 5295, pp. 192–208. Springer, Heidelberg (2008)
13. Leino, K.R.M., Wallenburg, A.: Class-local object invariants. In: First India Software Engineering Conference (ISEC 2008). ACM, New York (2008)
14. Liskov, B.H., Wing, J.M.: A behavioral notion of subtyping. ACM Transactions on Programming Languages and Systems 16(6), 1811–1841 (1994)
15. Manna, Z., Pnueli, A.: Axiomatic approach to total correctness of programs. Acta Informatica 3(3), 243–263 (1974)
16. Meyer, B.: Object-oriented Software Construction. Series in Computer Science. Prentice-Hall International, New York (1988)

Fixpoints and Search in PVS*

Natarajan Shankar

Computer Science Laboratory
SRI International
Menlo Park CA 94025 USA
shankar@csl.sri.com
http://www.csl.sri.com/~shankar/

Abstract. The Knaster–Tarski theorem asserts the existence of least and greatest fixpoints for any monotonic function on a complete lattice. More strongly, it asserts the existence of a complete lattice of such fixpoints. This fundamental theorem has a fairly straightforward proof. We use a mechanically checked proof of the Knaster–Tarski theorem to illustrate several features of the Prototype Verification System (PVS). We specialize the theorem to the power set lattice, and apply the latter to the verification of a general forward search algorithm and a generalization of Dijkstra's shortest path algorithm. We use these examples to argue that the verification of even simple, widely used algorithms can depend on a fair amount of background theory, human insight, and sophisticated mechanical support.

1 Introduction

Software is now a critical component of a range of systems from medical devices to aircraft flight control. Software defects are embarrassingly commonplace. Most of these defects are merely annoying, but some software defects can be very costly or even life-threatening. Formal verification, particularly computer-aided verification, has been touted as one solution to the problem of software unreliability. However, there is still a significant gap between the promise of verification technology and the practice of software engineering. We argue that this gap can be closed, but only with a long-term investment in the scientific foundations of software. We use the example of a formal development of fixpoint theory and its application to a widely used search algorithm, to illustrate this point.

Algorithms for graph search on weighted and unweighted directed graphs are employed in a number of applications. The general forward search (GFS) algorithm determines if a goal vertex g in a directed graph is reachable from a source vertex s. The algorithm is presented in Lavalle's *Planning Algorithms* [LaV06] without proof. The mechanized verification of GFS using PVS is presented here mainly to illustrate the challenge of proving the correctness of even simple, widely used algorithms. This

---

* This research was supported by NSF Grants CSR-EHCS(CPS)-0834810 and SGER-0823086 and by NASA Cooperative Agreement NNX08AY53A. Insightful feedback from the anonymous refereees and from Sam Owre were helpful in revising the paper.

proof relies on nontrivial invariants and a rich body of mathematical concepts and theorems. The mechanized verification illustrates a number of features of the PVS language
and prover.

The GFS algorithm explores the vertices starting from the source vertex by maintain-
ing two disjoint sets: the *live* vertices Q and the *dead* vertices D. Initially, D contains
the source vertex s and Q contains those successors of s that are distinct from s. In
each step, a live vertex v is removed from Q. If vertex $v = g$, then the search succeeds.
Otherwise, v is added to D, and the non-D successors of v are added to the set of live
vertices to continue the search. In order to demonstrate the correctness of GFS, we have
to show that the search succeeds exactly when vertex g is reachable from s.

Given a source vertex s in a directed graph G, the set R of vertices reachable from s
is the smallest set containing s that contains the target vertices of any edge in G whose
source vertex is in R. Such *inductive* definitions arise from fixpoint theory as fixpoints
of a monotonic operator on a given ordering. The Knaster–Tarski theorem is the key
result which asserts the existence of such fixpoints. It is fundamental to logic, database
theory, algorithms, program semantics, and program analysis. A *lattice* L is a partially
ordered set that is closed under the operations of taking the *least upper bound* (or *join*)
$\bigsqcup Y$ and *greatest lower bound* (or *meet*) $\bigsqcap Y$ of any subset Y of L. A *monotonic*
function f on the lattice preserves the order so that $f(x) \le f(y)$ whenever $x \le y$. A
fixpoint of a lattice is an element w such that $f(w) = w$. The Knaster–Tarski theorem
asserts that a monotonic function f on a complete lattice L has a complete lattice F of
fixpoints. In particular, it has a least fixpoint $lfp(f)$ and a greatest fixpoint $gfp(f)$.

Knaster [Kna28] first proved this theorem for the power set lattice which is the power
set of a given set ordered by the subset relation. Tarski [Tar55] generalized the result
to arbitrary complete lattices. Given a complete meet semi-lattice with a greatest lower
bound operator over a subset of lattice elements, it is easy to define the corresponding
least upper bound operator. Therefore a complete meet semi-lattice is really a complete
lattice.

The power-set lattice is a commonly used instance of the abstract theory of lattices.
It consists of all the subsets of a given set ordered by the subset relation. On the power
set lattice, $\wp(X)$, let S be a function from X to $\wp(X)$. We can then define a *strongest
post-condition* operator $post(S)$ on $\wp(X)$ so that $post(S)(Y) = \bigcup_{y \in Y} S(y)$. We can
define a cumulative version $cpost(S)(Y)$ of the strongest post-condition operator as $Y \cup
post(S)(Y)$, and an indexed version $ipost(S, Z)(Y)$ as $Z \cup Y \cup post(S)(Y)$. Note that
all the operations $post(S)$, $cpost(S)$, and $ipost(S, Z)$ are monotonic. Given some set
Z in $\wp(X)$, the set of elements *reachable* from Y using S can be computed as the least
fixpoint $lfp(ipost(S, Z))$. This is the smallest set R such that $Z \subseteq R$ and $post(S)(R) \subseteq
R$. Reachability in a directed graph $G = (V, E)$ can be defined as $lfp(ipost(\hat{E}, \{s\}))$
where s is the source node and $\hat{E}$ is the function defined so that for any subset of vertices
X, $\hat{E}(X) = \{v' \in V | \exists v \in V.(v, v') \in E\}$. We develop background fixpoint theory
starting from lattices in order to verify graph search algorithms. This formalization of
fixpoint theory contains definitions and theorems, such as those concerning fixpoints of
continuous operators, that are not really used in the verification.

Graph reachability can be formalized directly without building on fixpoint theory.
PVS has a notion of inductively defined predicates for just this purpose. However, GFS

is one in a class of algorithms including depth-first search, breadth-first search, Dijkstra's shortest path algorithm, and A* search. A more general treatment based on fixpoint theory can be used to extend the formalization of GFS to these other algorithms as well. We illustrate this with an abstract treatment of Dijkstra's algorithm where the graphs have non-negative weights associated with the edges and the objective is to find the shortest, i.e., lowest weight, path from a source to a target vertex.

The rest of the paper covers the formalization of fixpoint theory in PVS and the verification of the GFS and Dijkstra's algorithms. In Section 2, we briefly introduce PVS. Section 3 describes the formalization of fixpoint theory in PVS. This formalization is specialized to the Boolean or power-set lattice in Section 4. The verification of the GFS algorithm and a generalized version of Dijkstra's algorithm are outlined in Sections 5 and 6, respectively. Section 7 enumerates some of the lessons learnt from this formalization and lists the related work, while the conclusions are summarized in Section 8.

2   A Brief Overview of PVS

The Prototype Verification System (PVS) is a comprehensive framework for interactive and automated verification based on higher-order logic [ORSvH95]. PVS is used here as the medium for formalizing the concepts underlying search algorithms, and we do exploit several of its features. However, other verification systems such as Coq [BC04], HOL [GM93], or Isabelle [NPW02] would also function along roughly similar lines. PVS, as we mentioned, is based on higher-order logic, which admits variables not only over individuals, as in first-order logic, but also over functions, functions of functions, and so on. Higher-order logic uses types to avoid paradoxes due to self-application. Types are built from base types such as the Booleans `bool` and the real numbers `real`. The type [A→B] represents the type of functions with domain type A and range type B. For example, $[A \to \texttt{bool}]$ represents type of predicates over the type A, and we abbreviate this as `PRED[A]` or as `set[A]`. The type $[A_1, \ldots, A_n]$ represents the type of n-tuples where the i'th element has type A_i for $1 \leq i \leq n$. In addition, PVS has predicate subtypes which are of the form $\{x : T | e\}$ which contains the elements x of T satisfying e. With this, we can define subtypes for rational numbers, integers, even numbers, prime numbers, ordering relations, and order-preserving maps. For example, the subtype of even numbers can be defined as $\{\texttt{i : int | EXISTS (j : int)}$ $2*\texttt{j = i}\}$. With predicate subtypes, typechecking and theorem proving become interdependent since the demonstration that an expression like $6 + 4$ is an even number now requires a proof. The PVS typechecker generates proof obligations corresponding to predicate subtypes called type correctness conditions (TCCs). PVS also has dependent types such as $[x : A \to B]$, where the range type B can depend on the domain element x. For example, if B is the type $multiples(x)$ containing the integer multiples of x, then the dependent type $[x : int \to multiples(x)]$ contains those functions on the integers that map each integer x to some multiple of x. The PVS language has other features like parametric theories and recursive and corecursive datatypes that will be explained when needed. The PVS language and its type system can be used to embed other methodologies that require the generation of proof obligations, for example, Hoare logic [Hoa69, HJ00] or the B method [Abr96, Muñ99].

PVS also has an interactive proof checker that builds on various automated procedures for binary decision diagrams, satisfiability modulo theories, and rewriting. The proof checker uses a sequent representation for proof goals such that each step either completes the proof of a subgoal or generates new subgoals. Proof strategies can be defined to execute complex patterns of proof steps, like induction. Examples of the language features and the proof checking commands are given below.

3   Fixed Points over Complete Lattices

A complete lattice L over a partial ordering relation $\leq$ is closed under the operations of taking the *supremum* $\bigsqcup$ (join or least upper bound) and *infimum* $\bigsqcap$ (meet or greatest lower bound) of a given subset of elements of L. We first present a small PVS theory that defines the property of being an infimum operator. The theory lowerbound takes as parameters, the type T and a partial ordering relation <= over this type. The type (partial_order?[T]) corresponds to the set of ordering relations that satisfy the partial_order? predicate.

```
lowerbound  [ T: TYPE, <= : (partial_order?[T]) ]
: THEORY
  BEGIN

  X : VAR set[T]
  x, y, z: VAR T

  lowerbound?(X)(x): bool = (FORALL y: X(y) => x <= y)

  glb?(X)(x): bool = (lowerbound?(X)(x) AND
                      (FORALL (y: (lowerbound?(X))): y <= x))

  END lowerbound
```

It suffices to formalize complete lattices in terms of a meet or a join semi-lattice. This formalization of complete lattices in terms of the meet semi-lattice is developed in the theory meet_semilattice described below. The theory takes as parameters, a type T, a partial ordering <= on T, and an operator glb that maps subsets of the type T to the greatest lower bound in T with respect to the ordering <=. The theory lowerbound is imported within the parameter list of the meet_semilattice theory. Note that an element of the type set[T] is a predicate over type T.

```
meet_semilattice [T : TYPE, <= : (partial_order?[T]),
                  (IMPORTING lowerbound[T, <=])
                  glb : [X: set[T] -> (glb?(X))] ]
: THEORY
  BEGIN
    :
    :
  END meet_semilattice
```

Within the scope of BEGIN ... END, the theory enumerates a list of lemmas and definitions. The first sequence of lemmas record that <= is a partial ordering and that the glb operator computes a lower bound and the greatest such lower bound. These lemmas are are essentially extracted from the type of <= and glb (using the PVS proof command TYPEPRED), but by proving them, we allow the respective properties to be directly employed in other proofs.

```
x, y, z: VAR T

X, Y, Z : VAR set[T]

f, g : VAR [T -> T]


reflexivity: LEMMA
   x <= x

antisymmetry: LEMMA
     x <= y AND y <= x IMPLIES x = y

transitivity : LEMMA x <= y AND y <= z IMPLIES x <= z

glb_is_lb: LEMMA   X(x) IMPLIES glb(X) <= x

glb_is_glb: LEMMA
     (FORALL x: X(x) IMPLIES y <= x)
    IMPLIES y <= glb(X)
```

The first couple of definitions capture the notion of a monotone operator on the lattice
and of the fixpoint of an operator.

```
mono?(f): bool = (FORALL x, y: x <= y IMPLIES f(x) <= f(y))

fixpoint?(f)(x): bool =
   (f(x) = x)
```

Two key theorems then follow from the definition of the least fixpoint `lfp` as the greatest lower bound of the set of pre-fixpoints, i.e., the set of elements x such that `f(x)`
`<= x`. Then, `KT1` asserts that `lfp(f)` is a fixpoint of a monotone operator `f`, and `KT2`
asserts that it is the least such fixpoint.

```
lfp(f) : T = glb({x | f(x) <= x})

KT1: THEOREM
 mono?(f) IMPLIES
    lfp(f) = f(lfp(f))

KT2: THEOREM
   mono?(f) AND fixpoint?(f)(x) IMPLIES
   lfp(f) <= x
```

The proof of `KT1` is interesting. By anti-symmetry, we can reduce it to `f(lfp(f))`
`<= lfp(f)` and `lfp(f) <= f(lfp(f))`. For the first case, we know that
`lfp(f)` is `glb({x | f(x) <= x})`, so by `glb_is_glb`, it would suffice to show
that `f(lfp(f))` is a lower bound of `{x | f(x) <= x}`. Indeed this is the case
since for any element x, `lfp(f) <= x` by `glb_is_lb`, and hence `f(lfp(f)) <=`
`f(x)` by the monotonicity of f, and `f(lfp(f)) <= x` by transitivity since `f(x)`
`<= x`. Once we know `f(lfp(f)) <= lfp(f)`, the other case follows since this
means that `f(lfp(f))` is a pre-fixpoint by monotonicity, and `lfp(f)` is a lower
bound of the set of pre-fixpoints.

The PVS version of this proof shown below has eight steps. In the first step, the
universal quantifiers are replaced by Skolem constants, e.g., the universally quantified
variable f is replaced by the constant `f!1`. Also, the implication in the goal is flattened
into a *sequent*. A sequent has the form $\Gamma \vdash \Delta$ for a sequence of *antecedent* formulas Γ
and a sequence of *consequent* formulas Δ and asserts the validity of $\bigwedge \Gamma \Rightarrow \bigvee \Delta$. With

flattening, the monotonicity condition becomes the antecedent formula, and the fix-point equation becomes the consequent formula. Instead of splitting the equality using anti-symmetry, we introduce a case split on `f!1(lfp(f!1)) <= lfp(f!1)`. This corresponds to the second case of the informal proof above. The all-purpose `grind` command completes the first branch of the proof where the formula is assumed, i.e., added as an antecedent. Since the theory `meet_semilattice` (i.e., the part of the theory that precedes the occurrence of `KT1`) is given as a `:theories` parameter to `grind`, it rewrites the definitions of `lfp` and `mono?` and employs `glb_is_lb` and `antisymmetry` as rewrite rules. The interaction is more delicate on the other branch where `f!1(lfp(f!1)) <- lfp(f!1)` is added as a consequent. First, `grind` is applied without instantiation leaving us with the task of demonstrating

$$ \texttt{f!1(glb(\{x | f!1(x) <= x\})) <= glb(\{x | f!1(x) <= x\}).} $$

By applying `glb_is_glb`, we can use transitivity and monotonicity to show that `f!1(glb({x | f!1(x) <= x}))` is a lower bound for `{x | f!1(x) <= x}`.

```
("" 
 (skosimp)
 (case "f!1(lfp(f!1)) <= lfp(f!1)")
 (("1" (grind :theories "meet_semilattice"))
  ("2"
   (grind :theories "meet_semilattice" :if-match nil)
   (rewrite "glb_is_glb")
   (skosimp*)
   (rewrite "transitivity" + :subst ("y" "f!1(x!1)"))
   (grind :theories "meet_semilattice"))))
```

The theorem `KT2` is easily proved since `lfp(f)` is the lower bound of the set of pre-fixpoints. The PVS proofs of most of the theorems contain interactive steps that roughly correspond to their informal proofs, and make only modest demands on the automation available in PVS.

The meet-semilattice can be shown to be a complete lattice. by defining the least upper bound `lub(X)` as the greatest lower bound of the set of upper bounds of `X`. With this definition, `lub_is_lb` and `lub_is_lub` are easily verified as being the duals of `glb_is_gb` and `glb_is_glb`, respectively. Later, we exploit the duality between meets and joins by instantiating the `meet_semilattice` theory with its dual.

```
lub(X): T = glb({y | (FORALL (x: (X)): x <= y)})

lub_is_ub: LEMMA X(x) IMPLIES x <= lub(X)

lub_is_lub: LEMMA  (FORALL x: X(x) IMPLIES  x <= y)
   IMPLIES lub(X) <= y
```

We introduce some further definitions in the theory `meet_semilattice`. The maximal element in the lattice is defined as the greatest lower bound of the empty set.

```
top: T = glb(emptyset[T])
```

In order to define continuity, we introduce the notion of a descending sequence as one where each successive element is below its predecessor in the `<=` ordering. The type `sequence[T]` consists of the functions from the natural numbers to `T`.

```
i, j, k: VAR nat

A : VAR sequence[T]

descending?(A): bool =
  (FORALL i: A(i + 1) <= A(i))

dB, dC: VAR (descending?)
```

A function f is meet-continuous or infimum-continuous if for any descending sequence $A_0, A_1, \ldots$ with greatest lower bound $\underline{A}$, the infimum-image of f on A, i.e., greatest lower bound of the sequence $f(A_0), f(A_1), \ldots$, is $f(\underline{A})$. Note that the `glb` operation has been overloaded to apply to sets of lattice elements as well as sequences of lattice elements.

```
glb(A): T = glb({x | (EXISTS i: x = A(i))})

i_image(f)(A): T = glb(LAMBDA i: f(A(i)))

i_continuous?(f): bool =
  (FORALL dC: f(glb(dC)) = i_image(f)(dC))
```

A fairly lengthy argument (31 interactive steps) is required to show that a meet-continuous operator on the lattice is also monotonic. For a monotonic operator f, we define a descending sequence $\top, f(\top), f(f(\top)), \ldots$, as `dn_seq(f)`. The descending property of this sequence is established in the proof obligation generated by the *typing judgement* `descending_dn_seq`. The PVS typechecker employs the judgement as a forward-chaining rule when inferring types for expressions. The greatest fixpoint of a continuous function `f` is defined as `cgfp(f)`.

```
monotone_i_continuous: LEMMA
  i_continuous?(f) IMPLIES mono?(f)

dn_seq(f)(i): RECURSIVE T =
(IF i = 0 THEN top
   ELSE f(dn_seq(f)(i-1))
 ENDIF)
MEASURE i

descending_dn_seq: JUDGEMENT dn_seq(f : (mono?)) HAS_TYPE (descending?)

cgfp(f): T = glb(dn_seq(f))
```

The `meet_semilattice` theory also contains a definition of the dyadic `meet` operation, and various theorems about it that are elided from the formal presentation. These theorems assert that `meet` is commutative and associative with `top` as its identity element, and that it is the maximal lattice element lying below both its arguments.

```
meet(x, y): T = glb({z | z = x OR z = y})
```

Next, we show that the `meet_semilattice` theory contains its dual. This is done defining a new theory `comp_lattice` with the same parameters and assumptions as `meet_semilattice`. Within this theory, we import both the `meet_semilattice` as well as its self-dual `meet_semilattice[T, >=, lub]`. With the latter, we can prove the dual versions of KT1 and KT2 as KT3 and KT4, respectively.

```
comp_lattice[T : TYPE, <= : (partial_order?[T]),
                   (IMPORTING lowerbound[T, <=])
                   glb : [X: set[T] -> (glb?(X))] ]
: THEORY
  BEGIN
   IMPORTING meet_semilattice[T, <=, glb] AS MSL %meet semilattice
   IMPORTING meet_semilattice[T, >=, lub] AS JSL %join semilattice

   END comp_lattice
```

The operators in the dual lattice JSL are renamed so that gfp(f) is JSL.lfp(f), ascending?(A) is the same as JSL.descending?(A), and lub(A) is JSL.glb(A).

```
   gfp(f) : T = JSL.lfp(f)

   i, j, k: VAR nat

   A : VAR sequence[T]

   ascending?(A): bool = JSL.descending?(A)

   aB, aC: VAR (ascending?)

   lub(A): T = JSL.glb(A)
```

The duals of KT1 and KT2 are proved as KT3 and KT4. The theory also establishes join-continuity, given by the predicate u_continuous?, as the dual of meet-continuity, but we omit this part of the theory.

```
   KT3: THEOREM
      MSL.mono?(f) IMPLIES
      gfp(f) = f(gfp(f))

   KT4: THEOREM
      MSL.mono?(f) AND MSL.fixpoint?(f)(x) IMPLIES
      x <= gfp(f)
```

So far, we have shown that any meet semilattice is a complete lattice by defining a least upper bound operator and verifying that a monotone operator on a complete lattice has a least and greatest fixpoint. It remains to show that the set of fixpoints of a monotonic function itself forms a complete lattice. This is done by showing that for any monotone operator f, the set of fixpoints of f admits a greatest lower bound operator. The informal argument for this claim is quite subtle. For a given complete lattice L, let F be the set of fixpoints of a monotone operator f. We have to show that for any subset X of F, there is an element of $\hat{l}$ of F that is the greatest lower bound of X. First, let k be the greatest lower bound of X in L. Let L/k be the set of elements j of L such that $j \leq k$. It can be verified that L/k is a complete lattice. Furthermore, f is closed on L/k: for any element j of L/k and for all elements x of X, $j \leq x$ we have $f(j) \leq f(x) = x$, and hence $f(j) \leq k$. Any fixpoint of f in L that is in L/k is also a fixpoint of f in L/k, and vice-versa. By KT3 and KT4, there is a greatest fixpoint for f in L/k. Let $\hat{l}$ be this greatest fixpoint. It must clearly be the greatest lower bound of X in F.

The lattice structure of the fixpoints is developed in the theory KnasterTarski. We import the generic form of the theory comp_lattice since we plan to use specific instances of it. The specific instance comp_lattice[T, <=, glb] is imported separately and abbreviated as MSL since it is referenced frequently.

```
KnasterTarski[T : TYPE, <= : (partial_order?[T]),
                (IMPORTING lowerbound[T, <=])
                glb : [X: set[T] -> (glb?(X))] ]
: THEORY
  BEGIN

    IMPORTING comp_lattice

    IMPORTING comp_lattice[T, <=, glb] as MSL

  END KnasterTarski
```

First, for any lattice element x, we define the complete lattice formed by taking the elements y such $y<=x$. The greatest lower bound operator on this subset of the lattice is defined using the corresponding operator for the lattice. In this definition, we need a special case for the empty set since `lower(x)` is not a complete sublattice of the lattice. The greatest fixpoint operator on the smaller complete lattice is used in the proof. The theory instance `comp_lattice[(lower(x)), <=, lower_glb(x)]` generates proof obligations that are easily discharged.

```
lower(x)(y): bool = (y <= x)

lower_glb(x)(Y : set[(lower(x))]): (lower(x)) =
    (IF empty?(Y)
        THEN x
        ELSE glb(Y)
        ENDIF)

lower_gfp(x)(f: [(lower(x)) -> (lower(x))]): (lower(x)) =
    comp_lattice[(lower(x)), <=, lower_glb(x)].gfp(f)
```

Next, we need to show that the set of fixpoints of the lattice over `T` admits a greatest lower bound operator. For this, we prove a few lemmas. The first one, `lower_glb_closure`, asserts that if `X` is a set of fixpoints, then the set `lower(glb(X))` is closed under any monotone operation `f` on the lattice. This lemma is easily proved by invoking the definitions of `mono?` and `fixpoint?` and the assumptions `transitivity` and `glb_is_lb`.

```
lower_glb_closure: LEMMA
  (FORALL (X: set[(MSL.fixpoint?(f))]):
    MSL.mono?(f) =>
        (FORALL (w: (lower(glb(X)))): lower(glb(X))(f(w))))
```

The second lemma `lower_fixpoint` asserts that any fixpoint on the lattice `lower(glb(X))` is also fixpoint on the lattice over `T`.

```
lower_fixpoint: LEMMA
  (FORALL (X: set[(MSL.fixpoint?(f))]):
    MSL.mono?(f) AND
    lower(glb(X))(y)   AND
    meet_semilattice[(lower(glb(X))), <=, lower_glb(glb(X))].fixpoint?
        (restrict[T, (lower(glb(X))), T](f))(y)
  => MSL.fixpoint?(f)(y))
```

The lemma `lower_fixpoint2` is the converse of `lower_fixpoint`, and both are proved with a single proof command.

```
lower_fixpoint2: LEMMA
  (FORALL (X: set[(MSL.fixpoint?(f))]):
    MSL.mono?(f) AND
    lower(glb(X))(y)  AND
    MSL.fixpoint?(f)(y)
 => meet_semilattice[(lower(glb(X))), <=, lower_glb(glb(X))].fixpoint?
       (restrict[T, (lower(glb(X))), T](f))(y))
```

Finally, we can prove the main theorem `lattice_FP` asserting that the set of fixpoints of the operation `f` admits a greatest lower bound operator: to any set `X` of fixpoints, there is a fixpoint `y` which is its greatest lower bound. The proof here involves a fair bit of interaction (forty steps), mostly following the informal argument given above.

```
lattice_FP: THEOREM
  MSL.mono?(f) IMPLIES
   (FORALL (X: set[(MSL.fixpoint?(f))]):
      EXISTS (y: (MSL.fixpoint?(f))):
        (FORALL (x: (X)): y <= x) AND
        (FORALL (z: (MSL.fixpoint?(f))):
          (FORALL (x: (X)): z <= x) => (z <= y)))
```

In the remainder of the paper, we demonstrate an application of the fixpoint theory in forward search over a graph.

4   The Boolean Lattice

Many applications of fixpoint theory are based on the power set or Boolean lattice consisting of the subsets of a given set ordered by the subset relation. For graphs, the set of nodes reachable from a source node can be computed by taking the fixpoint of the image of edge relation. This lattice is formalized in the theory `set_lattice`. Recall that the type `set[T]` over a given parameter type `T` is just the type of predicates on `T`. The Boolean lattice is the imported instance of `comp_lattice`, where the greatest lower bound operator is $\bigcap$ given by the `Intersection` function from the PVS prelude theories.

```
set_lattice  [T: TYPE] : THEORY
  BEGIN

  x, y, z: VAR T
  X, Y, Z: VAR set[T]
  U, V, W: VAR set[set[T]]

   IMPORTING comp_lattice[set[T], subset?[T], Intersection[T]]

  END set_lattice
```

A transformer `P` maps an element of `T` to `set[T]`. The image or post-condition `post(P)(X)` of a set `X` with respect to a transformer `P` is the union of `P(x)` for each `x` in `X`. The cumulative post-condition operator `Post(P, X)(Y)` is defined to accumulate `X` and `Y` in addition to `post(P)(Y)`. The next couple of lemmas demonstrate that the operator `Post(P, X)` is monotonic and join-continuous. The latter proof is quite delicate and nontrivial, and it employs nearly a hundred interaction steps.

```
P, Q, R: VAR [T -> set[T]]

post(P)(X): set[T] = {y | EXISTS (x:(X)): P(x)(y)}

Post(P, X)(Y): set[T] = union(X, union(Y, post(P)(Y)))

mono_Post: LEMMA MSL.mono?(Post(P, X))

continuous_Post: LEMMA u_continuous?(Post(P, X))
```

Finally, we define reachability set `Reach(P)(X)` with respect to a transformer `P` and an initial set `X` as the least fixpoint of the transformer `Post(P, X)`. The lemma `init_Reach` asserts that the initial set is reachable, and the lemma `post_Reach` asserts that if `x` is reachable, then so is `P(x)`.

```
Reach(P)(X): set[T] = MSL.lfp(Post(P, X))

init_Reach: LEMMA
   (FORALL x: X(x) IMPLIES Reach(P)(X)(x))

post_Reach: LEMMA
   (FORALL x: Reach(P)(X)(x) IMPLIES subset?(P(x), Reach(P)(X)))
```

The theory `Reach_inclusion` captures the judgement that if the transformer `P` returns only subsets of a set `X`, then the set of states reachable from some subset of `X` is also a subset of `X`. The predicate `powerset` is defined in the prelude so that `powerset(X)(Y)` holds exactly when `subset?(Y, X)` does. Since the predicate is Curried, the predicate subtype `(powerset(X))` contains all of the subsets of `X`. The typing in the `Reach_invariant` is quite delicate: `P` has the type `[U -> (powerset(X))]` and not `[X -> (powerset(X))]`. Otherwise the domain type will not match the type `[T -> set[T]]` expected by `Reach`. The use of `U` instead of `X` in the type of `P` is not significant: a specific `P` can always be defined to return the empty set when applied outside `X`. The proof of this judgement follows easily from KT2 and `mono_Post`.

```
Reach_inclusion[U: TYPE, X : set[U]]: THEORY
BEGIN
  IMPORTING set_lattice[U]

   Reach_invariant: JUDGEMENT
   Reach(P : [U -> (powerset(X))])(Y : (powerset(X)))
   HAS_TYPE (powerset(X))

END Reach_inclusion
```

The next section employs the Boolean lattice in formalizing forward graph search.

5   General Forward Search

Thus far, we have defined a parametric theory of meet-semilattices which we instantiated with its dual lattice to derive complete lattices. We have verified the Knaster–Tarski theorem for complete lattices and instantiated the complete lattice theory for the case of the Boolean lattice. We have defined the concepts of post-condition and reachability over the Boolean lattice. We now use these concepts to verify the correctness of a general forward search algorithm. The algorithm is adapted from Lavalle's book *Planning*

Algorithms [LaV06] where it is presented without proof. The main invariant is fairly subtle, but the verification itself is not particularly difficult.

The theory `GFSrc` (for *general forward search*) is defined with a nonempty type parameter U, the set of possible vertices. The second parameter is a `select` operation that picks an element from a nonempty set drawn from the type U. In the theory `GFSrc`, the type of directed graphs is defined as a dependent record with two fields: the V field is a finite set of vertices, and the E field is a (necessarily finite) set of edges between the vertices in V. In PVS. the contents of the fields for a graph G are denoted by G`V and G`E, respectively.

```
GFSrc   [U : TYPE+, select: [X: (nonempty?[U]) -> (X)]]
                : THEORY

  BEGIN

  graph: TYPE = [# V : finite_set[U],
                    E : set[[(V), (V)]] #]

  G : VAR graph

   :
   :
  END GFSrc
```

Next, we establish that an element of the type `set[(X)]` is a finite set when X is finite.

```
  is_finite_set: LEMMA
    (FORALL (X: finite_set[U]), (Y: set[(X)]):
       is_finite(Y))
```

Then, importing the generic version of the `set_lattice` theory, we define the operation of taking the successors `image(G)(v)` in the graph G of a vertex v in terms of the `image` operator in the prelude that computes the image of a relation E with respect to a set Y as set $\{x : EXISTS (y: (Y)): E(x, y)\}$. The operation `graphReach(G)(vs)` is defined as the set of vertices that are reachable from an initial set of vertices vs.

```
  IMPORTING set_lattice

  image(G)(v: (G`V)) : {X : set[(G`V)] | (FORALL (x:(X)): G`E(v, x))}
  = image(G`E, singleton[(G`V)](v))

  graphReach(G)(vs: set[(G`V)]): set[(G`V)]
  = Reach(image(G))(vs)
```

The general forward search algorithm GFS(G, s, g)(D, Q) is defined to check if the goal vertex g is reachable from the source vertex s in the graph G. It makes use of two sets of vertices D and Q. Initially, if s = g, then g is clearly reachable from s. The set D consists of the *dead* vertices. It initially contains the source vertex s. The set Q contains the *live* vertices and is initialized to contain the successors of the source vertex s but excluding s itself. In each iteration, we remove a vertex v from Q. If there is no such vertex, the algorithm terminates with the set D as the set of vertices reachable from the source vertex. Otherwise, if there is such a vertex v either v = g, and g is reachable from s, or we place v in D, and add those successors of v that are not already in D ∪ Q to Q.

The algorithm terminates since the cardinality of D grows with each iteration, and the total number of vertices is finite.

The correctness argument relies on a pair of invariants on D and Q:

1. *All the vertices in Q are reachable from* s. This holds initially since Q contains the successors of s (excluding s itself). It is maintained in each iteration where a subset of the successors of vertex v in Q are added to Q. Since v is reachable from s, these successor vertices must also be reachable from s.
2. Q and D are disjoint, and the successors of any vertex in D are already in D ∪ Q. This holds initially since D contains only s and the successors of s excluding s are contained in Q. It is maintained in each iteration since for each vertex v removed from Q and added to D, the successors of v excluding those in $\{v\} \cup D$ are added to Q.

In addition, we require that D contains s but not g. With these invariants, one can show that algorithm GFS(G, s, g)(D, Q) returns TRUE iff g is reachable from s. This is because the algorithm terminates either by

1. Finding g in Q, and we know that the vertices in Q are all reachable from s by the first invariant, or
2. Emptying Q at which point D is closed under the successor operation and hence over-approximates the set of reachable states. Since D does not contain g, it must be the case that g is unreachable.

The two invariants on D and Q are captured by the Q_invariant predicate.

```
Q_invariant(G, (s: (G'V)), (D : set[(G'V)]))(Q : set[(G'V)]): bool
 = (powerset(graphReach(G)(s))(Q) AND
    (FORALL (v: (D)): NOT member(v, Q) AND
                      subset?(image(G)(v), union(D, Q))))
```

The main search procedure is defined below as GFS. Note that the type of the result returned by GFS captures the correctness of the algorithm. The type constraints in the definition of GFS generate proof obligations corresponding to the satisfaction of the result type, the preservation of the invariants on D and Q, and the termination. The termination argument is trivial, but a couple of the other proof obligations involve over fifteen interactions, mostly to carefully expand definitions, invoke lemmas, and selectively instantiate quantifiers.

```
GFS(G, (s, g: (G'V)))((D : set[(G'V)] | member(s, D) AND NOT member(g, D)),
                      (Q : set[(G'V)] | Q_invariant(G, s, D)(Q))):
  RECURSIVE {b : bool | b = (Reach(image(G))(s)(g))}
  =
  (IF empty?(Q)
    THEN FALSE
    ELSE LET v = select(Q)
         IN (IF v = g
               THEN TRUE
               ELSE (LET P = difference(image(G)(v), union(D, Q))
                  IN GFS(G, s, g)(add(v, D), union(remove(v, Q), P)))
               ENDIF)
    ENDIF)
  MEASURE card(G'V) - card(D)
```

Finally, the top-level search algorithm is defined as `GFSearch` below. It invokes `GFS` if g is different from s. The correctness of `GFSearch` is captured in the lemma `GFSearch_Reach` which asserts that the search procedure succeeds exactly when the goal vertex g is reachable from the source vertex s. It is trivially proved from the type associated with `GFS(G, s, g)(s, difference(image(G)(s), s))`.

```
GFSrc(G, (s, g: (G'V))): bool =
  (s = g OR
   GFS(G, s, g)(s, difference(image(G)(s), s)))

GFSrc_Reach: LEMMA
  (FORALL (s, g: (G'V)):
   GFSrc(G, s, g) = Reach(image(G))(s)(g))
```

6   Generalizing Dijkstra's Algorithm

The GFS algorithm computes reachability in a directed graph. Dijkstra's algorithm [Dij59] is a greedy method for finding the shortest path on a weighted directed graph where the edge weights are non-negative numbers. GFS can be seen as an instantiation of Dijkstra's algorithm for the case where all the edge weights are zero. We directly generalize both GFS and Dijkstra's algorithm to one that operates on a linearly ordered lattice. The general scheme is that these algorithms perform search by computing a fixpoint as a function mapping from vertices to values over a lattice. In the case of reachability using general forward search, the lattice consists of two elements: a bottom element **true** and a top element **false**. Initially, only the source vertex is marked as reachable. Successive iterations extend the set of dead vertices, i.e., ones that have reached their stable fixpoint values. The frontier set consists of those vertices that are non-dead successors of dead vertices. The fixpoint maps all the vertices reachable from the source to **true**.

For Dijkstra's algorithm, the fixpoint maps the vertices to the minimal cost of a path from the source to the vertex. The search starts with an initial map that assigns the cost 0 to the source vertex, and a maximal cost ∞ to the other vertices. As with GFS, the algorithm partitions the map between the dead vertices and the live ones. The dead vertices are those for which the shortest path has already been computed. The live or frontier vertices are the non-dead successors of the dead vertices, namely those that are mapped to the cost of the shortest path from the source in which all the intermediate vertices are dead.

The theory `function_lattice` formalizes the generalization of GFS and Dijkstra's algorithm. The function lattice lifts a lattice over type T to one over the function type [S→T]. Here we focus on a linearly ordered lattice T. The parameters of the theory `function_lattice` are the domain type S, the range type T, the lattice ordering `<=` on T with the associated `glb` operation, and a selection operation `select` which picks an element from a nonempty set drawn from the type S. The role of the argument f of the `select` operation will be clarified in the theory assumptions.

```
function_lattice  [S, T : TYPE, <= : (total_order?[T]),
                    (IMPORTING lowerbound[T, <=])
          glb : [X: set[T] -> (glb?(X))],
                    select: [X: (nonempty?[S]), f: [S->T] -> (X)]]
: THEORY
  BEGIN
    :
    :
  END function_lattice
```

The theory function_lattice has an extra type constraint and two assumptions on the theory parameters. These assumptions are listed within the section ASSUMING ... ENDASSUMING. The added type constraint is that the ordering <= must be a linear ordering which is captured above by requiring <= to be a total ordering. The type S is required to be finite as indicated by the theory assumption is_finite_S below. The Boolean constant is_finite_type[S] is defined in the PVS prelude library to assert the existence of an injection from the type S to some initial segment of the natural numbers. The select_minimal assumption states that select(X, f) when applied to a nonempty set X must return an element j that is minimal with respect to f(j) according to <=. In other words, for any i in X, f(select(X, f)) <= f(i) must hold. Note that when an instance of the theory is imported, the corresponding instances of the assumptions are generated as proof obligations.

```
ASSUMING

  x, y, z: VAR T

  X, Y, Z : VAR set[T]

  is_finite_S: ASSUMPTION is_finite_type[S]

  select_minimal: ASSUMPTION
    (FORALL (X: (nonempty?[S])), (f: [S->T]), (i: (X)):
        f(select(X, f)) <= f(i))

ENDASSUMING
```

The first step is to show that the functions of the type $[S \rightarrow T]$ form a lattice on a point-wise ordering. The definition of <=(f, g) captures this ordering by requiring f to be point-wise below g.

```
funlat: TYPE = [S -> T]

i, j, k: VAR S

f, g, f1, f2: VAR funlat

IMPORTING comp_lattice[T, <=, glb], meet_semilattice[T, <=, glb] AS msl

<=(f, g): bool = (FORALL i: f(i) <= g(i))
```

The greatest lower bound of a set of functions F, given by fglb(F) is defined as the function g such that g(i) is the greatest lower bound (on the lattice T) of the set { f(i) | F(f) }. The IMPORTING on comp_lattice[funlat, <=, fglb] generates the proof obligations demonstrating that the function lattice is indeed a meet-semilattice.

```
F, G: VAR set[funlat]

fglb(F)(i): T = glb({a : T | EXISTS (f:(F)): a = f(i)})

IMPORTING comp_lattice[funlat, <=, fglb] AS flat,
          meet_semilattice[funlat, <=, fglb] AS fmsl
```

The restriction of a function to a subset of the domain is used in defining the main search algorithm. It is defined so that `restrict(f, D)(i)` is `f(i)` when `D(i)` holds, and `top`, otherwise. The lemmas `restrict_union` and `restrict_meet` show that `restrict` distributes over these operations.

```
D, Q, D1, D2: VAR set[S]

restrict(f, D)(i): T =
  (IF D(i) THEN f(i) ELSE msl.top ENDIF)

restrict_union: LEMMA
      restrict(f, union(D1, D2)) = fmsl.meet(restrict(f, D1), restrict(f, D2))

restrict_meet: LEMMA
   restrict(fmsl.meet(f1, f2), D) = fmsl.meet(restrict(f1, D), restrict(f2, D))
```

The generic *post* operation is a parameter to the algorithm given by the variable P. It must satisfy several important restrictions. It must be monotonic, distributive with respect to the `meet` operation, and increasing in the sense that if g is `P(restrict(f, singleton(i)))` for some i in S, then `f(i) <= g(j)`. This is a generalization of the restriction in Dijkstra's algorithm that the edge weights be non-negative.

```
P: VAR (fmsl.mono?)

distributive?(P): bool =
  (FORALL f1, f2:  P(fmsl.meet(f1, f2)) = fmsl.meet(P(f1), P(f2)))

increasing?(P): bool =
  (FORALL f, i, j: f(i) <= P(restrict(f, singleton(i)))(j))
```

There are a few simple lemmas about the meet operation. The first of these asserts that the meet of two functions to an argument is the meet of individual application of these functions. The other two lemmas are obvious facts about the meet operation over a linear ordering.

```
function_meet: LEMMA
   fmsl.meet(f1, f2)(i) = msl.meet(f1(i), f2(i))

meet_linear: LEMMA
   msl.meet(x, y) = x OR
   msl.meet(x, y) = y

meet_if: LEMMA
   msl.meet(x, y) = (IF x <= y THEN x ELSE y ENDIF)
```

The "state" of the search algorithm consists of the set D of dead elements from S and the map f from S to T. The main invariant for the search algorithm consists of two parts. The first invariant `D_inv?(D)` asserts that the entries in the D part of the map all lie below those in the non-D part of the map. The second invariant `Q_inv?(D, P, f)` asserts that the post operation P applied to `restrict(f, D)` is identical to f. This captures the intuition that the successors of D are already reflected in f.

```
D_inv?(D: set[S], f): bool =
  (FORALL (i: (D), j: (complement(D))): f(i) <= f(j))

Q_inv?(D, P, f): bool = (P(restrict(f, D)) = f)
```

In each iteration of the search algorithm, the state consisting of the set D and the map f is extended to D' by adding an *live* element j, i.e., where NOT D(j) holds and f(j) is distinct from top, and merging the successors of j to f. The lemma post_restrict asserts that the application of P to restrict(f, D') yields a map f' which can be decomposed so that f'(i) is just f(i) when D'(i) holds, and the meet of old value f(i) and value P(restrict(f, singleton(j)))(i) arising from applying the post operation P to j.

```
post_restrict: LEMMA
  (FORALL (P | distributive?(P) AND increasing?(P)),
          D,
          (f | D_inv?(D, f) AND  Q_inv?(D, P, f)):
   (EXISTS i: NOT D(i) AND f(i) /= top)
   AND j = select({i | NOT D(i) AND f(i) /= top}, f)
  IMPLIES
   P(restrict(f, union(singleton[S](j), D)))(i)
    = IF union(singleton[S](j), D)(i) THEN f(i)
             ELSE msl.meet(f(i), P(restrict(f, singleton(j)))(i))
             ENDIF)
```

The search algorithm latsearch takes three arguments: the post operation P which must be distributive and increasing, the dead set D, and the map f which must satisfy the D_inv? and Q_inv? conditions. The result is required to be a map that is a fixpoint on the function lattice which agrees with the input map f on the input dead set D. As already mentioned, the live set consists of the non-D elements i such that f(i) /= top. If the live set is empty, then the current map f is returned. Otherwise, a minimal element j is selected and added to D to obtain D1 while updating the map f to P(restrict(f, D1)).

```
latsearch((P | distributive?(P) AND increasing?(P)),
          D,
          (f | D_inv?(D, f) AND  Q_inv?(D, P, f))):
     RECURSIVE
       {g | fmsl.fixpoint?(P)(g) AND restrict(g, D) = restrict(f, D)}
  = (IF (EXISTS i: NOT D(i) AND f(i) /= top)
       THEN LET D1 = union(singleton[S](select({i | NOT D(i) AND f(i) /= top}, f)),
                           D),
                f1 = P(restrict(f, D1))
            IN latsearch(P, D1, f1)
       ELSE f
     ENDIF)
    MEASURE card(fullset[S]) - card(D)
```

The preservation of the invariant on D and f is generated as a proof obligation. Its proof is quite difficult and delicate. It is then easy to show that the post-condition on the result follows from the invariant. The invariants and post-condition do not imply that the result that is computed is the least fixpoint. Indeed, the result is not the least, but the greatest fixpoint in the point-wise ordering on the function lattice. For forward search, the range type T for the function lattice is bool, and the ordering has TRUE <= FALSE. This way, the greatest fixpoint on the function lattice corresponds to reachability since as many vertices as possible are marked as unreachable. For Dijkstra's algorithm, the range type T is the disjoint union of the integers with a top element ∞, where the ordering is the usual numeric ordering on the integers with ∞ as a maximal element. The meet operation then corresponds to taking the minimum of two values according to this ordering. Note that the latsearch algorithm computes the fixpoint, whereas GFS stops as soon as the goal state is found, but this optimization is a fairly trivial one given the invariants.

7 Observations

To summarize, we have developed an abstract treatment of fixpoints over complete lattices, instantiated this theory for the Boolean lattice, and exploited this instantiation in a correctness proof for general forward search. The general forward search algorithm is itself generalized to cover shortest path algorithms such as Dijkstra's algorithm on weighted directed graphs. The point of the proof is primarily pedagogical. There is no intrinsic difficulty in the informal or the formal development of these ideas. The formalization within PVS nicely illustrates the use of some advanced features in the PVS language such as predicate subtyping, dependent typing, parametric theories, theory assumptions, and typing judgements. We expand on some of the pedagogical themes in the paragraphs below.

Abstraction plays a crucial role in the formal development. We have tried to formalize the concepts at the highest level of abstraction so that the results, and particularly, the proofs, can be widely reused. For example, we reused the meet_semilattice theory in formalizing complete lattices. This kind of abstraction is also the hallmark of good software engineering, but in programming, abstraction can be double-edged. The overhead of using the abstraction through layers of instantiation might outweigh the engineering benefits. In a formal development, however, abstraction is essential since it can be very tedious to repeat the same proofs in all the different instances. However, there is also an overhead associated with using abstractions. For example, Dijkstra's algorithm is relatively easy to prove correct for graphs with numeric edge weights, whereas the generalized algorithm in Section 6 is quite a delicate exercise. Furthermore, instantiating the abstract scheme to derive the concrete version of Dijkstra's algorithm requires a fair amount of work. One way to avoid the overhead associated with developing and using the abstraction is to use the abstract patterns and schemes as templates for synthesizing and proving concrete versions of the algorithm.

The level of automation impedes the wider adoption of this technology. Most of the proofs in this development were entirely straightforward, but a handful of the proofs required a serious degree of interaction ranging from twenty to forty steps. Interaction is of course integral to the success of any formal development: functions have to be correctly defined, types must be carefully expressed, theories have to be developed, and suitable lemmas must be stated and proved. Also, an interactive proof checker can be used both to discover a proof that is initially unknown to the user, or to check a known proof. In both cases, it is useful to be able to vary the level of interaction to gain a deeper understanding of some of the formal details. Still, many of the proofs are slightly less succinct than the informal arguments that we have given. It would be good to close the gap, particularly through better support for set-theoretic reasoning, quantifier instantiation, and selective definition expansion. One capability that would have helped considerably with these proofs is possibility of extending the decision procedures with new theories like lattices.

Our fixpoint approach to path search algorithms yields certificates validating the results of individual computations. Typically, when a search procedure succeeds, it is possible to instrument it to generate *evidence* in the form of a path from s to g in the graph. The more challenging problem is to provide evidence when the search algorithm fails. Our generalized correctness argument provides a method for certifying the negative result as well. The set D can be treated as a set of marked vertices. If one checks that the successors of each marked vertex are also marked, the source vertex s is marked, and the goal vertex g is not marked, then g must not be reachable from s. The fixpoint marking of vertices in D thus serves as evidence that can be easily checked by local computations on the graph. For example, with Dijkstra's algorithm, it is not enough to know the exact path since we also need evidence that this is the shortest path. Supposing the weight of the putative shortest path is w, then a fixpoint mapping $\hat{f}$ can be constructed where each vertex in D retains its assignment in f, and all other vertices are assigned a symbolic value $\hat{w}$ indicating that the cost to reach these vertices is at least w. It is easy to check that the resulting $\hat{f}$ is a fixpoint so that it constitutes evidence that there is no shorter path from the source to the goal vertex. When the goal vertex is unreachable, the fixpoint assignment f is itself a certificate of unreachability since it assigns the maximal value top to this vertex.

There is a fair amount of related literature on the formalization of fixpoints. Rajan, Shankar, and Srivas [RSS95] formalized the mu-calculus by defining least and greatest fixpoints over the Boolean lattice. Bartels, Dold, von Henke, Pfeifer, and Rueß [BDvH⁺96] formalized the fixpoint theory of monotonic and continuous functions over *complete partial orders*, which is a partial order with a least element in which every linearly ordered subset has a least upper bound. They then prove the existence of least and greatest fixpoints for monotonic and continuous functions over complete partial orders. They also prove the validity of fixpoint induction over admissible predicates. This theory is used to embed the semantics of a small imperative programming language. Agerholm [Age94] similarly develops fixpoint theory as a basis for embedding the Logic for Computable Function (LCF) [Sco93] using the HOL proof checker [GM93]. Regensberger [Reg95] has a more sophisticated embedding of fixpoint theory over complete partial orders in Isabelle/HOL [NPW02]. Paulson [Pau95] establishes the existence of fixpoints over the Boolean lattice using Isabelle/ZF. Rudnicki and Trybulec [RT97] have used Mizar to verify the full Knaster–Tarski theorem over complete lattices including the existence of a complete lattice of fixpoints.

Abstract global search algorithms for scheduling and constraint satisfaction have been formalized by Pepper and Smith [PS97]. These algorithms involve splitting, backtracking, and constraint propagation, and are different from the search algorithms considered above. General forward search and Dijkstra's algorithm fall under a class of greedy algorithms that can be handled by the abstract structure of greedoids [KL81]. The greedoid abstraction, though different from the lattice abstraction used here, is also interesting as a general schema for a large class of algorithms.

We have adopted a style of formalization that relies heavily on predicate subtypes and the generation of proof obligations. Some of these ideas go back to earlier specification languages like VDM [Jon90], which had a notion of datatype invariants, and Nuprl [CAB$^+$86] which employed a form of predicate subtyping that required type correctness to be established as part of a proof. The contract-based methodology of Eiffel [Mey97] uses pre-condition and post-condition assertions. In PVS [ORSvH95], contracts are captured by types and theory assumptions.

8 Conclusion

We have seen that fixpoint theory is a foundation for the verification and certification of a popular and widely used search algorithm. There are many ways to formalize the concepts underlying fixpoint theory in PVS. For example, the work of Bartels, *et al*, use subtyping to capture the concept of partial orders and complete partial orders. We have also made similar use of subtyping. With subtypes, the type information has to be made explicit within a proof, but fewer proof obligations are generated since the sub-type relations can be established by typing judgements that are automatically used by the type-checker. One alternative to subtypes is to use theory assumptions to explicate the constraints on <= and glb. Assumptions have the advantage that the properties of the structure are accessible through named formulas, though it is quite easy to record the type constraints as lemmas, as we have done with the theory meet_semilattice. Unlike types, proof obligations corresponding to the assumptions are generated whenever a theory instance is invoked since these assumptions are not automatically known to the type-checker.

The larger point is that even seemingly simple algorithms have interesting proofs. These proofs capture the key insights underlying these algorithms. These proofs can be used to generalize and extend the algorithms as well as in generating certificates for validating the results returned by these procedures. Model checking is itself a search paradigm that is based on the explicit representation and construction of fixpoint sets. We have argued elsewhere [Sha08] that such fixpoint sets can be used to certify the results returned by a model checker. In future work, we plan to explore the use of fixpoints in certifying results from model checkers and other inference procedures.

References

[Abr96]   Abrial, J.-R.: The B-Book: Assigning Programs to Meanings. Cambridge University Press, Cambridge (1996)

[Age94]   Agerholm, S.: A HOL basis for reasoning about functional programs. In: BRICS RS-94-44, Department of Computer Science, University of Aarhus, Denmark (December 1994),
http://www.daimi.aau.dk/BRICS/RS/94/44/BRICS-RS-94-44/BRICS-RS-94-44.html

[BC04]   Bertot, Y., Castéran, P.: Interactive Theorem Proving and Program Development. Springer, Heidelberg (2004), http://coq.inria.fr/

[BDvH$^+$96] Bartels, F., Dold, A., von Henke, F.W., Pfeifer, H., Rueß, H.: Formalizing Fixed-Point Theory in PVS. In: Ulmer Informatik-Berichte 96-10, Universität Ulm, Fakultät für Informatik (1996)

[CAB⁺86]   Constable, R.L., Allen, S.F., Bromley, H.M., Cleaveland, W.R., Cremer, J.F., Harper, R.W., Howe, D.J., Knoblock, T.B., Mendler, N.P., Panangaden, P., Sasaki, J.T., Smith, S.F.: Implementing Mathematics with the Nuprl Proof Development System. Prentice Hall, Englewood Cliffs (1986),
http://www.cs.cornell.edu/Info/Projects/NuPRL/

[Dij59]   Dijkstra, E.W.: A note on two problems in connexion with graphs. Numerische Mathematik 1, 269–271 (1959)

[GM93]   Gordon, M.J.C., Melham, T.F. (eds.): Introduction to HOL: A Theorem Proving Environment for Higher-Order Logic. Cambridge University Press, Cambridge (1993), http://www.cl.cam.ac.uk/Research/HVG/HOL/

[HJ00]   Huisman, M., Jacobs, B.: Java program verfication via a hoare logic with abrupt termination. In: Maibaum, T. (ed.) FASE 2000. LNCS, vol. 1783, pp. 284–303. Springer, Heidelberg (2000)

[Hoa69]   Hoare, C.A.R.: An axiomatic basis for computer programming. Comm. ACM 12(10), 576–583 (1969)

[Jon90]   Jones, C.B.: Systematic Software Development Using VDM, 2nd edn. Prentice Hall International Series in Computer Science. Prentice Hall, Hemel Hempstead (1990)

[KL81]   Korte, B., Lovász, L.: Mathematical structures underlying greedy algorithms. In: Gecseg, F. (ed.) FCT 1981. LNCS, vol. 117, pp. 205–209. Springer, Heidelberg (1981)

[Kna28]   Knaster, B.: Un théorèm sur les fonctions d'ensembles. Annals. Soc. Pol. Math. 6, 133–134 (1928)

[LaV06]   LaValle, S.M.: Planning Algorithms. Cambridge University Press, Cambridge (2006)

[Mey97]   Meyer, B.: Design by contract: Making object-oriented programs that work. In: TOOLS, vol. (25), p. 360. IEEE Computer Society, Los Alamitos (1997)

[Muñ99]   Muñoz, C.: PBS: Support for the B-method in PVS. Technical Report SRI-CSL-99-1, Computer Science Laboratory, SRI International, Menlo Park, CA (February 1999)

[NPW02]   Nipkow, T., Paulson, L.C., Wenzel, M.: Isabelle/HOL: A Proof Assistant for Higher-Order Logic. Springer, Heidelberg (2002),
http://isabelle.in.tum.de/

[ORSvH95]   Owre, S., Rushby, J., Shankar, N., von Henke, F.: Formal verification for fault-tolerant architectures: Prolegomena to the design of PVS. IEEE Transactions on Software Engineering 21(2), 107–125 (1995), http://pvs.csl.sri.com

[OS01]   Owre, S., Shankar, N.: Theory interpretations in PVS. Technical Report SRI-CSL-01-01, Computer Science Laboratory, SRI International, Menlo Park, CA (April 2001)

[Pau95]   Paulson, L.C.: Set theory for verification II: Induction and recursion. Journal of Automated Reasoning 15(2), 167–215 (1995)

[PS97]   Pepper, P., Smith, D.R.: A high-level derivation of global search algorithms (with constraint propagation). Science of Computer Programming 28(2-3), 247–271 (1997)

[Reg95]   Regensburger, F.: HOLCF: Higher order logic of computable functions. In: Schubert, E.T., Alves-Foss, J., Windley, P.J. (eds.) HUG 1995. LNCS, vol. 971, pp. 293–307. Springer, Heidelberg (1995)

[RSS95]   Rajan, S., Shankar, N., Srivas, M.K.: An integration of model-checking with automated proof checking. In: Wolper, P. (ed.) CAV 1995. LNCS, vol. 939, pp. 84–97. Springer, Heidelberg (1995)

[RT97]   Rudnicki, P., Trybulec, A.: Fixpoints in complete lattices. Formalized Mathematics 6(1), 109–115 (1997)
[Sco93]   Scott, D.S.: A type-theoretical alternative to ISWIM, CUCH, OWHY. Theor. Comput. Sci. 121(1, 2), 411–440 (1993); Typed notes circulated in 1969 (1969)
[Sha08]   Shankar, N.: Trust and automation in verification tools. In: Cha, S(S.), Choi, J.-Y., Kim, M., Lee, I., Viswanathan, M. (eds.) ATVA 2008. LNCS, vol. 5311, pp. 4–17. Springer, Heidelberg (2008)
[Tar55]   Tarski, A.: A lattice-theoretical fixpoint theorem and its applications. Pacific. J. of Math. 5, 285–309 (1955)

Multi Core Design for Chip Level Multiprocessing

Tryggve Fossum

Intel Corporation

1 CMP Concepts: Introduction and Some Background

Chip level integration continues to be a driving force in the computer industry. It lowers the cost and increases performance of computer systems, creating a remarkable rate of improvement in all processors, from handheld devices to supercomputers. Processor chips now (in 2009) contain up to two billion transistors. Gordon Moore outlined a roadmap for chip level integration in 1965, which has become known as Moore's Law. It predicts that the density of transistors in a silicon chip will double every process generation. It has become the heartbeat of the semiconductor industry. Nine years later, in 1974, Robert Dennard defined more specifically a scaling methodology for MOSFETs, which the industry has adopted for the most part. His rules and parameters are listed in Table 1.1. The process scaling factor is denoted by κ. If we scale all the relevant process parameters by $\kappa = \sqrt{2} \approx 1.4$, the transistor count in a fixed size chip will in fact double every process generation. Along the way, in order to achieve this, a myriad of complex problems have to be solved in physics, chemistry, and optics, making the improvements gradual. It is impressive how well the scenario outlined by Moore and Dennard continues to play out.

As they get smaller, the transistors switch faster, by the scaling factor, κ. This allows designers to increase the clock frequency of the processors or fit more gates in each pipeline stage. Note that this speedup happens even as the supply voltage is reduced by the same scaling factor.

Table 1.1. Robert Dennard's Scaling Rules for MOSFETs [1]

Scaling factor :	$\kappa = \sqrt{2} \approx 1.4,$ $1/\kappa \approx 0.7$
Device dimension tox, L, W:	$1/\kappa$
Doping Concentration, Na:	κ
Voltage, V:	$1/\kappa$
Current, I:	$1/\kappa$
Capacitance, εA/t,	$1/\kappa$
Delay time/circuit, VC/I:	$1/\kappa$
Power dissipation per circuit, VI:	$1/\kappa^2$
Power density, VI/A:	1

P. Müller (Ed.): LASER Summer School 2007/2008, LNCS 6029, pp. 162–187, 2010.
© Springer-Verlag Berlin Heidelberg 2010

Computer architects and designers have been busy putting this increasing number of faster transistors to good use. While the improvements in functionality and performance have been many and frequent, there have been some highlights in processor design. Much of the focus has been on interfacing to memory. As processors get faster, the relative latency of memory accesses grows.

For example, in the first processor I worked on, the VAX11-780, the processor cycle time was 200 nanoseconds, and memory access time was 1200 nanoseconds, so a memory access had a six cycle latency. Today, processors have a cycle time of 250 picoseconds and memory access time is about 100 nanoseconds, making the access latency 400 cycles. To remedy this, designers incorporate caches in the design to lower the effective latency and improve system performance. The idea of Reduced Instruction Set Computers, RISC, architectures is given credit for several benefits. It contrasts with Complex Instruction Set Computers, CISC. The RISC concept is based on the observation that most of the work in computers is done by a small set of operations, and hence it made sense to spend area and power to speed up those tasks rather than add functions that were rarely used. This phenomenon is well described in J. Emer and D. Clark's paper [4]. The initial RISC designs simplified the instruction set and the execution pipeline to the point where the whole processor could fit on a single chip. Removing the slow and costly cross-chip signals was a tremendous benefit. A process generation later, when there were enough transistors for CISC processors to fit on a single chip as well, the RISC performance advantage was reduced.

Moving the cache onto the chip was a major step forward. Cache accesses are important for frequently accessed memory data, needing short latency and high bandwidth. Which is exactly what integration provides. Initially, there was a drop in cache capacity due to limited on-die transistor count. Or maybe just the first level cache fit on the die. Later, the second level cache followed. Now, three levels of cache fit on the die, with a variety of cache organizations possible. Cache is the architectural gift that keeps on giving.

Out-of-order execution was another highlight in this history. Executing instructions out of order offers opportunities for performance increases. If an instruction cannot issue due to a dependency, later instructions whose dependencies are met, can be issued early. This utilizes spare issue slots and other hardware resources, and can in return free up instructions depending on their results to complete earlier than they would have in a strictly in order design. While this may sound simple, it turned out to be difficult for designers to deal with all the side effects of out of order execution. These out of order instructions require a place to store their speculative results, and recovery mechanisms to ensure correct operation in the event of exceptions, branches and memory conflicts.

Early single chip processor designs, starting with Intel's Pentium Pro, had remarkable success with out-of-order, much to the surprise of many architects who had started to look for alternatives like VLIW and software speculation. The additional data structures and control logic needed to support out of order execution, became much more manageable once everything fit on a single die.

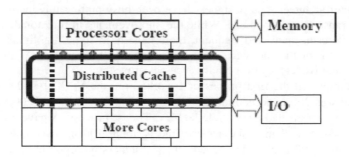

Fig. 1.1. CMP with Ring Interconnect

Today it is practical to fit multiple cores on a single chip. Fig 1.1. shows a simple example. Multiple processor cores are lined up in the top and bottom rows, with a distributed cache in the middle two rows. These cores and caches are connected with a ring interconnect, with a cache section and a core sharing a ring stop. Somehow, Memory and IO are attached as well.

Multicore is another inflection point in chip level integration. We are in effect integrating the interconnects, a long time challenge for designers. What will be the impact?

Threads which do not share data may have some benefits from running on cores on the same die. But the big benefit comes from chip level parallel processing, with threads running in cores on the same die, sharing data.

Attempts to do this with multi chip designs have had mixed success. The benefits of overlap in execution, was sometimes lost in communication delay and control complexity. Parallel processing has to balance computation overlap with communication delays. Coarse-grained parallelism refers to the case where each thread operates on data for a long time before synchronizing and communicating with other threads. Such an application can run well on a number of systems. Fine grained parallelism, on the other hand, requires frequent communication between threads, and has been difficult to exploit with multi-chip implementations. Multicore improves communication between cores by 1-3 orders of magnitude, both in bandwidth and latency. While busses between chips have bandwidth of multiple Gigabytes per second, on-die networks can reach multiple Terabytes per second. Data-sharing between processors in separate sockets can take hundreds of nanoseconds, while sharing data between cores on a chip can take a few nanoseconds.

Scaling Example: In 1995, the Alpha processor 21164 (EV5) was implemented in 0.5 micron technology with a die size of 3 cm². It ran at 300 MHz, with a supply voltage of 3.3 Volt, and had a power limit of 50 Watt. It was among the fastest micro processors at its time. It contained about 9.6 million transistors. Eight process generations later, using Moore's Law, and the scaling numbers in table 1.1, the same processor in today's leading edge technology of 32 nm, would be 1.2 mm² in area. Frequency would be about 4.8 GHz, voltage would be 0.2 Volt, and the active power per core would be 0.2 Watt. We could fit 250 EV5 size cores on a 3 cm² die in the 32 nanometer technology. Such a chip would still retain the original active power of about 50 Watt.

There are some issues with this design:

1. The 0.2 Volt supply voltage has not been achieved. This is due to various obstacles, both practical and physical limitations. An aggressive supply voltage at this time is more likely to be 0.5 Volt.
2. At 0.5 Volt, the power per core is about 1.2 Watt, and the total chip power is 300 Watt. This is very high for a single chip, even a big one. 100 Watt (or maybe much less) would be more acceptable. We could get there by reducing the core count to 64, running at a slower frequency of 1 GHz, limit activity level some other way, or a combination of these techniques.
3. Having all these cores on a single die is useless unless there is a way to connect them to each other, and to IO and Memory. We will need an on-die network. Which will take area and power away from the cores.
4. The need for high bandwidth between these cores and memory needs to be satisfied. Scaling the external bandwidth will be very expensive and maybe impossible. So we will need to satisfy some of the bandwidth requirements with on-die caches. The area and power allocated to this will reduce the core count further.

These are some of the problems we will look at in this course.

Research Problem: How many cores should optimally be placed on the same die in a CMP? If power and other resources are limited, the capabilities and performance of each core will be restricted by the total number of cores, and this needs to be balanced against the advantages of the cores being on the same die. The answer to this is likely to depend on the target applications and to evolve over time.

Processor performance in executing a program can be factored as:

Performance = instructions per cycle X cycles per second
Or: Performance = IPC X Frequency

Thus clock frequency is an important contributor to performance, and before processors became power limited, it was crucial to maximize frequency. Since dynamic power consumption grows linearly with frequency, it is now necessary to balance frequency with ways to increase instructions per cycle, IPC. This is especially the case with CMP, where on one hand parallel processing is an alternative to high speed, single stream computing, and on the other hand, all the cores share that total available chip power. This makes it less likely that we will see super-pipelined processors running at extremely high frequencies in the future, even though it may be theoretically possible.

There is a joke that the number of people predicting the end of Moore's Law doubles every two years. Eventually, they may be right. That will present new challenges to computer designers and software developers, since there will no longer be an automatic performance and density improvement due to process developments. The improvements will have to come from better designs, improved functionality, but with relative constant underlying materials. Efficient use of available chip resources will become even more important.

2   On Die Networks

Computer networks have existed for many years. They used to consist of cables between cabinets, then wires between circuit boards and backplanes, and more recently, wires between chips on boards. Now, we are looking at ways to best connect processor cores within a die. Many of the design considerations are similar, but they also change in important ways.

- *Communication pattern.* The goal on-die is to provide cores with access to shared resources, mainly memory. Cores communicate by writing to shared memory and reading from it. It is the core-cache-memory connections that are most important.
- *Bandwidth.* With cables or wires on a circuit board, the bandwidth is typically limited to 1-20 Gigabytes/per second. On die, one can get several orders of magnitude improvement, at 1-2 Terabytes/per second.
- *Latency.* Access to remote memories and caches in a multi socket system can take hundreds of nanoseconds. On die, it can be less than 10 ns.
- *Processor - Cache Communication, Sharing and Coherence.* Caches are designed to reduce the effective latency to main memory and to reduce memory bandwidth requirements. In multi processor systems with shared memory, the caches usually need to be kept coherent. This is commonly done with cache snooping or with directories keeping track of what data is stored in a cache. The coherence function can require multiple chip crossings. With CMP, it becomes practical for multiple cores to share a single cache, making cache coherence and data access much faster.
- *Memory Access – NUMA effects.* NUMA stands for Non-Uniform Memory Access. This can be due to several factors. A common reason is that a shared memory is distributed across multiple processor sockets. With CMP, memory access becomes uniform for the cores on the same chip. This can help thread scheduling and load balancing, and make code tuning simpler.
- *Pipelining.* Signaling on cables and across board wires is made more complex by the lack of storage elements. On die, it becomes easier to add storage latches to make signaling work at high frequencies.
- *Floorplan, Wiring, Layout.* The considerations for placing components on a planar chip are quite different from what happens on modules and in backplanes. But while there are multiple metal layers and lots of wires, the space is still two dimensional and restricted in several ways. A regular floorplan is important. Wiring can be massive, but it needs to be regular.

- *Power Management.* For large CMP chips, power quickly becomes a limitation. This can be due to current limits, power dissipation, or current spikes due to sudden changes in processing activity.
- *Clocking.* Clock skew will be smaller within a single die, although as the die becomes large, having a single clock domain can still be problematic. Some large die have multiple clock domains, with asynchronous communication between domains.
- *Modularity – Re-use, Standardization, Interoperability.* On die, these issues become surprisingly complex. By necessity, the industry does a decent job of standardizing interfaces between chips and boards and systems of major components. Once we get on the same chip, interoperability becomes even more important, but also harder to achieve. Managing the millions of signals inside a chip can be complex. The temptation to over-optimize for a particular situation can be hard to resist.
- *Visibility – Test, Debug, Performance Counters.* With fewer signals showing up on pins where they can be probed, visibility and analysis come to depend more on built in mechanisms like on chip logic analyzers and history buffers.
- *Reliability, Fault Tolerance.* Historically, chip-level integration has helped reliability by reducing the overall part count and the number of connectors in the system. This trend continues with CMP. But with the high transistor count per chip, there may also be more errors inside a specific die. Just as we added ECC to recover from memory errors, we will also need to increase the number of transistors used for error detection and recovery.
- *Sub-socket Partitioning, Isolation, Security, Virtualization.* These features remain important for CMP. The opportunities for added functionality grow with the transistor count. The plethora of resources makes partitioning and virtualization more desirable. Virtualization can make a single CMP chip appear as multiple computer systems to the users. It is important to be vigilant in avoiding security holes and making sure tasks are securely partitioned, minimizing the chance that actions in one partition affects another in a negative way. This is another task that will use more transistors in the future.

2.1 Intel's Polaris Chip, a Design Example

Intel's Research team developed the Polaris chip as an experimental chip to explore CMP designs [5]. It addresses important issues of the network interconnect: memory access, clocking, and power management. There are eighty cores, which together can execute at a rate of more than one Teraflop. The cores are connected in a Mesh network (see Fig 2.1.), meaning that each node is connected to adjacent nodes in the North, East, South, and West directions. In the Polaris design, there is also a vertical direction for connections to stacked memories. Stacked memories is an advanced packaging technology where Memory chips are stacked vertically, in a very dense package.

Along with the core in each node, there is a router which connects the core to the interconnects and routes the through traffic.

Figure 2.2 shows a die photo showing the individual cores on the Polaris chip.

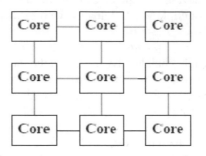

Fig. 2.1. Diagram of a 3 x 3, 2-Dimensional Mesh Interconnect

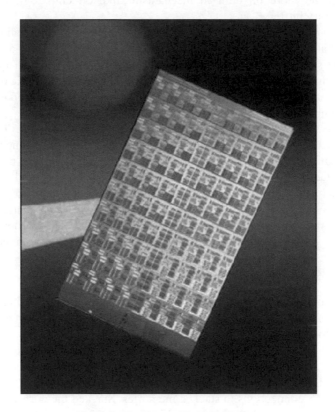

Fig. 2.2. Die Photo of Polaris CMP

The main purpose of the interconnect is to connect the individual cores to the on-die caches and hence to main memory. Even communication between cores usually go through memory, i.e. one core writes to a cache location and another core reads it. Thus quick, high bandwidth access from the cores to the collective caches is critical. Meshes have the potential to minimize the latency and provide high bandwidth, and is a popular interconnect between chips on boards and boards in cabinets, and even between cabinets in large scale systems.

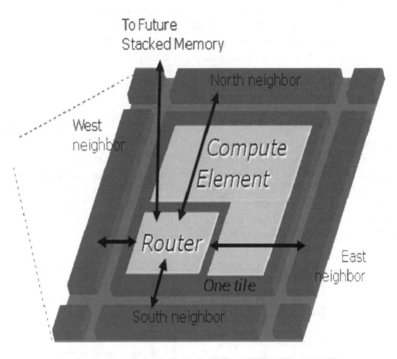

Fig. 2.3. Diagram of individual node in Polaris Chip

Figure 2.3 shows the individual node in the Polaris chip. In addition to the processor, there is a router which directs traffic along the four horizontal directions connecting the compute element to neighboring elements. There is also a vertical direction reserved for future connections to memory chips stacked on top of the processor chip. This represents an interesting opportunity for increasing memory bandwidth and reducing latency.

A toroidal mesh, see Fig 2.4, where the endpoints wrap around, can be especially effective in minimizing latency and improving bandwidth by providing an alternative path between nodes. Some computer networks organize their system in a circular fashion to maximize the benefits of the torus by making the wrap-around connections short as well.

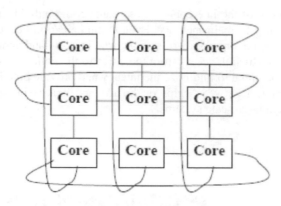

Fig. 2.4. A 3x3, 2-Dimensional Toroidal Mesh Interconnect

On die, the considerations change somewhat. The relative timing of communication to computation becomes quite different. The distances and propagation delays between cores are now very short. The time to arbitrate at switch points becomes a more significant factor. As does the time to store and forward a packet at a switch point if access through the switch is not granted. If the lanes in the mesh are not wide relative to the packet size (usually a cache line), there can be a large serialization and de-serialization (SERDES) effect. While these delays are factors in multi chip designs as well, the time is often dominated by transmission delays.

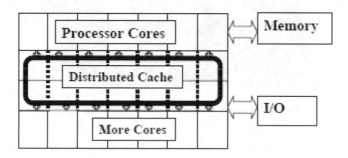

Fig. 2.5. CMP with a Ring Interconnect

Keeping these factors in mind, we have researched a ring based on-die multi-core design. Shown in Fig. 2.5. Ring interconnects have traditionally had problems with bandwidth and latency when used in large scale systems. Arbitration is simple, and routing is really easy. But few available paths and long distances create bottlenecks. This changes once you get on a single die. It becomes practical to have enough wires to transmit a whole cache line in a single cycle, eliminating SERDES effects. Arbitration remains simple: Once a message is on the ring, it has the right of way. There is of course a myriad of issues to be solved, and a ring may not be the right solution for all on-die interconnects. But in the case of a CMP, with cores accessing caches, we can make some simplifications to make the ring work well.

In our example, the cores are attached to the ring along the outside of the chip. A large cache occupies the inside of the ring. It is partitioned into pieces which are distributed along the ring, each cache piece sharing a ring stop with a core. To access the cache, the core uses the address to calculate which section of the cache may have the data. The core sends a request to the correct ring-stop. The cache section then either services the request, or, in the case of a miss, generates a memory request. Once the data returns from memory, a copy is sent to the requesting core, as well as stored in the shared cache for future use by any of the cores.

The effective bandwidth of the ring is the aggregate bandwidth of the ring segments provided, divided by the average amount used by a message. I.e.

Ring Bandwidth =
Frequency * Width * Number of Ring Stop / Average Ring Distance per Request

Setting the Frequency to 2 GHz, the width to be 512 bits, and a total of 20 ring stops, the Raw bandwidth equals 2.56 Terabytes/second. If requests are randomly distributed, we can set the average distance to 10 ring stops. The effective available bandwidth then becomes 256 GB/sec.

If we want more bandwidth than that, we can add more wires, increase the frequency, or reduce the distance messages have to travel.

As we add more wires, it soon becomes clear that adding another ring to go in the opposite direction will actually quadruple the available bandwidth. In addition to doubling the raw bandwidth, it also halves the average distance, since a message can now choose the ring with the shortest distance. So the average distance becomes one quarter the number of ring stops. In our example above, the available bandwidth becomes 1 TB/second.

The effect of adding a second, counter rotating ring is similar to the benefit of turning a mesh into a toroidal mesh. There are now two ways of getting from one point to another, and we can pick the shortest.

Note that in these calculations, the number of stops on a ring does not change its effective bandwidth since the raw bandwidth and the average distance grows by the same factor which then cancels out:

Let N be the number of ringstops.
Effective Bandwidth of a Bi-directional Ring =
Raw Bandwidth / Average Occupancy =
N * Raw Bandwidth per segment / (N/4) =
 Raw Bandwidth per segment * 4

For example: If a ring has 256 wires in each direction, and the ring cycles at 3 GHz, the Raw bandwidth per segment is 192 GBytes per second (96 GBytes per second in each direction) and the total available ring bandwidth is 768 GBytes per second.

If adding ring-stops lets the ring operate at a higher frequency, it will of course increase bandwidth proportionally. But mostly, one would add ring-stops because there is a functional unit to connect to, whether it is a core, a cache, a memory controller, or an IO interface.

So far, we have assumed that the ring traffic is uniformly distributed among the ring stops. In the case of processor to cache traffic, this assumption is very reasonable. The average ring distance that a message travels on the ring, depends on the distribution of data in the various cache segments. If we interleave the cache segments on cache line boundaries, and hash the addresses, the traffic can be very close to uniform in distance distribution and the average will be ¼ of the ring-stops in a bi-directional ring. This is good for general purpose applications, with a fair amount of data sharing. The small interleave step and the address hash helps avoid hot spots on the ring. It is also easy to calculate the destination ring stop from the address: just use the address bits next to the byte-within-cache-line address bits.

If there is little data sharing between threads, it may make sense to interleave the cache on virtual page boundaries. With page coloring, the OS can then allocate virtual pages such that the data is filled in the cache next to the requesting core. This scheme will do very well for average performance, but leaves the design vulnerable to hot spots when many threads access data residing inside a single page.

In the design we outlined, each piece of memory data can be found at exactly one cache segment on the ring. An alternative strategy is to have each cache segment be independent and let memory data be placed in any cache segment, typically in the segment next to the core which requested the data. This improves latency and ring performance when the core can fairly predictably hit in the local cache. If it misses, there has to be a coherence mechanism for finding the data in other caches, typically through snooping or a global cache directory. Either of these schemes can work well, depending on the target applications.

Yet another alternative is to mix the two methods by grouping the cores into subgroups sharing the caches inside the group, but not the caches outside the group. This makes most of the ring traffic local, which helps bandwidth, but still requires extra coherence traffic when a reference misses in the cache. Of course, the ring would be well suited to carry this coherence traffic. This scheme can work well when the number of ring stops gets very high and applications are well partitioned.

When choosing between the possible network topologies, we need to keep the applications in mind. Knowing what kind of traffic we will see lets us simplify the topology, the routing protocol, and the flow control, which is very important, since worst case scenarios can be very bad. Most networks perform poorly if a single node is involved in all transactions. The ring design would not do well in a tornado pattern, where every node just sends requests from the cache unit a few stops to the right.

Research Question: What are the tradeoffs between Ring and Mesh topologies as the core count on a chip grows? We need to consider scalability of bandwidth, latency, arbitration, power consumption, regularity of layout. Maybe include error handling.

3   Designing a Core for CMP

Having multiple cores on the die, makes it even more important that the core that is being replicated, is well optimized. Any inefficiency is likely to be multiplied by the number of cores. For many years, it was not possible to fit a full sized core on a single chip. The history of processor design is highlighted by milestones when important features were integrated into the processor chip. The Intel 486 CPU integrated the Floating Point Unit. The Pentium chip executed multiple instructions per cycle and added branch prediction. The Pentium III added SIMD instructions, called SSE. The Pentium Pro was the first major processor to execute instructions out of order. Itanium processors added large speculative execution to in order designs. Pentium4 added multi-threading. Pentium M added power management for power efficient execution. Xeon added 64 bit processing. Core 2 Duo is adding multiple cores per die, along with multiple levels of on-die cache.

Fitting the important processor features on the die was very important in minimizing interconnect delays due to chip crossings, and had a big performance impact. With Multi-core chips, we are integrating the interconnects as well.

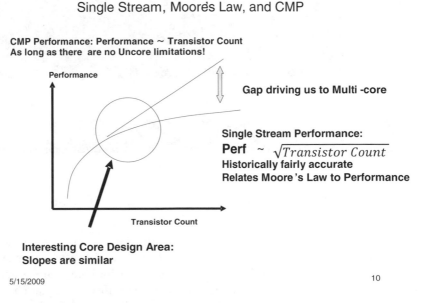

Fig. 3.1. Relating Moore's Law to Performance Growth

Empirically, it has been observed that single stream processor performance is proportional to the square root of the transistor count. It helps relate Moore's Law to performance as seen in Fig. 3.1. Considering that the circuit speed improves by the square root of 2 between process generations, the performance of the next generation processor, with twice the number of transistors, becomes:

$$New\ Performance = \sqrt{2 * Transistor\ Count} * Circuit\ Speedup = \sqrt{2} * \sqrt{2}$$
$$* \sqrt{Transistor\ Count} = 2 * Old\ Performance$$

Going forward with CMP, it seems plausible that performance can grow almost linearly with transistor count by just adding more cores, rather than increasing the transistor count per core. The gap between the straight line and the square root curve drives us toward CMP.

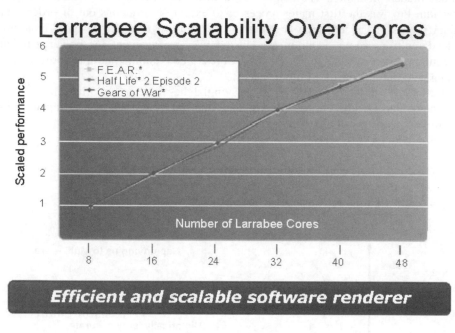

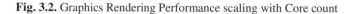

Fig. 3.2. Graphics Rendering Performance scaling with Core count

Fig 3.2 shows that on some applications performance can scale linearly with core count in a CMP. The graphs show projected performance of a software renderer running some popular video games on Larrabee, a multi core chip designed for processing graphics. [3]. One key to the excellent scalability of the Larrabee chip is good software use of the on-die caches and the available memory bandwidth. By blocking the data to fit in the caches, the chip does not run out of memory resources as the core count grows.

The point of the graph where the slopes of the curves in Fig 7 are equal, make for an interesting core design point. Improving core performance at this point improves both single stream and throughput performance. In practice, this is not a single point, since the performance curves will vary with the nature of the applications running on the core.

What is the optimal core architecture? Different designers have come up with different answers to this over the last sixty years. This diversity in opinion is due to several factors:

1. The underlying hardware technology changes. The core designed with vacuum tubes will be different from the one we design with many millions of MOSFET transistors. In between, we have had various semiconductor technologies, including TTL, ECL, and GaAs. These technologies had their specific set of strengths and weaknesses to be optimized for. Since the technology continues to evolve, we are unlikely to find agreement on the ideal core in the near future.
2. Compatibility requirements. More important than theoretical performance and functionality, is the ability to run existing software. Ideas which require the world's software to be re-written have a high hurdle to overcome.
3. What is the best design will vary with the applications. Out of order processing is good for irregular code which will be hard to schedule by a compiler due to dynamic effects like branches and cache misses. On the other hand, compute intensive code like graphics and scientific computing may be readily scheduled by a compiler and require less dynamic hardware.
4. The interesting design space for a core is enormous. While designers do performance modeling to refine their designs, it is not possible to do it exhaustively, and so we still have to rely somewhat on experience and judgement, and maybe even taste. Almost like fashion, design styles come and go.

While early computers were quite spartan by necessity, their architecture was often aimed at functionality rather than simplicity. There was a tendency to add a variety of hardware constructs to solve specific problems encountered in programming experiences at the time. It was OK if these designs spanned multiple chips, modules, and cabinets. The prevailing Complex Instruction Set Computers (CISC) tended to have a lot of functionality in their instructions. There is a wide choice of operands: registers, immediate, and memory. Memory operands can be addressed in a variety of ways, including indexing and indirection. CISC computers were designed to do transcendental functions, decimal string operations, and more in a single instruction.

By contrast, Reduced Instruction Set Computers (RISC) emphasized common simple operations, leaving it to software to build more complex functions. RISC designs were the first to fit full featured processors on a single die due to their simple instruction set and execution pipeline. This gave them a big performance advantage over CISC processors. But soon afterwards, CISC processors also fit on a single die, and the performance gap became smaller.

Some RISC advantages still exist. When single instructions both accesses memory operands and perform operations, it makes the cache access more time critical and makes it harder to pipeline the operations. Separating instructions that access memory from the instructions that operate on data is referred to as a LOAD/STORE architecture, and is a key RISC feature. It gives the compiler an opportunity to schedule other operations between a LOAD instruction and instructions which use the data. This puts less pressure on cache access, and the cache can be designed with better functionality, taking a couple of cycles to complete the operation.

RISC architectures tend to have fixed instruction lengths, i.e. each instruction has the same length, regardless of the operation it does. Usually, the length is 32 bits. This can be quite restrictive when you try to fit all the functionality you would like, and the instruction set designers have to make compromises. The fixed length is quite important when decoding instructions, especially when decoding multiple instructions in parallel as in super scalar designs. With variable length instructions, it is harder to know where the following instructions begin and end.

On the other hand, CISC instructions tend to have direct access to memory operands. This reduces the instruction count in a program, both static and dynamic. This again saves issue slots, and makes more effective use of the instruction cache. The difference in code density between CISC and RISC versions of a program can be a factor of 2-3.

CISC architectures often convert the most complex instructions into sequences of microcode operations. This lets the hardware be optimized for the simpler, higher frequency operations, and can bridge the gap with RISC.

Another big core design choice is whether the instructions are executed in order or out of order. Usually, out of order means issuing out of order, but completing instructions in order. The Tomasulo algorithm [2] uses register renaming to assign temporary registers to hold early results and make them available for use by later instructions. Instructions are assigned a free target register at issue time. When the instruction is committed at "retire" time, the assigned register becomes the architectural state. If the instruction turns out to be cancelled for some reason, the architectural state is backed up to previous registers. It is an elegant scheme and works very well.

The out of order mechanism is especially useful in dealing with dynamic effects which the compiler cannot easily schedule for, such as cache misses and branches, and procedure calls. Out of order execution makes the branch predictor more effective by letting instructions on the predicted path be issued early.

Out of order designs work well on programs like those in the SPECint benchmark suite. These programs have significant run-time effects due to cache misses and branch mispredicts. These are not easily handled by the compiler. And thus the dynamic re-ordering in out of order designs can give a 20-50% performance advantage. For other, vectorized or streaming programs, where the compiler has scheduled the code for the processor, in order designs can almost close the performance gap to out of order.

Very Long Instruction Word computers (VLIW) are in-order designs where the dependency checking of instructions are done by the compiler. Instructions are grouped into strings of three to thirty, which are issued together under software control. It can be a challenge for the compiler to find this many independent instructions to issue. Often, VLIW architectures include instructions for speculative execution which can mimic in software the effect of out of order execution. Control Speculation lets the compiler move operations past branches to help latency and fill in the issue slots. Data Speculation lets the compiler re-order memory references. This is most useful for moving loads up past stores in order to get them started early. The challenge is to detect when the speculation fails and find a way to recover. This may require hardware support.

Much of core architecture centers on branch operations and cache access. Both of these features have a dynamic behavior which requires speculation and recovery from incorrect speculation. Other operations are predictable and are more easily sped up by allocating additional of resources. For arithmetic, this can include vector operations, where a single instruction performs the same operation on an array of data.

A core can be designed to process instructions from multiple programs at the same time. This is referred to as simultaneous multithreading. These hardware threads of execution are just programs running in a processor core using shared hardware resources. It is achieved by adding general registers and a few other resources to hold the multiple process contexts. The rest of the hardware, including arithmetic units, can be a shared resource and used to execute instructions from either of the threads. Thus by adding a small amount of hardware, one can significantly increase aggregate performance. Since instructions from different threads tend to be independent of each other, it is more likely that they can be processed in parallel, even issued in the same cycle.

Instruction Issue Slots

Fig. 3.3. Issuing Instructions From Four Threads with Simultaneous Multi Threading

Multithreading can be an effective way of maximizing use of hardware resources to increase throughput. But since some resources are shared, they can sometimes be critical, resulting in contention between the threads. Thus the gain in throughput comes with some loss of single threaded performance. The major source of performance loss with multithreading is cache contention. The multiple threads will increase total cache activity. If the data is not shared between threads, there is less temporal and spatial locality, and the miss rate will increase. With multithreading, there is more tolerance for cache misses, since there are other threads to run while waiting for memory. But one has to be careful to not overwhelm the cache and memory system by trying to support too many threads.

Multithreaded Performance

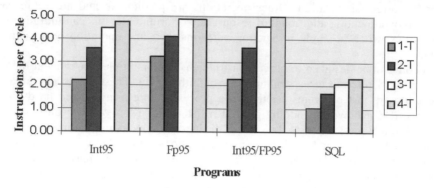

Fig. 3.4. Performance of Multi Threaded Programs in a Superscalar Alpha Processor

Fig 3.4 Shows the performance of multiple threads in an eight wide superscalar Alpha design with Simultaneous Multithreading. The aggregate number of instructions per cycle increases as we go from one to four active threads, but there is a diminishing return, especially as we go from three to four threads. In fact, for floating point benchmarks, the performance peaks with three threads due to resource conflicts. The best speedup is with a mix of integer and floating point applications, since they are less likely to stress the same resources.

Research Problem: We have looked at various ways of improving processor performance/ in a CMP. For applications you are interested in, which techniques will work best?

4   Memory Access and System Scaling

Memory access has been a challenge for computer designers for a long time. Providing high memory capacity and bandwidth along with short latency is difficult and expensive. Multiprocessing puts additional demands on memory bandwidth. Multiprocessing with cache coherence adds coherence traffic and more latency, further compounding the problem. With process scaling, per chip density increases follow Moore's Law, but the external wires, package pins, and connectors which connect them to the processor chips improve more slowly.

Fig 4.1 shows four processors connected to system bus along with a memory controller and a path to Input and Output (I/O). The memory is controlled centrally and accessed by the four CPU's via the system bus. Such systems have been made by many manufacturers and have worked well. The single system bus can be a bandwidth and latency problem, but clever designers have made it work. The key to success has been to have a cache with each of the CPU's. The cache may have been integrated or not, but it served to improve the effective memory latency and to reduce the bus bandwidth requirements. As the processors got faster, the caches got bigger

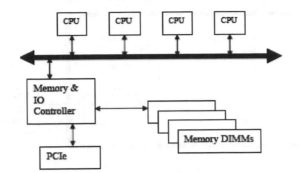

Fig. 4.1. Traditional Bus based Computer System

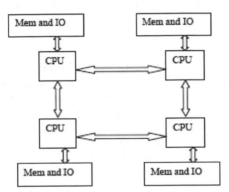

Fig. 4.2. Link based Computer System

and more sophisticated. As the cores got faster, the caches needed to get better. Typically, they had to scale faster than the rest of the core, because they also had to make up for slower scaling of the memory system.

Figure 4.2 shows a system where memory has been distributed and is co-located with the individual CPU's. Thus each CPU has local memory directly attached. Access to remote memory is via dedicated links. It is often referred to as a Non-Uniform Access Memory system, NUMA, since there can be a significant latency difference between local and remote memory. Such a system works best if most memory references are local, meaning that the Operating System has managed to co-locate a program and its data to the same socket. This can be difficult to achieve, but much effort has gone into making it work well for many important applications. Without good NUMA support in the OS, performance of such systems tend to be limited by link bandwidth rather than memory bandwidth.

With a link based system, it becomes more beneficial to integrate the memory controller in with the CPU chip (assuming we have the transistors). This eliminates two chip crossings in the path to and from memory, which reduces latency, especially for local memory. Similarly, we can integrate the connection to IO devices. So we have a CPU chip which looks like this:

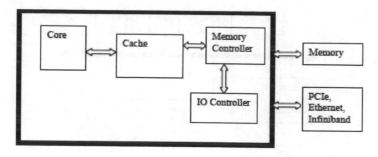

Fig. 4.3. Integrated CPU chip

Figure 4.3 shows a highly integrated CPU chip as we have seen come to market recently. Memory and IO have been left off for obvious reasons. The next logical step is to integrate multiple cores on the same die. How does this affect the memory system?

The raw processor performance of the cores grows with the core count. This results in increased memory traffic. The off-chip bandwidth may not increase proportionally. The traditional solution is to increase the on-die cache size. Again, the total cache will have to increase at a higher rate than the raw performance to account for the lesser scaling in the memory system. Another factor is the impact of multi-core vs. single core. Caches work well for most single programs because they have good temporal and data locality. How do they work for multi-core?

On one hand, multi-core processing will bring in multiple data sets into the cache, corresponding to the multiple threads of execution. This will increase pressure on the cache. On the other hand, there is potential for sharing between the threads, thus increasing the efficiency of the cache if it is shared. The sharing takes multiple forms:

1. Programs share data.
2. Programs can share instructions.
3. Programs can share the cache as a common resource.

Sharing data efficiently is the goal of many parallel programs. This has the potential for large performance improvements and in the long term it may be the most interesting aspect of multi-core processors. Data sharing has traditionally been classified as coarse grained or fine grained, depending on the frequency of communication between the threads. Coarse grained parallelism is most tractable since it puts less demand on bandwidth and latency. Fine grained has been difficult in multi socket systems since the cost of communication can easily outweigh the benefits of parallel computation. This tradeoff will change with multi-core since the communication delays decrease by two orders of magnitude.

Communication will still be a challenge in multi-core designs when data is shared between threads. This makes techniques like Transactional Memory interesting, as well as fast, efficient lock mechanisms. This is an important area for research. With Transactional Memory, programs can execute a code segment atomically, assuming there is no contention for access to shared data. If this assumption is false, the whole segment is undone, and none of the writes are made visible to the system.

Sharing instructions can be important if the programs running are large, as in Transaction Processing, the Operating System, and some personal productivity applications. If the working set of the program gets to be megabytes, it is important to keep one copy for all the cores rather than one copy per thread.

Even if the running programs have little in common, sharing a large cache is typically more efficient than splitting that cache into smaller, private caches. This is because working sets vary in size as programs go through phases, leaving opportunities for other programs to use spare cache locations.

There will of course be contention for cache space between threads. While caches seem to be very robust in general, the multiple threads can create interference and reduce cache hit rate. It is important to detect these cases and incorporate techniques for dealing with them. An example would be when a thread accesses a large data structure linearly and in effect sweeps the whole cache with little re-use. A simple counter can detect this case, and map the sweeping references to a smaller section of the cache, leaving the thread to thrash against its own data.

Associative caches, where a block of memory data can fit in multiple locations, become even more important with multi-core, since independent code streams are more likely to map data to the same index. The cache replacement algorithm, i.e. the process of deciding of which block to replace when a new block is being brought in, may need to consider the multi-core effect. The traditional LRU algorithm (Least Recently Used) works well for single stream, single level caches. In multi-core designs with multiple cache levels, the LRU may be less effective since it does not see all the cache traffic, and the various cores can have very different access patterns in the lower level caches.

The first level cache is often included in the last level cache for simplicity of design. Making it non-inclusive may make better use of the total cache space, but at the expense of some complexity and maybe delays. As the caches get bigger and become a significant portion of the total die area, it will make more sense to make them exclusive.

Research Problem: Caches present a window into main memory. It reduces the effective memory latency and increases available bandwidth. Their existence is normally invisible to the correct execution of a program, since hardware keeps the caches coherent with the memory contents. There is a significant amount of hardware which goes into doing this work, even when it may not really be necessary for correct execution. If software took over more of the function of keeping caches coherent, hardware could be simpler, performance would be higher, and power consumption would be lower. Transactional Memory is a step in this direction, and there are likely many other ideas to be found.

5 Power Management

We saw in the example in Section 1 how power consumption is likely to present a fundamental limitation for CMP designs. By Dennard's rules, power stayed fairly constant per area if the supply voltage is scaled down by the common scaling factor. Dynamic power is a direct function of the square of the voltage:

$$P = \text{constant} * V^2 * C * F$$

where P is the dynamic power of the chip, V is the supply voltage, C is the switching capacitance, and F is the frequency.

Since frequency is also a linear function of the voltage, the net effect is that dynamic power in a chip scales by the cubic power of the voltage. We see that a small increase in voltage creates a large increase in power. Conversely, lowering the voltage by just a little, can save significant amounts of power. Since frequency is proportional to the voltage, lowering the voltage normally necessitates a drop in frequency. This is referred to as voltage-frequency scaling. In a CMP, a small drop in frequency can often free up enough power to enable an increase in the core count. Thus voltage-frequency scaling has been a very efficient way of controlling power. It is now sometimes done in a single chip by dynamically scaling voltage and frequency to match the power budget with the activity level of the program. This is quite intriguing. Unfortunately, it may not be a long term strategy, as the voltage approaches the minimum level needed for transistors to function correctly.

Once we become unable to lower the voltage further, transistors may continue to shrink, but the power per area will not stay constant as it does in Dennard's table of design parameters. Power problems will surface in several areas: Power distribution, cooling, current limits, sudden voltage swings, etc. Many clever people are busy pushing back the limits we see in these areas, so we should not despair for the future. But an important theme in CMP design will be to make the best possible use of the available power. Given the problems we face with global warming, this is a sound policy in any case.

One idea is to try to match the power allocated with the activity level of each core. If we notice that a program has a low average execution rate (IPC), we can conclude that on average it uses less power. That could free up power for other cores who may be running programs with more instruction level parallelism. Since we cannot exceed the power budget, we need to guarantee that the behavior we observe continues. We can do that by limiting the issue rate of the core with the slow program to something less than maximum. We can then monitor how good a match the restriction is with the program as it executes. If it often wants to execute more instructions than we allowed, we can increase its allocation. If it usually has spare instruction issue slots, we can restrict it further and free up more of the total power budget.

Programs often have irregular behavior. There may be bursts of high activity even if the average is low. Cutting off these peaks by limiting issue width, can be a significant performance loss. If these bursts are short, they won't cause a power problem. Allocating a burst budget of extra instruction issue slots can be effective in allowing for the bursts of higher activity without compromising the overall power consumption. We found that across a wide range of applications, allocating a burst budget of just ten instructions, removed most of the performance impact of restricting instruction issue. Figure 5.1 shows an S-curve of a number of benchmarks showing the impact on performance by restricting the average issue width to 1.5, 2.0, 2.5, and 3.0, respectively, but with 10 credits to be used during short bursts of high program activity.

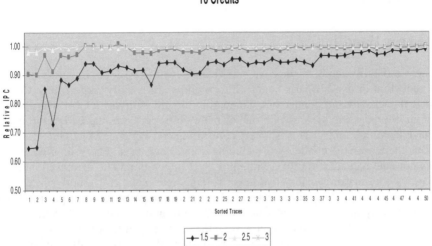

Fig. 5.1. Performance Impact of Restricting Issue Width in a Four wide Superscalar Design

A refinement of the issue limiting technique is to match the type of activity a program has with the type of restrictions put on it. Floating point operations consume more power than integer, multiplication more than addition, etc. If we know what kind of program is running, we can budget power accordingly.

Many programs spend a lot of time waiting for memory during cache misses, which can take hundreds of cycles. During this time, the cores can consume very little power. We can stretch our power budget and have more cores running at the same time if we can count on a certain cache miss rate. Again, a solution is to enforce the idling via a technique called core rationing. We notice that on average 30% of the cores are waiting for memory data, using very little power. We can use this to enable more cores. To keep from running out of power, we make sure 30% of the cores are idle even when there are fewer cache misses.

By keeping track of how often cores are forced to wait when there is no cache miss, and how often more than the expected number of cores are waiting for memory, we can adjust the formula for idling cores, to optimize performance at the available power budget.

Running experiments using these techniques, we found that the negative performance impact of core rationing is very low, and the potential for power saving is significant.

There are many other techniques for conserving power in computer chips. Clock gating and power gating are some of the most important ones. We have mainly focused on techniques specific to CMP design. The Polaris chip mentioned earlier, included extensive power and clock control of individual components to match their current function. For example, cores not currently computing, can have their voltage lowered just to the point where they can still retain information. This requires multiple voltage domains, which has a cost, but can be worthwhile as a way to match power to activity level.

6 Error Handling

System reliability tends to improve significantly with chip level integration, through the reduction in overall parts count. Silicon chips are usually more robust than mechanical packages and connectors. Comparing the reliability of a CMP chip with that of a multi processing system with one or more chips per core, the CMP chip is likely to have better reliability. This is a very comforting consequence of Moore's Law.

But there are still challenges, including some new ones. The reliability per chip does not automatically improve with chip level integration. The increased number of circuits, with finer dimensions and lower voltage, makes the chips more susceptible to soft errors, caused by random effects from cosmic rays of neutron particles. Also, customers may not be satisfied with a single chip multi processor. Rather, they may want the CMP to be part of a larger system that can be used to solve even larger problems. The reliability of very large systems, pushing the limits of software and power, will continue to be an error handling challenge. CMP makes it possible to design systems with thousands of cores.

Finally, the job of improving reliability is never done. As computers become an even bigger part of our everyday life, we will expect more from them in terms of functionality and performance, and the possible impact from failures will be greater. This gives chip manufacturers like Intel a great incentive to continue to improve the reliability of their components.

Besides doing all we can to make the underlying technology reliable, we will also use a larger portion of the available transistors to actually reduce or eliminate the impact of failures. This is already a well established strategy in the DRAM business, where parity and ECC (Error Checking and Correcting Codes) are successfully used for error detection and recovery. In this case, the added transistors increase the raw failure rate, by adding error correcting codes which may themselves be subject to errors. But the added logic is able to use the redundant bits to calculate the original values and recover from the error.

Similar techniques will be used in the rest of the design. But unlike memory chips, CMP's do not consist of only regular structures like RAM arrays. There is a variety of logic structures which cannot be checked by simple techniques like ECC and parity.

Parity refers to a technique of adding an additional checksum bit to a binary value by taking the exclusive OR of all the bits in the number. This parity bit is saved along with the data, and then used to check the number later on. If the parity of the data has changed, it is a sign that the value has been corrupted. This technique catches all single bit failures, in fact, any odd number of bit failures. It does not by itself offer a recovery mechanism. For that we can use ECC, which adds enough bits to the value to make it possible to pin point the bit in error and actually correct it. Current ECC methods will often detect up to two failures, and correct single bit errors. By adding more bits, this can be extended to both detect and correct more bits.

Parity and ECC are effective techniques for protecting arrays of data and wires transporting data. Unfortunately, they are not easily propagated through arithmetic and other complex transformations. Granted, for such computations, the window of vulnerability is less, since there is only a short window of time when a transient error can affect a result as it is being computed. The result is usually stored in a set of latches, where the data may be kept for several cycles. One technique is to make these latches radiation hardened by adding redundant copies of the data, or making them more resistant to neutron particles in some other way.

While an error during an arithmetic operation is highly unlikely, if there are thousands of processors in the system, with trillions of such operations per second, the probability of a neutron particle causing a fault sometime during a year can be non-negligible. Modulo arithmetic can be used to check arithmetic. Usually, one does the arithmetic modulo 3, since the value of a binary number modulo 3 can be calculated quickly and simply. It will also catch all single bit failures and many double bit failures. The idea is to store the modulo 3 value along with the operands, and do the same operation on the modulo 3 values as we do on the operands themselves. Then we compare the mod 3 result with the mod 3 value of the result.

There are several ad hoc techniques which can reduce the probability of a soft error affecting a computation. Since the likelihood of an error is roughly proportional to the size of the data structure, compression can be used to reduce the exposure. For example, if cache line or a page in memory is all zero, one can represent that fact with a single bit and use that bit to reproduce zeroes when the data is needed, rather than expose the data itself to neutron particles.

Main memory and disk storage is usually protected by ECC. If such data is used by the computation in a read-only fashion, it can be flushed and re-fetched when an error is detected. If there is no detection mechanism, one can periodically flush and re-fetch the data to keep errors from becoming visible.

In some applications, the occurrence of an undetected error can be catastrophic. The most reliable systems have traditionally been based on repeating the computation. This can be done by having redundant processors each computing the same program and comparing the results. Having two processors operate in lockstep and comparing all available signals has been used in some fault tolerant systems. In these systems it is extremely unlikely that an error goes undetected. In some applications this is important. The challenge in designing such systems is to limit the chance of false alarms, i.e. reduce the cases where there is loss of lockstep operation, but no program visible error has actually occurred. The sources of these false positives can be recoverable errors in memory. If a bit flipped and was corrected by ECC, it may still cause a timing change, which would affect lockstep. Asynchronous interfaces is another source. A signal may accidentally be clocked in different cycles by two processors, leading to a cycle-by-cycle miscompare.

With CMP, the opportunities for redundant computation to catch errors grow. Multiple cores and threads can run the same programs. Data in memory, IO and higher level caches do not need to be replicated, but instead covered by ECC and a single copy used by the redundant computations. Before written data is committed, the results offered by the two operations are checked against each other. Not replicating memory traffic is especially important when memory bandwidth or cache capacity is a critical resource for good performance. In a CMP, two cores can run the same program somewhat independently, using the same data in a shared cache. When they write data into that cache, the data (and address) is compared, and if identical, the cores are assumed to be correct and they are allowed to proceed. This scheme will have fewer false positives than lockstep operation, but they can still occur. One case could be that one core reads a cache line, which then gets invalidated by a third core before the second core has read the data.

If the timing of the two cores becomes too disparate, the cache controller which does the comparison may have problems buffering up intermediate results.

An especially intriguing version of the redundant computing scheme is to use two threads running simultaneously inside a single processor core. In an in-order design, they could run back to back, and the checking of a result could be very fast and timely. Running three threads could provide error recovery as well. Comparing the middle thread with both the first and the third thread, would indicate which of the threads is in error, and the results produced by other two can be used for recovery. In this scheme, data is not replicated. For applications where memory access and cache size is the limiting factor, redundant multi threading can be very effective.

One of the great opportunities with CMP is the flexibility the multiple cores offer for dynamic reconfiguration to implement important features like reliability, virtualization, security, as well as performance. New ideas are sure to show up in coming years.

Once a design has extensive error detection and recovery, it is tempting to rely on this to relax other design constraints, such as timing and power margins. Executing closer to the edge of what the design can tolerate, can result in higher performance and lower power. As long as the occasional error is always detected and recovered from, this can be a good tradeoff. The Razor design developed at the University of Michigan [6] is an example of such a design. At every critical stage in the pipeline, there are two sets of latches: one for early clocking and on for late clocking. The early latches capture the data and passes it onto the next stage, while the late latches capture the data conservatively and checks it against the early set. If they do not match, an error has occurred and the computation needs to be redone. A mechanism like this can relax margins based on manufacturing and environmental factors, and other parameters normally assumed to be worst case.

7 Summary

We have presented some of the motivation for Multi-core designs and how this is becoming a key feature of CPU's. Multi-core designs presents challenges for the designers in architecting a scalable, high performance interconnect and an optimal processor core. These processors require new inventions in the memory system, with effective, multi-level caches, and high bandwidth to main memory. If the supply voltage stops scaling downward at some point, it will be even more important to manage power efficiently. Finally, we looked at how designers will need to use a larger portion of transistors to guarantee reliable operation of large systems.

Maybe the biggest challenge presented by multi-core designs will be developing software which takes advantage of the performance opportunities in parallel processing. Hardware needs to support this with visibility and determinism for debug and performance tuning, and features like transactional memory to make a difficult programming task a little easier.

Acknowledgements

These notes are based on work done over several years with many people, too many to mention here. The novel ideas on the Ring interconnect for CMP were developed with Steve Felix, George Chrysos, and Matthew Mattina. Thanks to Steve Lang for reading these notes and giving me suggestions for improving both style and content.

References

1. Dennard, R., Yu, II.-N., et al.: Design of ion-implanted MOSFETs with very small physical dimensions. IEEE Journal of Solid State Circuits SC-9(5) (October 1974)
2. Tomasulo, R.M.: An Efficient Algorithm for Exploiting Multiple Arithmetic Units. IBM Journal of Research and Development 11(1), 25–33 (1967)
3. Seiler, L., Carmean, D., et al.: Data in graph. In: Larrabee: A many-core x86 architecture for visual computing, SIGGRAPH 2008: ACM SIGGRAPH 2008 Papers. ACM Press, New York (2008)
4. Emer, J.S., Clark, D.W.: Characterization of Processor Performance in the VAX-11/780. In: Proceedings of the 11th International Conference on Computer Architecture (May 1984); Reprinted in Readings in Computer Archictecture (2000)
5. Bautista, J., et al.: Polaris Description, at Intel Resesearch Group
6. Austin, T.M., et al.: Making Typical Silicon matter with Razor. IEEE Computer (2003)

Author Index

Printing: Mercedes-Druck, Berlin
Binding: Stein+Lehmann, Berlin